Critical Muslim 3
Fear and Loathing

Critical Muslim 3, July–September 2012

Editors: Ziauddin Sardar and Robin Yassin-Kassab
Deputy Editor: Samia Rahman
Publisher: Michael Dwyer
Managing Editor: (Hurst Publishers) Daisy Leitch
Cover Design: Fatima Jamadar

Associate Editors: Abdelwahhab El-Affendi, Muhammad Idrees Ahmad, Iqbal Asaria, Nader Hashemi, Vinay Lal, Hassan Mahamdallie, Ehsan Masood

Contributing Editors: Waqar Ahmad, Merryl Wyn Davies, Nader Hashemi, Aamer Hussein, Iftikhar Malik, Parvez Manzoor, Usama Hasan

International Advisory Board: Karen Armstrong, William Dalrymple, Farid Esack, Anwar Ibrahim, Bruce Lawrence, Ebrahim Moosa, Ashish Nandy, Bhikhu Parekh

Critical Muslim is published quarterly by C. Hurst & Co (Publishers) Ltd on behalf of and in conjunction with Critical Muslim Ltd and the Muslim Institute, London.
All correspondence to Muslim Institute, CAN Mezzanine, 49–51 East Road, London N1 6AH, United Kingdom
e-mail for editorial: editorial@criticalmuslim.com

C. Hurst & Co (Publishers) Ltd.,
41 Great Russell Street, London WC1B 3PL

ISBN: 978-1-84904-222-2
ISSN: 2048-8475

To subscribe please contact the following to place an order by credit/debit card or cheque (pounds sterling only):
Subscriptions Department
Marston Book Services Ltd
PO Box 269, Abingdon, Oxon
OX14 4YN, UK
Tel: +44 (0)1235 465574
Fax +44 (0)1235 465556
Email: subscriptions@marston.co.uk
Or subscribe online at www.marston.co.uk/encrypted/mbs/Subscription_Renewals_Orders.htm
A one year subscription, inclusive of postage (four issues), costs £50 (UK), £65 (Europe) and £75 (rest of the world).

THE BRITISH MUSEUM

Discover the Islamic World at the British Museum

From early scientific instruments to contemporary art, explore how Islam has shaped our world through objects for centuries

britishmuseum.org
Great Russell Street
London WC1B 3DG
🚇 Holborn, Russell Square

Mosque lamp. Enamelled glass.
Syria, c. AD 1330–1345.

OUR MISSION

Critical Muslim is a quarterly magazine of ideas and issues showcasing ground-breaking thinking on Islam and what it means to be a Muslim in a rapidly changing, increasingly interconnected world.

We will be devoted to examining issues within Islam, and Muslim societies, providing a Muslim perspective on the great debates of contemporary times, and promoting dialogue, cooperation and collaboration between 'Islam' and other cultures, including 'the West'. We aim to be innovative, thought-provoking and forward-looking, a space for debate between Muslims and between Muslims and others, on religious, social, cultural and political issues concerning the Muslim world and Muslims in the world.

What does 'Critical Muslim' mean? We are proud of our strong Muslim identity, but we do not see 'Islam' as a set of pieties and taboos. We aim to challenge traditionalist, modernist, fundamentalist and apologetic versions of Islam, and will attempt to set out new readings of religion and culture with the potential for social, cultural and political transformation of the Muslim world. Our writers may define their Muslim belonging religiously, culturally or civilisationally, and some will not 'belong' to Islam at all. *Critical Muslim* will sometimes invite writers of opposing viewpoints to debate controversial issues.

We aim to appeal to both academic and non-academic readerships; to emphasise intellectual rigour, the challenge of ideas, and original thinking.

In these times of change and peaceful revolutions, we choose not to be a lake or a meandering river. But to be an ocean. We embrace the world with all its diversity and pluralism, complexity and chaos. We aim to explore everything on our interconnected, shrinking planet — from religion and politics, to science, technology and culture, art and literature, philosophy and ethics, and histories and futures — and seek to move forward despite deep uncertainty and contradictions. We stand for open and critical engagement in the best tradition of Muslim intellectual inquiry.

CM3

July–September 2012

CONTENTS

FEAR AND LOATHING

WHAT WE FEAR

Merryl Wyn Davies

Old aphorisms never die, they simply fade with over-use, suffering a fate common enough with sacred text: oft repeated words of high sentence, seldom reasoned with, or mined for fresh meaning. To become a rhetorical flourish is not necessarily to remain a burst of illumination. Take, for example, Franklin D Roosevelt's clarion call: 'We have nothing to fear but fear itself.' How often is the idea — the fear of fear — used to invite an examination of the nature, structure and manipulation of fear in our time?

When I was young, BBC television used to preface certain programmes with a warning that what followed might not be suitable for people 'of a nervous disposition'. It usually indicated the kind of drama one had to watch from behind the sofa with half-closed fingers over one's eyes. The warning was 'Auntie' BBC fulfilling its mandate by protecting an unsuspecting public from fear. I was just such a person. However, I was never disposed to dutifully shield my nervousness from the frights on offer. The youngest in a family of people who considered themselves of decidedly non-nervous dispositions, it was a point of honour for me to resist all additional warnings — such as, it was past my bedtime or that I would get terrified and be upset. My defiance was more than a desire to avoid the disdain of my older brother; it was a curiosity to know what was unsuitable, a need to keep testing the limits of my nervousness and the irresistible allure of temptation, daring to do precisely what I knew was thoroughly unwise.

So did I learn by bitter experience that I had nothing to fear except the fear inherent in my own disposition? I did not. I had nightmares, a horror of the dark, of things that might lurk in shadows and of nightly noises that made me hold my breath and cower under my bed sheets. I was frequently overcome by fear of approaching menace. Gradually, I began to perceive there was something worse than the dramatised frights — the embellishments provided by my own imagination. Then I began to notice that the worst fears, the programmes that most assaulted my nervous disposition, had nothing to do with drama and never seemed to carry a prudential warning. Forget my nervous disposition, forget the power of imagination, whether mine or some dramatist's — I found there was a great deal more to fear in fact than fiction.

Once I realised it was the real world not that of the imagination that was the realm of fear, I ceased to have any interest in simulated horror. It has not escaped my notice, however, that public fascination with and consumption of fear has become ubiquitous. Holiday respite? Go and ride the latest mega machine offering fear with the frisson of a near-death experience. Or try sky diving or bungee jumping. Or relax at the pictures or become a couch potato and watch the infinite variations of fear by apocalypse or catastrophe complete with awesome visual effects. Who are the heroes now? Serial killers, vampires, witches. The undead, aliens and monsters are always on the march. The malevolent macabre is our secularised satan, evil is socially acceptable, we have made diverting companions of quaint folk who just happen to exist by devouring human flesh and drinking our lifeblood. A satiated world is offered the thrill of fear as a pleasurable release: nothing like a good scream!

Fear as entertainment seems the inevitable consequence of fear as the condition of normality, the inescapable accompaniment to the complexities of modern life. Everything has a fear factor — don't eat this or that because, headline news regularly informs us, it will kill you with cancer, obesity or addiction. Statistical projections, popularised as causal relationships, make headlines that force us to confront our fragile mortality and the possibility of death, the ultimate fear. The 'must have' consumer society is haunted by fear of losing it all. Technological mastery and material abundance are no consolation but the very source of our insecurity. The more we can do, the more we have, the more we are driven from fear to fear by fear in a state of constant anxiety. The threats we face coalesce into climates of fear — what is there not to fear?

Once again we teeter on the brink of doom. Indeed the prevailing climate of fear is not unlike that which prompted Roosevelt to counsel abandoning the fear of fear for the sake of something better. Today, the global economy seems ready to implode. However, its complexities now provide no obvious remedy for financial mismanagement. Outright cupidity has to be refinanced and continue to be rewarded beyond any thought of moral hazard. In our time the economy is too important to be reformed, let alone be infused with any sense of ethics and morality. The only hope is to reignite this engine so it can splutter back to life, driven by increasing consumer excess — the much sought-after 'economic growth'.

And once again there is a looming storm on the horizon, an ever-present threat, the rise of an adversary that is the antithesis of everything the liberal democratic capitalist dispensation stands for and all it makes possible: Islamism, the totalitarian fundamentalist threat par excellence. We are conditioned to know we have reason to fear.

Given our circumstances, the thought that we have nothing to fear but fear itself is reduced to empty rhetoric with no relevance to actual conditions. Unless, that is, the phrase is taken as the proposition that fear needs to be critically examined to find its origin and purpose. What are we afraid of? Why? Where do contemporary fears come from? What consequences flow from these fears and whose interests do they serve? How is fear deployed and to what ends? What structures of action or inaction arise from or rely on fear? We cannot rid ourselves of fear until we understand how this hydra-headed chameleon operates, how this shape-shifting changeling is capable of undermining us at every turn.

If we started to ask questions we might be reminded of the advice given to Roosevelt's successor Harry S Truman. Concerned by the expansion of the Soviet sphere of influence in the aftermath of the Second World War, and fearful of a potential Communist electoral victory in Italy, Truman knew something had to be done. But how could he persuade a war-weary nation to deliver the taxes necessary to fund combating the global threat of communism? Senator Arthur Vandeburgh had a simple answer. Truman had to 'scare the hell out of the American people'. Thus fear became the foundation of the Cold War world. Fear and insecurity were strategic instruments in the accumulation of the greatest array of military, economic, political and cultural power in human history and its projection on the global stage.

By 1958 America was homing in on Vietnam, reclassifying a nationalist yearning for autonomy as the new frontline against Communist encroachment on American freedom. Despite being well aware that Russia and China had no intention of coming to the aid of North Vietnam, the 'domino theory' became the official mantra, a fear that had to be defended against all logic. It was, said the authors of the bestselling cautionary tale *The Ugly American* — a lucid dissection of the failure of American foreign policy in Southeast Asia published in that year — 'a condition of avoidable ignorance'. Avoidable, that is, if the well publicised climate of fear was intelligently questioned, subjected to scrutiny by press, public and politicians. Instead 'avoidable ignorance' served the cosy mutual self interest of government, military elite and the growing industrial complex. Fear was manufac tured and manipulated to author policy that made escalation into war inevitable. Fear operated through and structured the failure of knowledge and judgement that was the dominant order of global affairs for the following four decades. No alternatives to the squandering of blood and treasure on all sides could stand against the orthodoxy imposed by the structure of fear. By the time the public was alerted to the failures occasioned by 'avoidable ignorance', they were trapped in the intractable quagmire of conflicting fears, damned whatever they did or did not do.

In the post-9/11 world there is every indication the entire procedure is being repeated once again by manipulation of the same levers of fear. Priming the engines of fear are the neocon Orientalists examined by Abdel Wahab El-Affendi. Orientalism, 'the prism through which the West viewed the Muslim world for centuries' has seized the opportunity offered by 9/11 to forge a new alliance. Drawing in acolytes driven by right wing 'paranoia' and 'grand conspiracy theories' as well as from the supposedly 'liberal' 'progressive left', it is exclusively dedicated to promoting fear in our time. The uniting factor for the disparate adherents, writes El-Affendi, 'became hatred and fear of Islam, Muslims and Arabs'. The new aggressively-resurgent right, neo-conservatism plus Orientalism, has converged with the renegade, Islamophobic left in recognition of 'Islamic terror'. Also known as Muslim Rage and 'the clash of civilisations', it is projected as an irrational reaction to liberalism which originates in the same impulse as totalitarianism in both its Bolshevik and fascist manifestations. Familiar contours of argument and policy are re-established. Barely six weeks after 9/11 the 'liberal' New York intellectual Paul Berman, could write of an 'infection' that only an all-out war with no quarters given, coupled with an equally merciless ideological struggle, could eliminate.

By late 2001 the organisation formed in 1995 by Lynne Cheney, wife of the then Republican vice president and Democratic Senator and former vice presidential candidate, Joe Lieberman, the National Alumni Forum (renamed the American Council of Trustees and Alumni) issued a report entitled *Defending Civilization: How Our Universities are Failing America, and What Can Be Done About it*, which accused American academic institutions in general (and not just Middle Eastern Studies) of being the 'weak link' in America's response to foreign threats, and of living in isolation from the public at large. 'We learn from history,' the report affirmed, 'that when a nation's intellectuals are unwilling to defend its civilisation, they give comfort to its adversaries'. Academia was an 'enemy within'.

There is ample evidence that this new Orientalism is dedicated to the path of 'avoidable ignorance' and promoting the same old failures of knowledge and judgement. El-Affendi cites Shmuel Bar's frank counsel that we might as well return 'straight to the Middle Ages' and accept 'the fact that for the first time since the Crusades, Western civilisation finds itself involved in a religious war'. The new alliance of intellectuals forms, appropriately enough, a kind of secular priesthood anxious to fulfil the polemic and propagandist role of monasteries in that earlier era. They propose establishing a direct relationship between knowledge and power in which academics are 'harnessed directly to the dictates of policy' and 'remain at the beck and call of government' in a way that Edward Said, the bête noire of the new orthodoxy and dubbed by some 'Professor of Terror', 'did not dare to accuse Orientalists of being'.

At the epicentre of neocon Orientalists stands the doyen of the field, Bernard Lewis. Indeed, as El-Affendi notes, the best advice of many members of the new orthodoxy is simply to read and reread Lewis' works. As Peter Clark writes, 'over the second half of his career Lewis has become a bitter, strident and tendentious critic of Muslims, seeing the different countries that make up the Muslim world as somehow dark, negative and "anti-western".' Indeed Lewis is increasingly an angry old man propounding his 'extraordinarily vague and simply misleading, if not erroneous, view of the world'. But he is not just any old controversialist. As Michael Hirsh noted in an article for *Washington Monthly* in 2004, Lewis not only had the ear of the Bush administration which he used to stiffen their resolve on the invasion of Iraq, but more strategically he has, over the years, trained many who served in the ranks of various US administrations.

Lewis' pre-eminence stems from his work on Ottoman Turkey, particularly his book *The Emergence of Modern Turkey*. Underlying the whole book is the idea that there is a western civilisation that is separate from (and better than) the civilisation of Turkey's 'Muslim neighbours'. The expression 'the clash of civilisations', 'the idea of an inevitable conflict between Islam and the West', is attributed to the famous Samuel Huntington 1993 article in *Foreign Affairs*, later expanded to book length and published as *The Clash of Civilizations and the Remaking of World Order* in 1996. But it first appears in Lewis's book where he refers to 'the ancient clash of Islam and Christendom'.

For Turkey, Lewis suggests, the history of the last century has been one of progress, a steady emergence from the darkness of the Ottoman Empire to the sunny secular uplands of the pro-western modern Turkish republic. It is a story of steady 'westernisation', an unquestioned ideal, as if a country without westernisation is somehow lacking, like an adolescent who has not reached maturity. This begs a thousand questions. Indeed it seems that whatever Lewis approves of is *ipso facto* 'western' and 'good'. Of course, the threat to democracy in Turkey now comes from 'creeping re-Islamisation of society under the present government'.

Given such a simplistic structure of fear, the failures of policy and judgement that produced the debacle in Iraq after the 2003 invasion seem inevitable. It is worth noting that Rajiv Chanderasakaran's 2007 book *Imperial Life in the Emerald City: Inside Baghdad's Green Zone* documents a reprise of the errors, failings and sheer avoidable ignorance committed by America in Southeast Asia half a century earlier. When fear rules and sets policy, attitudes need never change, lessons need never be learned. Armed with a febrile worldview of bi-polar antipathy, sensitivity to actual conditions is unnecessary. Far from illuminating reality, fear obscures it and blinds its manipulators to everything they do not want to know.

America predicated its policy in Iraq on the sectarian divide as the essential nature of the country. Indeed, sectarian conflict is an enduring fear and perennial topic of debate among western observers, especially in light of the unpredicted and worryingly unpredictable events of the Arab Spring. Fear of encroaching Islamism is compounded by sectarian imponderables. In analysing how sectarian identity operates in Arab perceptions, Fanar Haddad makes it clear that 'the first step to understanding sectarian relations is to recognise their fluidity'. Instead of being intransigent and unchanging, 'sectarian identity is subject to erratic fluctuations', 'can lose political relevance and lie dormant for many decades' and 'can be awoken by a number of drivers' before eventually being relegated once again under other forms of self-definition. Bludgeoning understanding into predetermined immutable categories is an avoidable ignorance, obscuring and deforming perception of reality. It begs the question El Affendi sees as a proper intellectual challenge: 'why [has] American policy in Iraq ... turned Islamic groups which had resorted to terrorism in the past into "moderate" allies, and turned former allies into deadly enemies?'

Haddad argues that the complex, overlapping layers of sectarian and ethnic identity exist in tension with overarching myths and national narratives. The Sunni-Shia sectarian divide is only one among many though it is the strongest in the Middle East in terms of historical legacy, demographics and, most importantly, political relevance. 'In the current climate, it intertwines itself with nationalism' and 'is conflated with ethnic divisions'. Yet Haddad 'will never tire of repeating: nothing can be said about all Shias or all Sunnis as both groups are far from monolithic'; sectarian identity competes with other group identities in multi-layered definitions of self and 'reacts to social, political and economic stimuli'.

The sectarian divisions were exacerbated by the Iraq invasion to generate differential responses to the events of the Arab Spring, most notably in the case of Bahrain. The post-2003 sectarian climate explains the reality 'that Bahrain did not and never will qualify' for popular endorsement and support 'for the same reason that Hezbollah's Hassan Nasrallah, the Iraqi government and Iran quite correctly highlighted the plight of Bahraini protesters and yet failed to show any solidarity with embattled protesters in Syria. On the contrary: they condemned the protests there.'

The Arab Spring has not displaced the centrality of the structure of fear defined as Islamism. From the perspective of the West it is the fundamentalism, the predominant existential threat, and as such blots out reasoning with the challenges posed by any and all other fundamentalisms. Vinay Lal and Gordon Steffey beg to differ. They give alternative images and reversals of the imaginings projected onto Islamism that construct and manipulate 'hatred and fear of Islam, Muslims and Arabs'.

Steffey takes us on a visit to the 'Christian fundamentalist madrasa' founded by the late Jerry Falwell: Liberty University in Lynchburg, Virginia. The institution embodies Falwell's 'obsessive reality': 'I truly believe the only way I can evangelise the world in my generation is to train Young Champions for Christ at Liberty University.'

At the university bookshop Steffey and his enigmatic travelling companion pick up a copy of *The Unlikely Disciple* in which Kevin Roose chronicles his semester at Liberty University. It is 'study abroad' for a non-evangelical. 'Right in my time zone, was a culture more foreign to me than any European capital, and these foreigners vote in my elections!' Roose cannot fathom 'how well-intentioned Christian kids' are transformed into 'zealots' 'shouting hellfire and damnation to the masses'. This is 'battleground evangelism', an essential training for a true fundamentalist. Repeated rejection is 'a way to get used to the feeling of being an outcast in the secular world' the self-affirming experience that makes each of them a 'Champion for Christ'. As Steffey observes: 'Angry zealots are not born that way, but "born again"?'

Liberty University used to boast its own 'best Muslim', one Ergun Mehmet Caner, an ex-Muslim appointed as Dean who pledged to produce 'special forces' for the 'frontlines', 'specially trained generals' because 'a general understands the mind of the adversary, as well as the rules of engagement'. Caner offered 'unambiguous confirmation' of popular fears: 'I hated you,' Caner insisted, where 'you' means American and/or Christian. He hated them as a product of his upbringing in the culture of 'Islamic jihad' in his native Turkey then the Beirut madrasa where he trained in anticipation of answering the Ayatollah Khomeini's summons to islamise the United States. His improbable journey from jihad to Jesus, 'delighted many audiences precisely because it aggrandised so many'. In 2005 Caner provided pre-deployment training to Marines in North Carolina, inviting them 'to look very carefully at my face' and see 'the face of a declared enemy', a comment that can only work as a neat invitation to associate racism with fear of Islamism.

Caner's journey was not only improbable but also untrue. He was revealed as a fraud. Born in Sweden as Ergun Michael Caner, he settled in Ohio as a toddler. Tutored in Islam by his father, Caner was reared principally by his non-Muslim mother after his parents' divorce and converted to evangelical Christianity as a teenager. For the true fundamentalist, appro-

priating the mantle of 'hatred' is not so much imaginary projection as statement of their own fears as the reality of the other, the enemy. All
fundamentalists need enemies to sustain their own convictions of virtue.
That's precisely why Richard Dawkins, the fundamentalist atheist and
scourge of creationism, a necessary part of the curriculum at Liberty University, visits the university to indulge in mutual harangue. No doubt both
sides emerge vindicated by the encounter.

Incidentally, Peter Morey offers an assessment of another 'Muslim of
choice' who came to media prominence after 9/11: Irshad Manji, the Canadian Muslim journalist. The media is always on the lookout for Muslim
spokespeople prepared to 'tell it like it is', or more accurately reiterate the
dominant orthodoxy of the structure of fear. Manji's preferred self-designation is as a 'Muslim Refusenik' or 'Muslim Dissident', which, as Morey
observes, immediately recalls 'those victims of another totalitarian horror
show, the Soviet Union'.

Manji confirms convenient neoconservative framing of Muslims: 'they' hate
'us' because 'they' really want to be like 'us'. She offers another standard
argument of the neocon Orientalists: many Muslims 'hitched their futures to
Hitler,' she writes. Word association does the rest: 'Axis Powers', 'Axis of
Evil'. Manji constructs a 'mainstream Islam' that needs forcible cleansing. As
Morley argues, 'there is nothing neutral about Manji. All is personalised
through her self-mythologisation as an embattled speaker of truth to Muslim
power. How much better for ratings if the inconvenient truths she tells in the
end confirm the rightness of our defensive western mindset?'

Vinny Lal confronts a much more complex challenge: 'How is one to
speak of Hindu fundamentalism, when Hinduism recognises no one single
text as supremely authoritative, has multiple centres of priestly authority all
of which a practitioner of the faith may however ignore without peril,
counts '330 million' gods and goddesses in its pantheon, and is certainly
without a historical founder?' He manages nevertheless to take us on a
fascinating journey through the diverse ways in which fundamentalism can
be expressed and sustained.

While imagined Nazi associations are part of the denunciation of Islamic
fundamentalism the popularity of Hitler among Hindu fundamentalists has
escaped general notice. *Mein Kampf* remains a runaway bestseller in India.
For aspiring middle-class Indians, Hitler is a model of 'leadership qualities'

and 'discipline'. Germany is an example of what discipline, efficiency, and strenuous devotion to work can accomplish. Oh, and one more thing – 'the treatment meted out to Jews was, from the standpoint of those desirous of forging a glorious Hindu nation, an object lesson on how Hindu India might handle its own Muslims.' 'Germany has also shown how impossible it is for races and cultures, having differences going to the root, to be assimilated into one united whole, a good lesson for us in Hindusthan to learn and profit by.' Among such fundamentalists Gandhi is viewed as a backward-looking luddite who emasculated India and would have set the country hopelessly adrift in a nation-state system where national interest and violence reign supreme. Whereas 'Hitler's idea of a virile nation set on a course of domination appears as an attractive alternative.'

Hindu fundamentalism is not confined to the boundaries of even the much-vaunted 'Greater India'. Indian American Hindus are adept at deploying discourses of multiculturalism to 'simultaneously stake their rights in a pluralistic America and interrogate the loyalty of Indian Muslims to the Indian nation-state.' Meanwhile, they give vast physical form to their determination 'to usher Hinduism into a new era of monumental architecture and modernist achievement'. Temples across North America and north London regularly proclaim themselves the 'world's largest Hindu temple outside India' complete with 'certification from the Guinness Book of Records'. 'Hinduism need not just be the 'oldest' religion in the world, it must also display some of the energising and self-aggrandising features that many middle-class Hindus otherwise associate with Islam.' Lal argues that Hindu nationalists still seek 'approbation from the West' while there is 'constant endeavour to suggest that the findings of Hinduism and modern science are compatible.'

The overt racial strand in Hindu fundamentalism is mirrored by the covert racial undertones other contributors have noted in the structure of fear dedicated to 'Islamism'. The subject of racism is taken up by Kundnani and MacFarlane. Old familiar fears are, as Haddad reminded us, fluid they morph, shift and adapt to circumstances and need. And they can be manipulated and deployed to obscure, distract and divert attention from reality and thereby construct avoidable ignorance that is the prelude to failures of knowledge and judgement. This is essentially Kundnani's argument in respect of the rise of the English Defence League, a rebranding of the older strands of far right extremism that has become an increasingly aggressive and violent presence on British streets. Their unabashed racist nationalism embraces a street level version of twenty-first-century crusade that found academic expression in the writing of Shmuel Bar.

McFarlane asks us not to be distracted by the subtly implied and deployed use of the language of racist stereotypes in the coverage and debate about the riots that shook Britain in August 2011. Behind the marshalling of old familiar fear he argues there stands an important 'interconnectedness' with direct bearing on the condition of the global economy and consequences stemming from its current disarray. McFarlane was in Egypt when the riots began in his home patch of Tottenham, north London. In Egypt the Arab Spring 'exposed the connection between economic and social injustice and the revolt against tyranny — the same inequality and lack of control experienced by large numbers of people in Britain'. The body politic is at sea, 'the point is that everyone can see it, even poor unemployed and disaffected young people in Tottenham, north London.' Rebellion against social injustice is in the air, 'and there is no wall between that and the wider political challenge it presents to our global ruling elite'.

Finally, we have two contributions from a Malaysian perspective both pointing to the way that fear makes fools of us all. The structures of fear at work in our world, represented by the revitalisation of new Orientalism in the climate of fear prevailing since 9/11, serve to make Islam a known and definite quantity for everyone. You either know, without need to question, what you hate and are hated by, or on the other hand, know what you love and must defend, without question, no matter what strangulating intellectual or emotional gyrations are required, to the last diacritical against the unreasoning onslaught of the massed battalions of detractors. As both Shanon Shah and Farouk Peru make plain, the result not only silences discourse but it also atrophies any semblance of critical reasoning. The world is delivered into the hands of stereotypes (so we know our enemies), straw men/persons (they'll burn readily), and construction barriers (so convenient for barricades). It is distracted from distraction by the distraction of insoluble animosities that service the self interests of the few. The beneficiaries are the tyrants who were bastions against the deluge, the academics and think tanks with un-insightful axes to grind, and the proliferating security/military industrial complex. And we never, ever, get to consider alternatives, ways of being better.

Both Shah, in his discussion of homosexuality, the Islamophobe's favoured baiting issue *du jour*, and Peru, considering apostasy and Malay Muslim identity, are confronted with Islam as 'a singular, monolithic entity capable of speaking independently of human mediation and interpretation'. This is exactly the Islam of 'tradition' and the Islam imagined and projected by the structures of fear and in both cases they argue it is an avoidable ignorance, a failure of knowledge and judgement. And there is an alternative. When we see things in context we can embrace the fluidity, the openness to debate and critical thinking that existed in the early history of Islam. And thereby discover the more rational angels of our nature and more humane responses to our time.

When you know the origins and purpose of fear it may indeed be possible to dispense with the fear of fear itself in favour of something better.

NEOCON ORIENTALISTS

AbdelWahab El-Affendi

Barely six weeks after the 9/11 attacks in America, a prominent New Yorker and 'liberal' intellectual, Paul Berman, published an essay in American Prospect with the title 'Terror and Liberalism'. It was later turned into a book by Berman with the same title and became a much-talked-about bestseller. The message in both works was a stark one for a supposed left-wing intellectual, as it echoed (albeit in a sophisticated way) the already well-known theses of Bernard Lewis on 'Muslim Rage', and its derivative in Samuel Huntington's 'clash of civilisations' argument.

Berman accuses liberals of being too naive to see 'Islamic terror' for what it was: a species of an irrational reaction to liberalism which originates in the same impulse as totalitarianism in both its Bolshevik and fascist manifestations. The common impulse is a perception of an apocalyptic threat to the purity of the community, emanating both from foreign enemies and their accomplices at home. It is an 'infection' that 'will require bloody internal struggles, capped by gigantic massacres' in order to root it out. Movements generated by this impulse are by their very nature irrational, and the error of liberals is to believe that one could reason with them. However, the truth is that only an all-out war with no quarters given, coupled with an equally merciless ideological struggle, could eliminate this threat.

In doing his bit for this 'ideological jihad', Berman follows Lewis's example by enumerating possible grievances Muslims may have against America, Israel or former colonial powers, before dismissing them as explanations for Muslim hostility. He admits that these are many, but argues that Palestinian hostility to Israel had nothing to do with dispossession and brutal repression. Similarly, anger against America has nothing to do with supporting Israeli injustices and all sorts of tyrannies, or with causing the death of millions of Iraqis. For even if Israel and America stopped robbing Palestinians and attacking Arabs, they would still be hated, because they were 'liberal' countries. So they might just as well get on with it.

The bad news, Berman argues, is that this irrationality is not restricted to a small faction of extremists, but is harboured by broad currents of Islamists and nationalists. In a sense, every Muslim or Arab is a potential Islamist or Baathist, and any of those is a potential terrorist. So we must prepare for an endless war against this implacable enemy.

In this and later works (including his diatribe against Tariq Ramadan in *The Flight of the Intellectuals*), Berman goes into meticulous detail as he maps the links between fascism and Islamism. Hassan Al-Banna, founder of the Muslim Brotherhood, was friends with the Mufti of Palestine, who in turn had met Hitler; Sayyid Qutb read authors with fascist sympathies; and so and so on. But after reading enough of Berman and the host of authors who converged onto this route, one gets the rather uncomfortable feeling that the boot may be on the other foot. These attacks on 'naïve liberals'? This desperate unearthing of secret links and conspiracy circles? These 'apocalyptic' warnings about 'apocalyptic' happenings? They sound troublingly familiar. The circle was closed when, in July 2011, a Norwegian right wing fanatic cited the writings of many such a 'liberal' intellectual in his manifesto before going on his killing spree against 'naïve' Norwegian liberals who did not appear to sufficiently appreciate the gravity of the threat of Islam.

Return of Orientalism

The 9/11 terror attacks offered pretexts for many dubious deeds, from exhortations to 'bury bad news', to invading countries, to recycling discredited literature and claims. Among the intellectuals, and in a context where attempts at an explanation were seen at worst as unpatriotic, and at best as naïve and misguided, the battle inevitably shifted to the level of theory and meta-theory: a struggle over which explanatory framework was more viable. And since Islam was a key term in this discourse, this in turn revived the old debate over Orientalism, that beleaguered discipline/ideological formation which represented the prism through which the West viewed the Muslim world for centuries. In a revealing coincidence, the terror attacks gave a boost to a determined and aggressive campaign by neoconservative intellectuals seeking to revive the fortunes of Orientalism in tandem with the overall right-wing shift in American politics.

Orientalism had earlier fallen victim to a constellation of developments that included a paradigm shift in social theory, the emergence of cultural criticism, a progressive radicalisation of academia, an increased sensitivity to other cultures, more compassion for oppressed or disadvantaged groups (known popularly as 'political correctness'), and the retreat of the conservative, ethnocentric perspectives which characterised earlier periods of modern western scholarship dealing with other cultures. As a result, the discipline/formation suffered a serious blow to its status and credibility following a series of critiques, not least by Ziauddin Sardar, from inside and outside Western academic circles.

However, Orientalism experienced what looked like a revival in response to the phenomena of 'Islamic resurgence' in the 1970s and 1980s, and continued to fend off its numerous critics, influence scholarship and even gain new adherents, including the likes of V S Naipaul and Salman Rushdie, dubbed as 'Orientalised Orientals' by Sardar.

In the meantime, a new related phenomenon emerged in the US, the so-called neoconservative trend, with its paranoia, enmities, and conspiratorial grand plans. The two trends started first working separately on launching an 'intellectual offensive' against the 'enemy within': academia. In 1995 an organisation called the National Alumni Forum was set up by Lynne Cheney (wife of the then Vice-President) and (former Democratic vice-Presidential hopeful) Senator Joseph Lieberman. Later re-named the American Council of Trustees and Alumni (ACTA), the Washington DC-based group claimed to be 'dedicated to countering political correctness and keeping its eye on campus radicals'. Late in 2001, it issued a report entitled *Defending Civilisation: How Our Universities are Failing America, and What Can Be Done About it*, which accused American academic institutions in general (and not just Middle Eastern Studies) of being the 'weak link' in America's response to foreign threats, and of living in isolation from the public at large. 'We learn from history', the report affirmed, 'that when a nation's intellectuals are unwilling to defend its civilisation, they give comfort to its adversaries'.

In the same year, Daniel Pipes, another neoconservative figure with links to the Middle East, co-authored an article in which American Middle Eastern Studies were accused of succumbing to a 'pronounced leftist bias and the proclivity toward apologetics for enemies of the United States'. In addition to these faults which the discipline 'shares with other area-studies', Middle Eastern scholarship displayed a 'tendency to overemphasise the Arab-Israeli conflict, to engage in severe factional infighting', and to adopt a jargon-ridden discourse. The field was also 'dominated' by scholars of Middle Eastern origin who tended to identify more with the countries they studied than with America. In general, the argument went, the field had become a preserve for 'unpatriotic' scholars bent on blaming America for every ill under the sun, and acting as apologists for Islamism and other anti-American trends.

'The Treason of Academia'

The events of September 11 provided the die-hard adherents of both trends, now firm allies, with a golden opportunity to launch a long-awaited Orientalist comeback. The determined fightback was spearheaded by figures such as Martin Kramer, former director of the Moshe Dayan Centre at Tel Aviv University, and his close associate, Daniel Pipes, director of the Philadelphia-based Middle East Forum, a right-wing think tank. They were helped in this by a host of neoconservative figures, including Fouad Ajami of John Hopkins University, Robert Satloff of the Washington Institute, and Bernard Lewis, the reputed 'doyen' of Orientalists who managed, at the age of 85, to produce a best-selling book immediately following the September 11 terror attacks. The determined intellectual onslaught was accompanied by various forms of public activism, including appeals to Congress, media campaigns and the formation in 2002 of a watch-dog named Campus Watch to name and shame 'delinquent' academics. It was also wholeheartedly embraced by top officials in the Bush administration, putting the Middle Eastern Studies establishment on the defensive.

Kramer blames the decline of Orientalism squarely on the influence of the late Edward Said (1935-2003), who was Columbia University's Professor of Comparative Literature, and especially on his famous book *Orientalism* (1978). 'For most academic commentators on things Islamic', Kramer writes in *The Islamism Debate*, '1978 is a watershed — not because a stern Shiite cleric inspired a revolution, but because a stern Columbia literature professor published a book. Edward Said's *Orientalism* persuaded them that their only legitimate role was to apologise and sympathise'.

Said's work, however, was preceded by earlier interventions, including some from within the 'Orientalist' tradition itself, most notably Marshall Hodgson, but mainly the input of an increasing number of scholars from within the Arab and Islamic traditions. Its impact was enhanced by its appeal to critical audiences in the period between the end of the Vietnam War (and the concurrent democratic revolutions in Greece, Spain, Portugal and Southern Africa) in the mid-1970s and the eruption of the Islamic Revolution in Iran and the Sandinista revolution in Nicaragua at the end of the decade. It was thus significant that the fight-back to rehabilitate Orientalism coincided with the ascendancy of the New Right in the Thatcherite-Reaganite era and the subsequent collapse of the Eastern Bloc.

The counterattack built on earlier critiques from authors like Bernard Lewis, Ernest Gellner and even Maxime Rodinson (who was lavishly praised in Said's book). However, these critiques and the insistent subse quent tirades did not dent the influence of Said's seminal text, which maintained the status, to the consternation of these numerous critics, as Joshua Teitelbaum and Meir Litvak put it, of 'a nearly sacred doctrine in the American academy'. In attempting to exploit the September 11 attacks, the critics added to the long list of sins ascribed to Middle Eastern scholars the charge of having failed to predict 9/11. This charge was made in Kramer's *Ivory Towers on Sand: The Failure of Middle Eastern Studies in America*. Like Lewis' book (which was a collection of lectures delivered a couple of years before), Kramer's book had also been long in preparation and was providentially released just after the 9/11 attacks. It thus made a powerful case by trying to link the alleged theoretical shortcomings of the discipline to its failure to be of use to American foreign policy makers. An energetic media campaign brought the book to the attention of academics and policy-makers alike. When Campus Watch was launched by Daniel Pipes in 2002, and Congress took steps to implement its recommendations shortly after that, academics had additional reasons to sit up and listen to this voice coming from beyond the tower walls.

While the political message regarding the unpatriotic bent of scholars was powerfully driven home, the intellectual one was not so easy to discern. As one perceptive reviewer noted, it was difficult at first sight to gather what

Kramer wanted to say, as his work was riddled with 'major inconsistencies': 'he accurately criticises those who study Middle Eastern politics for their marginalisation within the social sciences, then unfairly chastises them for adopting disciplinary paradigms remote from their regional subject matter. He finds those who refuse to speak to the immediate concerns of US foreign policy dangerously disengaged but questions the motives of policy-relevant researchers with whom he disagrees. He scorns the current structure of academic Middle Eastern studies — multidisciplinary institutes outside regular academic departments — yet suggests no alternative. And his sweeping charges often ignore work in the field dealing with precisely the issues he contends are misunderstood or ignored.'

There are also additional inconsistencies not noted in the above review. For example, Kramer alleges that the over-theorised discipline ignores reality and is, for this reason, scorned by policy makers, who tend to rely more on the better funded and more healthily staffed think tanks outside campuses for policy relevant research. However, he also claims that policy makers have been misled by these 'irrelevant' scholars!

Kramer was also criticised by Zachary Lockman for blaming Edward Said 'for everything that he believes has gone wrong with Middle East studies from the late 1970s onward' and, in the process, 'ignoring both the extensive critiques of modernisation theory and Orientalism that preceded the publication of that book and the complex and often critical ways in which Said's intervention was received and developed'.

However, in an interesting way, Kramer appears to vindicate Said in his attempt to undermine him. While Said accused Orientalism of being the handmaiden of imperialism, his main purpose was to direct attention to what he regarded as the subtle and complex interaction between knowledge and power in terms of blind spots, insidious ethnocentric prejudices and unquestioned presuppositions and paradigms. The field, he argued, rested on the artificial construction of rival and mutually exclusive identities for the purpose of exclusion and domination, and was inextricably connected to, and reproduced by, existing power structures of domination which in turn it helped to reproduce. Kramer, by contrast, sees Middle Eastern studies as an arena subject to the crude influences of funding bodies, personal academic ambition or factional affiliations. More interestingly, Kramer calls for more of the same: he wants academia to be harnessed directly to the dictates of policy and to remain at the beck and call of government in a way that even Said did not dare to accuse Orientalists of being.

Ironically, the neoorientalist counterattack thus becomes a parody of the original sin. Instead of the Foucauldian 'discursive police' being deployed together with disciplinary regimentation to maintain and reinforce relations of domination, the actual uniformed police were being summoned to do the disciplining (as in the famous 1989 article in *Commentary* which dubbed Said 'Professor of Terror'), while appeals were made to Congress to 'discipline' the disciplines. It is as if those who lost the match on the playing field decided to draw their guns to even the scores.

An Intellectual Challenge

At this point an intriguing question poses itself: why do the neoconservatives appear so fixated with achieving dominance over an academic world which they constantly disparage as irrelevant and lacking in influence? One answer could be that the neoconservatives view the world of academia as a dangerous bastion of hostile 'liberal' forces in the same way British Conservatives under Prime Minister Margaret Thatcher regarded the trade unions as a major threat that needed to be neutralised. The tactics advocated against academia (the mobilisation of hostile media and public opinion, the resort to legislation, the creation of watchdog organisations to monitor them and the setting up of rival think tanks) do indeed mirror the Thatcherite strategy of using a combination of legislation and political, economic and propaganda tactics to break the unions.

The neoconservatives themselves make the argument that this activism is dictated by the concern that the nation's intellectuals must be enlisted in the defence of a threatened civilisation. In this case, as with contest over the media, there are echoes of the old church-state battle. The intellectuals (and the media) are seen as the new priesthood, and those in power cannot afford to have them singing a different tune from the pulpit to the one being sung from the throne.

There is, additionally, the inherent attractiveness of a great intellectual debate. Professional intellectuals, as Joshua Micah Marshall argues, crave the Chinese curse of living in interesting times: 'Like doctors who want to treat the most challenging patients or cops who want to take down the worst criminals, it's only natural for people who think seriously about political and moral issues to seek out the most challenging and morally vexing questions to ponder and confront.' That is why intellectuals dread as a nightmare the 'end of history' vision of a bland and uninteresting post-communist era of eternal bourgeois rule 'in which there would be no more great debates or challenges, but rather a bourgeois millennium of endlessly growing investment funds, a brave new world of consumer appliances'. (In the current economic climate, one might be inclined to add the remark: you wish!)

It was David Satloff, a leading neoconservative figure and one of the key protagonists in this contest, who, in a talk delivered at the Moshe Dayan Centre in 1996 (and later published in a book edited by Kramer), hailed the 'Islamism debate' as 'one of the few remaining intellectual debates in US foreign policy'. This debate (which Satloff sums up in the question 'how did we lose Iran'?) was seen as at once providing a fascinating intellectual challenge and carrying great risks for senior bureaucrats, where providing the wrong answers could destroy careers. And while US policy towards Islamism has, in Satloff's view, evolved positively (towards successful containment) it has done so 'despite an analytical framework that is flawed, overly simplistic and at times curiously counterproductive'.

In the same volume, Kramer takes up the issue of this 'flawed analytical framework' in a rehearsal of his *Ivory Towers on Sand* arguments, railing against what he describes as the 'dominant paradigm' in academic thinking about Islamism. This paradigm, Kramer argues, insisted on viewing Islamism as 'the functional equivalent of democratic reform movements' in other parts of the world. If the Islamic movements do not look to us very democratic, that is only 'a consequence of our own age-old bias against Islam'. This paradigm, Kramer concludes, has failed. 'It has mistaken virulent forms of hyper-nationalism for social and political reformism. It has misleadingly classified Islamist movements into "moderate" and "extreme" categories that do not exist. It has made hopelessly naïve assumptions about the effect of power on Islamist behaviour. And it postulated the inevitable triumph of a movement which is now in the throes of a crisis.'

Why, then, Kramer asks, is this paradigm still standing in spite of its composite failures? And the answer is, again, the influence of Edward Said, who had made apologetics fashionable: 'Today it is difficult to find a scholarly discourse that is more self-conscious than the scholarly discourse on political Islam. Indeed many practitioners have only one eye on the movements they purport to study. The other eye is fixed squarely on disciplinary dogma, which holds that any feverish act done in the name of Islam should be shown respectful deference, repentance for historic wrongs done by the West against Muslims. This has been a major obstacle not only to understanding, but to open debate itself.'

Until 9/11, Kramer believed that he had remained a voice in the wilderness. But out of the heat of the burning towers, a new, more receptive atmosphere emerged. No more political correctness, naïve credulity or guilt-ridden empathy. The truth can now be told straight.

But what would the shape of this new truth be? What is the new paradigm which we are being offered to replace the erstwhile 'dominant' but now discredited one? Not, much apparently. It is intriguing that when one closely examines Kramer's contribution in his *Ivory Towers on Sand* and other writings, there is no sign of the promised new paradigm that would replace the one being disparaged, apart from repeating endlessly his mantra that 'the perils of Islamism had been underestimated, the potential of civil society had been overestimated' in the 'dominant paradigm'. What we are advised to do is to read and re-read Lewis over and over again, the same way Muslims recite the Qu'ran, with a similar hope of getting eventual enlightenment. In fact, as one key proponent of this approach, Shmuel Bar, frankly avers, the counsel is to return not only to pre-Enlightenment ways, but straight to the Middle Ages, and accept 'the fact that for the first time since the Crusades, Western civilisation finds itself involved in a religious war'.

The policy implications of this position are thus *a priori* and irrelevant to the alleged scientific purport of the proposed approach. In so far as some correct assertions and criticisms are made, they are mainly truisms, such as the claim that Muslim and other non-Western communities may not necessarily evolve into copies of America.

Equally, the claim about Middle Eastern studies failing to predict revolutions and other cataclysmic occurrences in the region misses the point, since academic discourse is not a hermetically sealed area, using as it does policy statements and deeds as raw material. When policy fails, that is the failure of the bodies responsible for policy, not of academics. If anything, academics should be more critical towards current policies in order to improve the scholarly input into policy making, a legitimate objective. For example, one has to examine the reasons why American policy in Iraq has turned Islamic groups which had resorted to terrorism in the past into 'moderate' allies, and turned former allies into deadly enemies. And this would of necessity involve a very critical look at US policies. In this at least, the neoconservative pundits were right: it was inconceivable for one to speak of anti-Americanism in Iraq prior to March 2003 any more than it was to speak to anti-Israeli sentiments among Lebanese Shiites prior to the 1982 Israeli invasion of Lebanon.

In this regard, it might be extremely dangerous (literally) to overload the debate with rigid ideological *a priori* positions as the neoconservative crowd counsels, and even more dangerous to try to use bullying and intimidation to stifle debate on these vital issues. The functional differentiation between various levels and arenas of analysis must be respected, preserved and even promoted, not bludgeoned into conformity. The tasks of policy makers, intelligence analysts, free media, policy think tanks and the not-so-dispassionate academic institutions, diverge both in approach and purpose. Things should remain that way. It is for some good reason that even though government departments and policy think tanks address the same areas of concern, their functional differentiation is seen as beneficial and essential. The *9/11 Commission Report* implicitly criticises the CIA's perception of itself as 'a university gone to war' (it would be even more daft and counterproductive to turn universities into the 'FBI on campus', as some appear to advocate).

Orientalism Meets the 'War on Terror'

The depth of feelings manifested in the 'Orientalism debate' is in itself revealing. The debate engages with some of the most fundamental questions of human existence and human knowledge, and raises a host of important philosophical and epistemological questions.

The core issue in this debate is the very status of 'social science' and the claims staked on its behalf. The crisis faced by Orientalism's tenuous claims to the status of a science is symptomatic of a deeper malaise infecting modern 'scientific' discourse in general. As Edmund Burke III has noted, 'as a species of Enlightenment discourse, orientalism has been a carrier of basic Western notions of the European self and the non-Western other which generated unfalsifiable propositions about the superiority of Europeans to non-Europeans. In this way, orientalists participated in the elaboration of modern European cultural identity.'

The assertion of the uniqueness of the September 11 attacks is in a sense a moral statement: the enormity of these acts is such that they cannot (and should not) be contemplated with detached objectivity. But it is also a function of the overall narrative of self that defines modernity and the West's central position in it. The self-description of the West's uniqueness inhabits the multiple narratives which define Western identity, whether in Toynbee's historical narrative of a civilisation that appears to be immune from decline, in Weber's or Marx's take on the uniqueness and apparent finality of modern capitalism, or the related 'end of history' theses from Hegel onwards.

This self-narrative of uniqueness is a reflection of Pierre Bourdieu's 'unthinkable' assumptions about self and the world which are so self-evident to those involved that they need not be spelt out explicitly. They are also inherent in the concept of modernity, which, as Sardar notes, 'is nothing more than extrapolation and abstraction of certain specifics of the historic process of Western development'. The Western experience is thus used as the only yardstick with which to measure other experiences. This means also that the inbuilt prejudices of ages past were also built into the methodology and premises of the disciplines. When a typical Orientalist statement is made (for example, Elie Kedourie's claim that 'democracy is alien to the mind-set of Islam'), one accepts a host of assumptions and beliefs about 'Islam', 'the West', 'democracy', religion, society, history, culture and civilisation, which remain largely unexamined because they are taken for granted. It is the internal erosion of these certainties which had worked to undermine classical Orientalism.

The crisis was accentuated, to use the words of Burke III, by the rise of neoorientalism in 'the superheated ideological climate of the Reagan/Bush years', a turn that was characterised by an 'increased ideologisation of relations between the Middle East and the West' and 'a fear campaign which created the new category of "the Islamic terrorist", a useful supplement to that old standby, "the Arab terrorist"': 'overnight, Islamic culture became highly toxic as a subject of intellectual investigation. One way of understanding what happened to Middle East studies in the 1980s is to say, using the language of Pierre Bourdieu, that these changes inscribe the massive invasion of the intellectual field by the political field. In more familiar terms used by Said, it was an assertion of Orientalism (the discourse of power) over orien-talism (the discipline).' This can also be seen as a reflection of the general crisis of the post-Enlightenment 'state-centred liberal project' with its obses-sive tendency 'to quantify, map and control' and the implication that the 'kind of sociology of Islam that emerged is shaped to the deeply problematic history of the encounter in the West between religion and the state'.

This crisis has also precipitated, and was impacted by, what Richard Rorty describes in *Philosophy and Social Hope* as the 'important cultural war' in America (and elsewhere), pitting the 'progressivists' against the 'orthodox'. The former are those who continue to push for the US to progress along the trajectory defined by the Bill of Rights, the New Deal, the civil rights legislation and the feminist movement. The latter could be seen as 'the same honest, decent, blinkered, disastrous people who would have voted for Hitler in 1933'. Rorty, inspired by Thomas Kuhn, argues that scientific disciplines can be seen as alternating between movements 'leftward in revo-lutionary periods and rightward in stable, dull periods where you get what Kuhn called "normal science". One could add that the social sciences, like the media, also pass through phases where social turmoil and looming threats cause them to lose autonomy, but regain more autonomy in periods of relative stability and prosperity. The significant autonomy enjoyed by the social sciences (and humanities) in the past few decades is responsible for the proliferation of a variety of 'progressivist' opinions and approaches, including the much-debated postmodernist tendencies. The right wing has been attempting to fight this effervescence of 'unconventional' views for many years, and 9/11 has afforded a rare opportunity to mount a concerted attack on the gains of the 'progressivists'.

Orientalism and Liberal Paranoia

Then something amazing happened: the 'progressivists' (or at least some of them) decided to join hands with those potential Hitler voters. As we have seen, this convergence has preceded 9/11, as was symbolised by the Liber-man/Cheney alliance. And the focus and uniting factor became hatred and fear of Islam, Muslims and Arabs. The intersection of new aggressively-resurgent right with the old ethnocentric colonial frame of mind (neoconservatism plus Orientalism), now converged with the renegade, Islamophobic left. This marriage of convenience is not as outrageous as it appears, since the bulk of neoconservative elite were also ex-Trotskyites.

The onslaught of these forces on academia has highlighted another important feature of the supposedly self-constituted and socially legitimated 'scientific communities: that some of them are far less autonomous and free to pursue their own agendas than others. While most scientific communities have to justify their practices in terms of social utility, this utility in the case of the social sciences is much more closely linked to prevailing ideologies or even reigning regimes. The constitution of the communities and the selection of those who have a right to engage authoritatively in the debate are also more directly influenced by power.

As we have seen, the onslaught on 'Middle Eastern Studies' has taken the form of a 'guerrilla war' and quasi-terrorist sniping by rank outsiders and agitators, mainly politicians, assisted by people who confess to having been marginalised in the internal conversation within the disciplines. They are using tactics other than the usual 'scientific' approach of writing papers and debating in conferences, resorting instead to intimidation through media campaigns, mobilisation of mass opinion, manipulation of funding and appeals to the authorities, including the police, to intervene on their behalf. Here, ideology and power came out in the open in the bid to influence 'scientific' practice, with right wing pro-Israeli intellectuals launching an offensive against academia as a whole to bring it in line with the dominant political ideology.

This development has been helped along by a trend I would describe as 'liberal paranoia'. The trend is largely a liberal/leftists backlash against Islam which has its roots in the controversy surrounding the publication of Salman Rushdie's novel *The Satanic Verses* in 1988, and vociferous (sometimes violent) Muslim protests against it. The novel, described by Sardar as 'pure Orientalism aspiring to be art', popularised the familiar Orientalist anti-Islam diatribes, recasting them in a playful postmodernist guise. In this the novel reversed the trajectory of another fellow-British novelist-turned-Orientalist, V S Naipaul, who was more content with reproducing his own straight non-fiction Orientalist lore in the form of travelogues such as *Among the Believers* (1981). But then Naipaul was a right-wing author in any case, unlike Rushdie who claimed to belong to the progressive camp.

The progressives duly rallied to Rushdie's side, and chastised the Muslims for their backward rejection of the freedom of expression. But as Rushdie himself confirms in his *Vanity Fair* obituary of Hitchens, (February 2012), the latter, just like Berman, 'came to believe that the people who understood the dangers posed by radical Islam were on the Right... so... he made what looked to many people like a U-turn across the political highway to join forces with the warmakers of George W. Bush's administration.'

A number of other incidents confirmed the liberals in their anti-Muslim, and increasingly Islamophobic inclinations. Some, like Tony Blair (who many might no longer regard as liberal and even fewer as intellectual) bought the Orientalist ware lock, stock and barrel, and now religiously peddles the discourse on terrorism as a product of Islamic theology and culture. This position, as we have seen, was pushed to the limit in Paul Berman's description of the war against Islamist insurgencies as a war against totalitarianism.

Less weighty contributions from the likes of the *Daily Mail* columnist Melanie Phillips and the novelist Martin Amis moved in the same direction, combining traditional right wing contempt for poor immigrants and people from other cultures with purported defence of lofty liberal values those immigrants could never relate to. In one fell swoop, it has become fashionable to hold fascist views and claim to be the foremost defender of liberalism. These new 'liberals' see the impoverished immigrant and the persecuted people of Gaza (once described by Pipes as 'miserable... and deserve to be') as both the epitome of barbarism and backwardness and part of a conspiracy to Islamise America and the world! It is an astonishing combination of arrogance and insecurity not seen since the days of Hitler.

Orientalism has thus come to indirectly enjoy the support of the right and left in an overlapping consensus, which is not that strange. While the right wing departs from its usual prejudices and xenophobia vis-à-vis Islam, the left is hostile to religion in general. It was prepared to accept Muslims as an 'ethnic' group and defend them, as long they obliged by leaving their religious identity behind. But the left is even more intolerant of religious identity politics than the xenophobic right. No wonder then their attacks on Islam and Muslims have become even more virulent and blatantly racist than the attacks from the right.

What is intriguing about the shifts in recent intellectual debates about Islam is this remarkable role reversal, where racism becomes fashionable and respectable, and even presents itself as 'liberal' anti-totalitarian stance in defence of 'civilisation'. The attacks on multiculturalism (joined in late 2009 and early 2010 by the leaders of Germany, Britain and France who all made speeches about its 'failure') became, as Bhikhu Parekh rightly pointed out, a code for attacking Islam:

These developments reveal a deeper intellectual shift, putting the critique of post-Enlightenment social science on its head. Redundant became Said's Foucauldian systematic unmasking of the knowledge-power nexus at work at the mythic foundations of modern social science. There is no need to unmask anything anymore, since the "terror" inherent in this presumed social science, and the one being deployed to bring it under control, are coming together out there in the open for all to see, just as it was in the good old days of the Inquisition. In this contest over the "sacred" bastions of academia, all the gloves are off, and the social sciences are being enlisted openly as a form of sophisticated spin that is not even permitted to follow its own rules of production from which it derives legitimacy.

And this was only part of a global dumbing down of the intellectual conversation. In the preface to the 2007 edition of his book *Ideology*, Professor Terry Eagleton likened the views of Amis (who had joined him as 'Professor of Creative Writing' at Manchester University), to those of a British National party thug. This analogy may not be that wide off the mark. In an era where it has become acceptable, even fashionable, to hurl vulgar slurs at whole communities, even advocate ethnic cleansing, and still call oneself 'liberal', the BNP might sue for defamation. More to the point, the bullying tactics of the new paranoid 'liberals' are not restricted to making outrageous remarks and claims. As we have seen above, actual bullying also became the order of the day. From calling Said the 'Professor of Terror', to using tabloids, pressure groups and congressional Inquisitions to intimidate academics, the main objective of the new Islamophobic discourse is not winning intellectual arguments, but rabble-rousing and blatant incitement.

We only began to have the rudiments of what later came to be known as Western Civilisation when learning circles in Europe took a hint from their Muslim neighbours and stopped resolving intellectual disputes by burning the other guy on the stake.

It is not that there is not a lot in need of criticism in the House of Islam, for there is. But we all know the fine line between condemning Israeli excesses and sliding into anti-Semitic diatribes. The tirades of the Islamo-phobic do not help address the problems facing Muslim cities, and are not intended to do so. In fact, they exacerbate the crisis and are exploited by extremists to point to Western duplicity, where those preaching Western liberal values to others were the first to act in contravention of those values. In the famous Qu'ranic phrase, they recommend virtue to others, but over-look themselves.

But the Muslims are changing from within. Luckily for all of us, the Arabs are again teaching everybody how to fight for freedom. And about time too.

BERNARD LEWIS

Peter Clark

Fifty years ago, Oxford University Press, under the auspices of the Royal Institute for International Affairs (Chatham House), published Bernard Lewis's *The Emergence of Modern Turkey*. I read it at the time and was enthralled. I was about to live and work in Turkey and it furnished my mind with a comprehensive and comprehensible framework within which I viewed the country of my hosts and employers. While I was on that first visit to Turkey I travelled to the countries of the Arab Middle East. My own absorption in the region has continued ever since. I worked for many years in Arab countries, learnt the language and translated contemporary Arabic texts; I read, listened, observed, reflected and occasionally wrote on the history and politics of the region. Over the years I read most of Bernard Lewis's other work, and about every ten years I reread *The Emergence of Modern Turkey*. As I read and reread this last work I became increasingly irritated by it until I finally threw my copy at the wall in exasperation. I have since bought another copy with an introduction to the third edition which is revealing and, I think, justifies my disillusion.

Lewis has a most engaging style of writing. There are phrases that linger in the mind and it is not difficult to see how, as a young man, new to the area, I was beguiled. Indeed words and style are part of the key to understanding Lewis, for he has been a poet, originally a passionate lover of Hebrew poetry. One lesser known but relatively recent work of his is a collection of his own verse translations of classical Arabic, Hebrew, Turkish and Persian poetry into English. He has sensitivity to language and to the nuances of words. I have not been disillusioned by his writings on language or his argument concerning the need for historical Arabic dictionaries. Words have different meanings in different contexts. I continue to be impressed, but not necessarily convinced, by his writings such as *The Politi-*

cal Language of Islam. He is enlightening on words that have been used in political discourse in both Turkish and Arabic.

Lewis has also been excellent when writing monographs on medieval or early modern Islamic history, whether it is on the Assassins or on Ottoman marketing practices (as in *Studies in Classical and Ottoman Islam 7th–16th Centuries*). In a later volume of essays, in condemning a lot of *parti pris* history writing, he states that the first task of the historian is to find out what happened, then to ask how it happened and then why it happened. No one can disagree with that, although I do not think he has lived up to the standards he has set himself. He has also been illuminating on some nineteenth-century Europeans, not least Jewish Europeans, who have written on Arab and Islamic matters. There are some illuminating essays on this subject in the first 1973 edition of *Islam in History*. (Several amendments were made in the later 1993 edition). These Europeans defy the 'Orientalist' stereotype as defined by Edward Said. There were also westerners who made great non-judgmental efforts to understand the dynamics of the Ottoman Empire and its Islamic sources. I share Lewis's appreciation of Adolphus Slade.

However, over the second half of his career, Lewis has become a bitter, strident and tendentious critic of Muslims, seeing the different countries that make up the Muslim world as somehow dark, negative and 'anti-western'. It was he who in 1990 first promoted the term 'clash of civilisations', an extraordinarily vague and simply misleading, if not erroneous, view of the world. He has increasingly become an angry old man, albeit an elegant controversialist, a *feuilletoniste*. Books such as *What Went Wrong?* and *The Crisis of Islam* have been applauded by now discredited right wing elements in the United States. Was it academic vanity that allowed Bernard Lewis to be taken up by the neocons and the George W Bush government, to applaud the invasion of Iraq, expecting the Iraqi streets to welcome their American liberators with bouquets and open arms, and to herald Ahmed Chalabi as a potential Atatürk? Can we date the change in Lewis to the breakdown of his marriage and his emigration to the United States in 1974?

But let us get it all into context. Bernard Lewis was born in Stoke Newington, north London, in May 1916. Precocious and gifted, he considered a legal career but studied at the School for Oriental Studies, later the School of Oriental and African Studies (SOAS), and obtained a brilliant degree in 1936 at the age of twenty. He studied in France under the legendary Louis

Massignon and was appointed to the staff of SOAS in 1938. After war service in the British army and in intelligence he returned to SOAS in 1949 to become the first Professor of Near and Middle Eastern History.

His first research was on the Ismailis, and after the war he wished to continue his studies in Syria. But after the foundation of the State of Israel in 1948 there was suspicion of foreign pro-Israel Jewish researchers who were viewed as potential spies for the new state. Lewis therefore chose to undertake research in Ottoman history. The Ottoman archives had recently been opened up. They were (and are) an extraordinary treasury of information at all levels of Ottoman society, and have been quarried by Turkish and international scholars ever since. Lewis was one of the first to identify their value. During the 1950s he was commissioned by Chatham House to produce a work on modern Turkey and *The Emergence of Modern Turkey* was the result. Most of what was available to westerners interested in the developments in Turkey was to be found in journalism. A very few accounts by Turks, notably Halide Edib (*Memoirs*, 1926; *The Turkish Ordeal*, 1928; *Turkey Faces West*, 1930) and Mahmut Makal (*A Village in Anatolia*, 1954), explained what it was like for a Turk to undergo the revolution. Atatürk's *Speech* justifying the changes he had initiated was available in English, French and German translation, and some scholars, such as Kemal H Karpat and Geoffrey L Lewis, were beginning to publish work based on Turkish sources.

In the last fifty years there has been an exponential expansion in Turkish studies by Turkish, American and European scholars. So many corners of modern history have been explored. Bernard Lewis's book is still a considerable landmark in Turkish studies, and has moulded attitudes and influenced research since 1961. There was a second edition of *The Emergence of Modern Turkey*, with revisions, in 1967, and a third in 2002. He has in recent years followed up the book with a coffee-table hagiography of Mustafa Kemal, published in Turkey. *The Emergence of Modern Turkey* is still worth reading but with a health warning: reading this book can seriously damage your perspective.

Bernard Lewis's approach is like that of an old Whig historian of English history — G M Trevelyan or perhaps Macaulay. (One sentence, describing the eclipse of Istanbul when Ankara was declared the capital of the Turkish Republic is pure Macaulay: 'For nearly five centuries Istanbul had been the capital of an Islamic Empire; the pallid ghosts of a splendid past still flitted unhappily through the halls of the Saray and the Sublime Porte.') The title of the book is instructive. The history of the last century has been one of progress, a steady emergence from the darkness of the Ottoman Empire to the sunny secular uplands of the pro-western modern Turkish republic. The supreme act of political maturity was the voluntary transfer of power in 1950 by the Republican Peoples Party, the party of Kemal Atatürk, who had died twelve years earlier, to the Democratic Party, as a result of openly-contested democratic elections.

Atatürk is Turkey's William of Orange, even though he did not see the consummation of his revolution. There is much that is valid and positive in the career of Atatürk, and he has rightly been a beacon to other political leaders, and Lewis's celebration of Atatürk reflects the Kemalist orthodoxy of Turkey today. But there is also much in the book that is totally misleading and simply wrong.

The introduction to the third edition of 2002 has an extraordinarily tendentious political message attacking those who challenge this Kemalist orthodoxy: 'Opposition to the pro-Western foreign policy alignment came initially from what one might call modish pan-leftism — fashionable ideologies and postures, imported from Paris, London, and New York. These ideologies were of course opposed to the United States, to NATO, to capitalist economics, and to military bases other than those maintained at the time by the Soviet Union in its satellite territories. Such views commanded considerable support in intellectual and, more particularly, academic circles, where they achieved an ascendancy not unlike that which they, for a while, enjoyed in France.'

Here is the angry snarl of a grumpy old neocon. The term 'modish pan-leftism' is meaningless political rhetoric. The words 'fashionable' and 'postures' are void of meaning. The alleged positions ('postures') of the presumed opposition to Kemalism were all targets for the right wing ideologues of the United States of ten years ago. There is no attempt to examine what the opposition to Kemalist ideology is, or why it might be supported by large swathes of Turkish opinion, for all sorts of different reasons. He is insulting to people who do not share his rigid point of view. Above all, the paragraph lacks subtlety.

In the nine years since that introduction was written, the 'pan-leftist' case has become irrelevant. Opposition to Kemalism has taken many forms.

Many Turks have been unwilling to see their country responding to the wishes of foreign policy makers. The mildly Islamist government currently in power in Turkey, whose earlier manifestation under Necmettin Erbakan is reviewed by Bernard Lewis, has realigned Turkish foreign policy. For centuries Turkey was the hub of a political world that included the Turkic world, the Arab world and Iran. Modern Turkey is redefining its role in its own interests and not through the distorting lens of American power and domination. Turkish foreign policy in recent years has become pragmatic and mature. Good relations were built up with Iran and Syria. This did not mean that the Turkish government or the Turks endorsed the Shiite Iranian revolution or the Baathist policies of Syria. There were shared interests and these were pursued. There was no point in emphasising areas of divergence. Secular Syria has taken a similar approach to Islamist Iran.

It may be that Bernard Lewis has modified his stance. In an interview given to *The Wall Street Journal* in May 2011, he argued that the threat to democracy in Turkey was the creeping re Islamisation of society under the present government. (Lewis is in step with the American right in seeking a bipolar view of the world; instead of 'pan-leftism', the enemy is now Islamism.) Turkey and Iran could change places in ten years time, Lewis thinks. By which time Lewis will be 105.

Back to the book. Bernard Lewis is fair in tracing the antecedents to the Atatürk revolution. There were Ottoman reformers and the Young Turks of the period between 1908 and the First World War who anticipated some of the major reforms of the 1920s. But it was the implosion of the Empire that gave Mustafa Kemal (from 1935 Kemal Atatürk) his chance to reshape the country in a secular way, and on western European models. Yet he was initially ready to co-opt the forces of Islam, both politically and personally. He was keen to ensure he had mullahs' blessings in Ankara in the first years of the revolution, and when he divorced his progressive wife, it was under Islamic law and not according to western codes.

Of course, much of *The Emergence of Modern Turkey* has been superseded by research and newer perspectives. In the last fifty years there has been greater emphasis on social history. Lewis writes well about administrative history, in particular the changes in government procedures from the nineteenth century through to the 1940s. This may be a result of his early legal interests. He is also reasonable on Sultan Abdülhamid II, who always had a bad press.

He was not the monochrome oppressive reactionary of liberal journalists of his time. This Sultan was a reformer, presiding over a wide expansion in education and public services – as well as an expanded secret police sector. But if his reformism had European models it was the work of Metternich or Bismarck, rather than the politics of the French Third Republic.

But the research of scholars such as Suraiya Faroqhi, Selim Deringil, Caroline Finkel, Donald Quataert, Mükrü Hanioğlu, Halil İnalcık, İlber Ortaylı, Feroz Ahmad, Zeynep Çelik, Erik J Zürcher, Stefan Weber and many others have made many of Lewis's judgments of later Ottoman society seem simplistic and superficial.

For example, seeing the Ottoman world as simply an aggregate of 'minorities' in a millet system is misleading. Society was as much horizontal as vertical. Poor people of all communities shared the same space. Elites also shared the same space. Of course confessional allegiance was important. There were community leaders who were expected to speak and negotiate on behalf of the community. There were also instances when there was a breakdown of sectarian coexistence. But such instances were the exception. The Eastern Mediterranean world for at least two thousand years has been multi-ethnic and multicultural and has flourished best when there has been an acceptance of the other. The Ottoman Empire for hundreds of years formalised this mutuality. Confessionalism determined where you worshipped and whom you married, but not always where you lived. People of a working-class quarter of Istanbul like Balat – Jews, Armenians, Muslims and Greeks – had far more in common with each other than the people of each community had with their confessional elites. In the Balkans poor Christians and Jews often had recourse to Islamic courts, which were seen as more humane than the courts of their own communities. This was especially the case with issues of divorce. In nineteenth-century Damascus, wealthy Muslims, Christians and Jews all adopted 'western' dress and furnishings at about the same time.

Lewis talks about 'minorities'. In twentieth-century political discourse this immediately delegitimises the Christians and Jews of the Empire. Yet the expression would have meant little to any theorists of the Ottoman Empire. The preferred term to describe Muslims and non-Muslims was 'elements', *anasir*. The non-Muslim communities until the nineteenth century did not have to be defensive, as minorities. They had an integral role in the working of the Empire.

Lewis, in his distaste for Muslim traditions, also misses what seems to me to be one of the most significant social phenomena that promoted cohesion in Ottoman society, the *külliye*. This was the huge Muslim complex — Süleymaniye in Istanbul is the supreme example and model — around a mosque, with schools, hospitals, soup-kitchens, caravanserais, baths, and a souk. All would be *waqf* property, an inalienable endowment. (Jews and Christians could also have *waqfs*.) The *waqfiya*, the document stating the conditions of the endowment, would prescribe how revenue from the shops and baths should be distributed. Revenues from Aleppo, for example, were assigned to other places in the Empire – the capital, the holy cities of the Hijaz or the birth-city of the founder of the *waqf*. It was a mechanism for redistribution of wealth. (The best explanation of how it worked is in Heghnar Zeitlian Watenpaugh's book on Aleppo: *The Image of an Ottoman City*, 2004.) Indeed Lewis does not see how architecture, urban space and social developments were closely and positively linked. He has nothing, for example, about fountains and the provision of fresh water, socially beneficial endowments or the surviving visual evidence of the 'unwestern' links between public works and Muslim legal provisions.

In his account of the nineteenth-century Ottoman realms he tells the story of the steady 'westernisation'. Throughout there is the idea that 'westernisation' is an unquestioned ideal, as if a country without westernisation is somehow lacking, like an adolescent who has not reached maturity. This begs a thousand questions. Indeed it seems that whatever Lewis approves of is *ipso facto* 'western' and good.

There is also the assumption of a 'decline' in the Ottoman Empire. This view is vindicated, it is inferred, by the Ottoman defeat in the First World War. The Empire's collapse after its defeat needed Atatürk to reassemble what he could of the fragments. Decline is thus seen primarily in terms of military strength. Of course the First World War was disastrous for the Ottoman Empire (as Mustafa Kemal realised at the time). From the Turkish point of view it was not a four year war, but a period of continuous warfare from 1911 to 1923. Although there was a strong German political and military presence in Turkey in the years up to 1914, it was not absolutely certain that Turkey would be on Germany's side. There had also been British support for the Ottoman navy. And the Ottomans did not perform too badly during the war. They repelled a combined British-French-Australian-New Zealand assault on Gallipoli, captured a British-Indian army in Mesopotamia, pushed back Russia in eastern Anatolia, and extended the Empire's territory in southern Arabia. Moreover the Ottoman Empire was not alone in collapsing: two other multi-ethnic Empires had a not totally dissimilar experience during and after the First World War – the Habsburg and the Romanov.

Underlying the whole book is the idea that there is a western civilisation that is separate from (and better than) the civilisation of Turkey's 'Muslim neighbours'. The story of Turkey's emergence has been its ability to shake off the shackles of this implicitly fatally flawed lesser civilisation. The contrast between the two civilisations is illustrated in 'the difference between the Western novel and the Oriental tale, Western portraiture and Oriental miniature, Western history and Oriental annals, Western government and Oriental rule – and perhaps between Western restlessness and Oriental repose'.

Lewis constantly denigrates some Ottoman achievements that have no western source. Recent research by Gábor Ágoston (*Guns for the Sultan*, 2005) has modified Lewis's idea of Ottoman technical ignorance and inferiority. And Lewis's comments that 'the beginnings of Western music in Turkey were military' reveals extraordinary ignorance. Yes, Donizetti Pasha trained the Turkish military bands. But the Turks needed few lessons in music and the military. Sultan Mehmet II's soldiers were spurred on to take Istanbul in 1453 by military bands.

In the Ottoman Empire, Lewis argues, 'Muslims knew only four professions – government, war, religion, and agriculture. Industry and trade were left in large measure to the non-Muslim subjects.' But the economies of many, if not most, of the cities of the Empire were dominated by Muslim trading families. It was the 'non-Muslim subjects' who cornered the external trade, but most economic activity was within the Empire. Moreover, there is nothing alien to Islam in commerce. Take the example of the Prophet Muhammad!

Underlying all is the idea of an inevitable conflict between Islam and the West. The expression 'the clash of civilisations' appears early in *The Emergence of Modern Turkey*, when he refers to 'the ancient clash of Islam and Christendom'. He is more explicit and nonsensical when he writes that 'the clash of civilisations in history does not usually culminate in a marriage of selected best elements, but rather in the promiscuous cohabitation of good, bad, and indifferent alike.' Throughout the book Lewis uses loaded language about movements or ideas that he personally disapproves of. He does not explain why people may think or act in a particular way. He cannot empathise with diversity or streams of thought or activity that deviate from the whiggish narrative that he imposes on the story of Turkey over the last two centuries. So there are loaded dismissive words and phrases — that could equally be applied, *mutatis mutandis*, to him. He writes of 'the seductive power of Western revolutionary ideology' and 'heady visions'. Sultan Abdülhamid's pan-Islamist policies led to him sending 'emissaries' who were 'stirring up Muslim opinion' and 'taking full advantage'. There is a danger from Islamist revivalism: 'If simple reaction has its way, much of the work of the last century will be undone, and Turkey will slip back into the darkness from which she has so painfully emerged.'

After my latest reading of Bernard Lewis's pioneering book, I have resisted the temptation to throw it at the wall in spite of all I have said. *The Emergence of Modern Turkey* — notwithstanding certain sections that are instructive — is in the end a distortion of scholarship, a corruption of history. Perhaps Bernard Lewis should have stuck to the law, or to poetry.

GLOBAL PALESTINE

John Collins

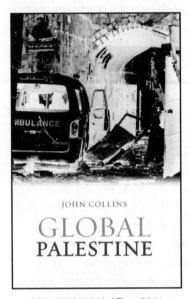

JOHN COLLINS

GLOBAL PALESTINE

9781849041812 / Dec. 2011

£15.99 paperback / 240pp

'*Global Palestine* tackles an obvious but under-studied question: why is Palestine so internationally significant? The answers provided herein blend sharp analysis of global politics, deep knowledge of local struggles and transnational solidarity movements, and clear understanding of the ways in which the Israeli state wields its power at home and abroad.' — **Lisa Hajjar, Associate Professor of Sociology, University of California, Santa Barbara**

Global Palestine offers a unique perspective on one of the world's most enduring political controversies by exploring a deceptively simple question: what does Palestine mean for the globe? The book begins from three overlapping premises. First, contemporary Palestine is the site of an ongoing project of settler colonisation. Second, as a growing movement of international solidarity indicates, Palestine's global importance seems to be increasing in inverse proportion to the amount of territory actually controlled by Palestinians. Third, understanding why and how Palestine matters globally requires situating the 'local' struggle over Palestine in relation to a series of global processes that shape the conditions within which all of us live our lives, including the four processes that underpin this book: colonisation, securitisation, acceleration, and occupation. Far from simply being influenced by these processes, Palestine has served as a laboratory for many of them, pushing them forward in profound ways, and Collins' analysis reveals clues to a series of emerging global conditions. Approaching Palestine in this way enables us to take a fresh look at the world's politics of violence, resistance, and solidarity from the perspective of what Walter Benjamin called 'the tradition of the oppressed.'

41 GREAT RUSSELL ST, LONDON, WC1B 3
WWW.HURSTPUB.CO.UK
WWW.FBOOK.COM/HURSTPUBLISHERS
020 7255 2201

TWENTY-FIRST-CENTURY CRUSADERS

Arun Kundnani

In September 2009, as the organisation was preparing for a major demonstration in Manchester the following month, the English Defence League (EDL) released a video on YouTube entitled, 'English Defence League response to the lies of the UAF and some elements of the press'. (The UAF, Unite Against Fascism, is an anti-fascist group active in countering English Defence League demonstrations.) The video was filmed in a disused warehouse in Luton. Lined against one wall of a large empty room are around twenty men dressed in black, their faces concealed behind balaclavas. One reads a prepared statement, while another sets fire to a Nazi flag that has been hoisted in front of the men. The EDL spokesman says burning this flag will prove his organisation is not a far-Right group motivated by racism but simply opposes those he calls 'Islamic extremists'. Addressing himself to these extremists, he announces: 'We the English Defence League will contest your kind, as our forefathers did, relentlessly pursuing you in our quest to see all sharia banished from our great democratic country. Long live the free.' Anyone can join the EDL if they share this stance, he says, even anti-extremist Muslims. Behind the men hang placards with the slogans, 'Black and white, unite and fight' and 'We support Israel's right to exist'. After the spectacle of the flag-burning, the camera zooms in on one section of EDL members, to demonstrate from the skin colour of their forearms that this gathering includes black men as well as white. In the description that accompanies the video on YouTube, a supporter has written: 'How anyone can call this group far right fascist Nazis is beyond belief. Since when were Nazi groups multi-race?!? It's not racist to oppose Islamic Extremism!'

The EDL had been in existence for just a few months when this video was released. It had been formed in response to a demonstration in Luton in March 2009, organised by Anjem Choudary, the leader of a small group that has had various names since its original incarnation, al-Muhajiroun, was disbanded in 2004. Choudary's protest against a parade through Luton town centre of British troops recently returned from Afghanistan prompted a furious reaction from bystanders; a coalition of angry locals, members of football 'firms' and seasoned far-Right activists came together. Making good use of the online and offline networks that already linked football firms and the far Right across the country, and picking up a significant number of young people who seemed to relate, via Facebook and YouTube, to its style of politics, the EDL was soon organising demonstrations in several towns and cities across England, attracting up to 2,000 people. The slogans at these early demonstrations included: 'Muslim bombers off our streets', 'Extremist Muslims go to hell', 'British voters say no to sharia law', 'LBC [Luton Borough Council] sell out cowards', 'Our troops are heroes', 'We demand a St George's Day parade', 'Ban preachers of hate', 'NF [National Front] go to hell' and, more prosaically, 'We are sick of this shit'. Their demands included a ban on the building of mosques, a ban on the wearing of the burka, a ban on renaming Christmas and a new criminal offence of calling for the introduction of sharia law.

The EDL's September 2009 video is striking for a number of reasons. Firstly, the image of a burning flag, accompanied by a line of balaclava-clad men, one of whom reads a prepared statement declaring the group's commitment to fighting a mortal enemy, places the YouTube clip within a genre of video communiqués issued by various terrorist organisations since the 1970s. In its style of presentation, the EDL video imitates the very extremism it ostensibly opposes. And there is more unintended mimicry when one of the reporters who has been invited to the warehouse suggests the EDL's appearance in balaclavas might seem intimidating. The EDL leader replies by saying: 'It's exactly the same as a burka.'

Secondly, in its graphic imagery of anti-Nazism, its reference to 'forefathers' who also fought against extremism (presumably in the second world war) and, most strikingly, in its appropriation of the socialist slogan, 'Black and white, unite and fight' (no longer against the bourgeoisie but against Muslim radicals), the video plunders anti-fascist imagery in an attempt to construct a popular front against 'Islamic extremism'. Similarly, the reference to Israel's right to exist aims at announcing a rejection of the anti-Semitism that was central to far-Right politics in the twentieth century, and at establishing a new alignment of forces to confront the Islamic extremist enemy. Hence the formation within the EDL of a 'Jewish division', a 'gay division' and the prominence of a Sikh activist, Guramit Singh, on EDL demonstrations. The EDL thus went to great lengths to present itself as an organisation that was not racist, and able to include within its ranks groups who are normally the targets of far-Right violence. The concept of 'extremism' was central to this positioning. By claiming to attack Muslim extremism rather than Muslims per se, the EDL hoped to dispel the suspicion that it was just another fringe, racist, far-Right group.

In another EDL video, released around the same time to promote its October 2009 demonstration in Manchester, another set of symbols is mobilised. To a pounding soundtrack, the video opens with pictures of sword-wielding crusaders, the red crosses on their shields and breasts mirroring the St George cross that forms the EDL logo. 'The English lion has awoken,' announces the video. 'The time has come to defend our land from 1,400 years of Jihad that has finally washed up upon our shores.' This is followed by a series of images of newspaper headlines, which are arranged to suggest that Britain is on its way to 'Islamification' within thirty years. 'Do you want your children and grandchildren to grow up under Islamic rule in this your Christian homeland? Second class citizens in the place your forefathers fought and died for for you to live free.' The viewer is told that 'Islam religiously teaches Moslems to convert Nations into Islamic rule', and that the government has been too politically correct to face up to this danger. Only a movement of English patriots taking to the streets can save the nation from sharia. The Manchester demonstration will be a 'day of reckoning'.

Apart from its crusader imagery (which, given the anti-Semitic violence of the crusades, tends to undermine the EDL's claim to be inclusive of Jews, let alone non-extremist Muslims), the power of this video lies in its sampling of newspaper headlines. There is little in the way of commentary or interpretation added to the headlines. Indeed, none is needed – the *Express*, *Mail* and *Star* newspapers articulate a narrative wholly consistent with the EDL's own, with their daily diet of cartoon Muslim fanatics, secret sharia courts, forced Islamic conversions, no-go areas for non-Muslims, all tolerated by a politically correct, liberal, multicultural elite that has even abolished Christmas so as not to offend the enemy within.

Muscular liberals?

Most discussion of the EDL centres upon the question of whether it is just another right-wing extremist organisation, opportunistically using popular concern over Islamist radicalism to mask an old-fashioned racist and violent politics, or whether it represents, at least for some supporters, a legitimate attempt to oppose totalitarian Islamism. In a report for the liberal think-tank Demos, for example, Jamie Bartlett and Mark Littler conclude that, though some EDL supporters use opposition to militant Islam as 'a cover for more sinister or intolerant views', many are genuine anti-extremists who carefully distinguish between moderate and extremist Muslims; therefore, main-stream politicians should 'engage with those who are sincere democrats, and isolate those who are not'. Labour Party advisor Maurice Glasman seems to agree with this position, saying in an interview with *Progress* magazine in April 2011 that we should listen to supporters of the EDL.

There is ample evidence that the EDL's opposition to Muslim extremism goes hand in hand with overt racism. Since its formation in 2009, there have been Nazi salutes, racist chanting and racial violence at EDL demonstra-tions. Activism for the EDL overlaps significantly with membership of the racist British National Party (BNP). Indeed, both of the EDL's senior lead-ers, Stephen Yaxley-Lennon (aka Tommy Robinson) and his cousin Kevin Carroll, are former members of the BNP and have been convicted of crimi-nal violence. The 'West Midlands Division' of the EDL have taken photo-graphs of themselves standing in front of Ulster Volunteer Force flags, carrying imitation firearms.

When EDL leaders claimed in 2009 that they had no problems with Mus-lims who rejected extremism, it was hardly reassuring. Two years later, they were making threats of violence against all Muslims. At a demonstration on 3 September 2011 through the largely Muslim area of Tower Hamlets, east London (a favourite location for far-Right mobilisation since the 'Battle of Cable Street' in 1936), Yaxley-Lennon told the crowd:

We are here today to tell you, quite loud, quite clear, every single Muslim watching this video on YouTube: on 7/7, you got away with killing and maiming British citi-zens. You got away with it. You better understand that we have built a network from one end of this country to the other end. We will not tolerate it. And the Islamic community will feel the full force of the English Defence League if we see any of our citizens killed, maimed or hurt on British soil ever again.

Again, it is notable that the logic of Yaxley-Lennon's statement is identical to that of his purported enemies. In the video message of Mohammed Siddique Khan, leader of the suicide bombers who carried out the 7/7 attacks on London's transport system, he says: 'Until we feel security, you will be our targets.' Both Khan and Yaxley-Lennon use the same argument to justify violence against a whole population that is deemed responsible for the violence of some of its members.

By late 2011, the EDL's alibi of anti-extremism had worn thin. On 16 November, it posted on its official Facebook page a message that differed little from the familiar script of the far right:

In the last 66 years we as a nation, as a race have had our national identity stolen from us by politicians who have forced us to accept multiculturalism. They have and still are practicing cultural genocide on their own people, despite warnings that we will not accept it. They have forced us to accept the dilution of our heritage and history by the implementation of laws which will stop us from rising up, even if that's just to voice an opinion. Any action which has the aim or effect of depriving us of our integrity as distinct peoples, or of our cultural values or ethnic identities. Any form of population transfer which has the aim or effect of violating or undermining any of the rights of the native or indigenous people. Any form of assimilation or integration by other cultures or ways of life imposed on us by legislative, administrative or other measures is cultural genocide. And unless we find our backbone and stand up to the ones who are committing crimes against the English people we shall continue to be subjected to slavery by a British elite aided by outside influences whose only intention is to destroy us from within and wipe us out as a race.

Any pretence of trying to organise a multi-ethnic opposition to Islamist extremism is here abandoned. Instead, the language of race is openly employed, post-war immigration is presented as cultural genocide, and a pro-multiculturalist elite is held responsible for destroying the English race. From the perspective of this post, there is little to separate the EDL from more traditional far-Right parties.

Whatever overlaps exist, it would be wrong to see the EDL as simply a mask for more familiar forms of far-Right, racist politics. Equally, it would be a mistake to think the EDL's distinction between moderate and extremist

Muslims, even when properly upheld, does not involve it in a politics of race. What both these positions ignore is the way racism itself has changed over the last twenty years, as a result of the end of the cold war and the launching of a global war on terror. Following the collapse of the Soviet Union, Islam became, as Samuel Huntington put it, the 'ideal enemy'. 'Radical Islam' was more than just a new totalitarian threat that could, like communism, be invoked by Western governments and commentators to justify militarism and denials of civil liberties. Whereas communism was an ideological enemy emerging from within the traditions of the European Enlightenment, 'Islamic extremism' seemed to offer new cold warriors an enemy that was not only an ideological alternative to liberal capitalism but also a cultural rejection of Western modernity itself, combining the cold war fear of political extremism with the Orientalist fear of 'fanaticism'.

From the perspective of the new cold warriors, traditional Muslims live hermetically sealed within their cultures, their lives entirely determined by them, whereas 'we' exist outside of any specific culture in the neutral space of universality, able to consume culture but not be consumed by it. Muslims enclosed in their culture can only ever produce a politics of communal backwardness; only those who have freed themselves from cultural deter-minism are able to join liberal civilisation. Political conflicts over foreign policy, discrimination, poverty, freedom of speech and religion, are thus no longer regarded as matters of power, interests and social structures but seen as symptoms of an inevitable, underlying conflict between Islam's regressive cultural identity and Western liberal values. The only acceptable agency for Muslims is the rejection of their cultural practices in order to become 'free like us'. As Gavan Titley and Alana Lentin note in their recent study of 'crisis of multiculturalism' discourses in Europe, this culturalist framework assumes liberal values, such as gender equality, are 'a property of a "com-munity" of white European secularism; that those in but not of Europe are always already excluded from this state of being, and lack the capacities to define and organise their own liberations'. Using the language of culture in this way to define a 'Muslim problem' produces the same outcomes that more obviously racial discourses once achieved; cultural tropes, such as wearing a hijab, 'can just as easily serve as racial signifiers as skin colour'. It also has the effect of projecting political and social conflicts, for example over the Iraq war or the claims of Western Muslims to equal citizenship, onto a cultural plane, where they can be dismissed more easily as the product of Islamic extremism.

This racialisation of 'Muslimness' is at the heart of the global war on terror. It is perfectly possible within this culturalist framework to erect a distinction between 'moderate' and 'extremist' Muslims, and thereby repudiate charges of a generalised prejudice against all Muslims: on this view, moderates are defined as those Muslims who have left behind their own traditional Islamic culture to adopt 'our values' of liberal reason. There are a variety of ways of phrasing this idea, from talk of needing to promote 'moderate Islam' over 'extremist Islam' to the more essentialist slogan: 'There is no such thing as moderate Islam, only moderate Muslims.' But, however it is worded, this framework is always a trap for Muslims labelled moderate. Constantly scrutinised for evidence they really have freed themselves from the cultural baggage of their Islamic origins, the moderate Muslim cannot win: fully embracing liberal reason as an equal citizen is fine, so long as one's reason does not lead to actual criticism of the state and society of which one is a part; at that point, the anxieties of the culturalist are stirred and accusations of infiltration or disloyalty follow. On the other hand, trying to fuse liberal and Islamic perspectives in some form of multicultural accommodation provokes accusations of duplicity and hidden agendas. This leaves one way out: to circumscribe one's critical faculties so that 'citizenship' means the enthusiastic expression of loyalty to Western societies and states. Thus, the liberalism that culturalists demand allegiance to is not so much a set of Enlightenment principles but a 'way of life', a Burkean 'inheritance' of founding moral habits, to which all political differences must be constrained for the sake of preserving Western identity. An exaggerated dividing line between an 'alien' Muslim identity and this liberal 'way of life' serves as the basis for reifying populations into fixed, immutable 'natural' identities – the hallmarks of a process of racism. That the solution to the problem presented by this alien Muslim identity is always to be found in the use of coercion indicates that it has been made into a symbol of racial difference and that its bearers are not being accorded their own rationality and citizenship. Yet precisely because this framework differs from familiar patterns of racialisation associated with skin colour, it can associate itself with the defence of a liberal 'way of life' and appear 'post-racial'. This culturalist discourse is central to the EDL's programme and explains the paradox of an apparently far-Right organisation that is able to tentatively include black supporters and invoke 'liberal ideals', such as women's rights, gay rights, 'democratic accountability' and 'human rights', in fighting against a totalitarian 'political and social ideology'.

According to conventional wisdom, the mobilisation of far-Right groups in Europe has pressured centrist politicians into adopting more xenophobic positions, leading to far-Right ideas entering the mainstream. But the example of the EDL suggests the flow of ideology is more in the opposite direction. The EDL is a movement that takes the culturalist ideology of the official war on terror and gives it organisational form on the streets. It takes literally the government's proposition that there is a war on Islamic extremism. From the government's Preventing Violent Extremism programme, it absorbs the notion that the enemy in this war is not a few individuals engaged in violence but an ideology embedded in Muslim communities. Likewise, the notion that Muslims can be categorised as extremist or moderate, according to their allegiance to Western values, is taken from statements of government policy. And from the repeated ministerial speeches attacking an imagined multiculturalist orthodoxy (most recently David Cameron's February 2011 speech in Munich), the EDL has taken its belief that state multiculturalism is holding back the fight against Muslim extremism. All it adds of its own is the thought that the politicians running the war are too soft and cowardly, still too caught up in multicultural platitudes, to fight it properly, particularly on the home front – the streets of England – where it will fill the gap with its own form of militancy. In its criticism of the state, the EDL uses the state's own discourse against it. This suggests the most appropriate analogy for the EDL is not the BNP but the anti-communist John Birch Society and Minutemen militia of the 1950s and 1960s, who appropriated the US's official cold war ideology and turned it against the government with the accusation that communist infiltration had weakened its willingness to take on the enemy, and out of this parasitical populism forged an often violent, far-Right movement. Just as the activists of the John Birch Society were convinced that fluoridation of water was a communist plot (a theory wonderfully mocked in Stanley Kubrick's *Dr Strangelove*), so the EDL bloggers warn of the 'creeping sharia' of halal food being offered on England's high streets. Conspiracy theory is essential to the EDL ideology because only if the government can be presented as secretly in league or complicit with the enemy is there any need for the EDL to fight their own version of the war on terror.

From Jewish conspiracy theory to Islamic conspiracy theory

Post-war British fascism was never just a matter of hating minorities. It was also an ideology that sought to explain and give order to social dislocation and the depredations felt by the working class, through a rival narrative to that of the Left. To achieve this, it presented non-white immigration as an alien corruption of the purity of the nation; but it paid equal attention to the ruling class that had allowed this to happen, a betrayal which far-Right ideology explained in terms of a Jewish conspiracy theory. What appeared to be a British ruling class was, in fact, a mirage; real power lay with the secret Jewish cabal that pulled the strings of international finance, the media and the revolutionary Left, as supposedly revealed in *The Protocols of the Learned Elders of Zion*, the forged Tsarist document purporting to show how Jews manipulated world events to their advantage. While far-Right street activism involved racist violence against non-whites, far-Right ideology saw the real problem as lying elsewhere: the Jews and their hidden agenda of destroying national identity by fostering the immigration and mixing of other races. As David Edgar put it in his 1977 analysis of the politics of the National Front (NF), the far Right 'blames the Jews for the blacks'. Even as popular racism against Asians and African-Caribbeans was the means by which young people were recruited, anti-Semitism remained a necessary ideological component, because only Jews could play the role of the secret source of economic and political power that had weakened and corrupted the nation. To this extent, British fascist parties such as the NF and the BNP were correctly described as Nazi in their ideology.

Since assuming the leadership of the BNP in 1999, Nick Griffin has sought to downplay this neo-Nazi legacy. Perhaps he still believes that Jews secretly control the media – as his 1997 pamphlet *Who are the Mindbenders?* argued. But publicly he has tried to re-model the party along the lines of more successful European counterparts such as the Front National in France, using the language of defending British cultural identity (rather than white racial identity) against a ruling elite that wants to destroy it through immigration, multiculturalism and appeasement of the Muslim enemy within. Instead of talk of a Jewish conspiracy, there is the idea that those in power are too 'cosmopolitan' to have the real interests of the British people at heart, while Islamic militancy is invoked to illustrate the dangers of immigration, capitalising on the Islamophobia of post-9/11 Britain. This message, of course, resonates effectively with many voters – it is, after all, no different from what has been shouted from a thousand newspaper columns since 9/11, and echoed, albeit in a more genteel form, by both Labour and Conservative ministers. Since 2001, the narrowing gap between the rhetoric of the BNP and mainstream political discourse has meant that, despite the BNP's active membership remaining dominated by long-standing neo-Nazis and violent racists, it has been able to dramatically increase its electoral support in local council and European parliament elections. By June 2004, the BNP was able to secure 808,200 votes across the UK in elections to the European parliament; by 2009, the BNP had won two seats in Brussels.

The significance of this can best be grasped if we recall the BNP's first election success, in 1993, when Derek Beackon won a seat on Tower Hamlets council in east London with the slogan 'rights for whites'. At the time, his election was considered shocking enough to prompt a mass campaign that united mainstream politics against him, removing him from office the following year. A key part of that campaign was the argument that voting for the Labour Party rather than the BNP was a better way of addressing issues of concern, such as housing. Since 2003, the BNP has had at least ten councillors in office at any one time, with the real possibility of winning control of a borough or city council, such as Burnley's. But the response of the political mainstream over the last decade has been different from the early 1990s. The Labour Party, having 'modernised' from 1994, has lost credibility as a vehicle for addressing working-class political concerns; activists on doorsteps who want to dissuade would-be BNP voters are thus unable to offer a positive alternative. Moreover, the current message from mainstream politics and popular newspapers is not that the BNP is fundamentally wrong but that it is exploiting 'legitimate grievances' that are better addressed by responsible politicians within the mainstream. If the best mainstream argument against the BNP is that it is irresponsible, then it is hardly surprising it attracts substantial support among the large numbers of people who see mainstream politics itself as devoid of moral responsibility. The weakness of this strategy was illustrated when Labour minister Jack Straw debated Nick Griffin on the BBC's *Question Time* in 2009. While Griffin himself was discredited, Straw was unable to attack the BNP's policies on multiculturalism and immigration. As Gary Younge noted in the *Guardian*, 'since New Labour's politics enabled the BNP, it is in no position to disable it.' In the last few years, the BNP's organising capacity has been severely reduced, firstly by the leaking of its membership list and, secondly, by the financial burden of defending itself against a legal challenge to its racist membership policy. But these tactics targeted the messenger not the message, allowing others to pick up from where the BNP had left off.

As it turned out, the EDL was well placed to do so. It has not organised as a conventional political party and has no formal members, so it is less vulnerable to the tactics that have been partially effective against the BNP. More significantly, the EDL has been able to tailor its ideology to current circumstances, because it owes its entire outlook to the war on terror. The BNP's opportunistic exploitation of Islamophobia since 9/11 carried it to a level of electoral support unimaginable in the 1990s. But, by virtue of its core membership, the party remains tethered to the neo-Nazi tradition and so, unlike the EDL, cannot fully realise the potential of the post-9/11 context.

Given anti-Semitism's centrality to the European far Right of the twentieth century, the EDL's new relationship to right-wing Zionism is the most striking indicator of its break with conventional fascist ideology. Along with counterparts in other parts of Europe, the EDL not only eschews anti-Semitism but actively embraces militant Zionists in the defence of the West against its Islamist enemy. Historically, the far Right in Europe tended to prefer the Palestinian cause, for purely anti-Semitic reasons. But the new culturalist politics of the war on terror has reversed this position, with Israel seen as a Western bridgehead within enemy territory.

In Belgium, the Flemish nationalist Vlaams Belang (VB) party – formed by members of the neo-fascist Vlaams Blok after it received a 2004 ban for promoting racism – has built links with the Israeli Right and succeeded in gaining the support of a minority of Antwerp's Jewish voters. Yet the VB is rooted in anti-Semitism and neo-Nazism: in 1988, the party's leader, Filip Dewinter, paid his respects to the Nazi soldiers buried in Belgium and, in 2001, he opened a speech with an oath used by the SS. But now Islamophobia has substituted for anti-Semitism and Dewinter visits Israel to meet right-wing members of the Knesset. In 2005, he told the Israeli newspaper *Ha'aretz*:

Islam is now the No. 1 enemy not only of Europe, but of the entire free world. After communism, the greatest threat to the West is radical fundamentalist Islam. There are already 25–30 million Muslims on Europe's soil and this becomes a threat. It's a real Trojan horse. Thus, I think that an alliance is needed between Western Europe and the State of Israel. I think we in Western Europe are too critical of Israel and we should support Israel in its struggle to survive. I think we should support Israel more than we do because its struggle is also very important for us.

In the Netherlands, Pim Fortuyn pioneered a new form of far-Right populism founded on defending liberal values against 'Islamification', his own open homosexuality indicating the distinctiveness of this politics from the traditional far Right (an innovation the EDL's 'LGBT division' later drew on). Fortuyn's party became the largest on Rotterdam's council before he was murdered by an animal rights activist in 2002. Geert Wilders, the leader of the third largest political party in Holland, has continued this new form of politics with the Islamophobic video *Fitna* and his call for a ban on the Qur'an. Wilders is another regular visitor to Israel, where he argues for annexing the West Bank and creating a Palestinian state in Jordan. 'Without Judea and Samaria, Israel cannot protect Jerusalem,' he says. When Wilders visited London in March 2010, the EDL organised a demonstration to welcome him. A group also travelled to Amsterdam to meet him there but were chased away by Dutch anti-fascists.

Like Wilders and Dewinter, the EDL has highlighted its Jewish support as a badge of 'post-racialism'. But the EDL's Jewish division is of more than just symbolic value. Its leader Roberta Moore connected the EDL to far-Right Jewish groups in the US, such as the Jewish Task Force, led by Victor Vancier (national chairman in the 1970s of the terrorist Jewish Defence League), and gave it the credibility to forge links with Pamela Geller, the New York-based Islamophobic blogger, and her Stop the Islamisation of America group. In September 2010, EDL leaders attended protests in lower Manhattan against the Park 51 community centre, named the 'Ground Zero victory mosque' by Geller; construction of the centre was abandoned, largely as a result of her campaign. A month after this visit, Rabbi Nachum Shifren, a Tea Party activist who believes that 'the Muslim onslaught is at the gates', came to

London to speak at an EDL rally, where he announced: 'We will never surrender to the sword of Islam.' Around the same time, the EDL was noticed by US neoconservatives. The Hudson Institute, part of the Israel lobby in Washington, DC, published an article describing 'members of the EDL holding their flags with pride, putting their arms around men and women of every age and ethnicity,' adding, 'it seemed that the nationalism of the EDL was a cousin of American nationalism, in which everyone can be proud of his nation, and of being a citizen, under the flag of the nation.'

To US Islamophobes, Britain had long appeared the most 'Islamised' nation in an 'Islamising' continent. For them, London had become 'Londonistan', a city given over to Islamic domination and a warning sign of what would happen in the US if 'creeping sharia' was not halted. The protests of the EDL seemed a welcome revolt against Islam by the native English and a confirmation that the kind of politics Geller was advocating could bring thousands to the streets. From 2007, activists had begun to talk about a trans-Atlantic 'counter-jihad' movement, involving various far-Right groupings across Europe, and held together by US-based blogs such as Pamela Geller's *Atlas Shrugs* (named after Ayn Rand's libertarian novel), Robert Spencer's *JihadWatch* (a subsidiary of the David Horowitz Freedom Center) and Ned May's *Gates of Vienna* (referencing the seventeenth-century Ottoman defeat). Geller and Spencer had attended a 2007 'Counter Jihad' conference in Brussels, along with Vlaams Belang leaders and Bat Ye'or, author of the *Eurabia* conspiracy theory (of which more below). By the end of 2010, the kinds of campaigns against mosque construction that had earlier erupted across Europe were in full swing across the US, despite its constitutional principle of religious freedom; the American Civil Liberties Union reported that forty mosques across the US were facing organised opposition. Meanwhile, twenty-three US states introduced legislation to ban sharia from their courtrooms, on the presumption that America was on the verge of being 'Islamised'.

In the US, promoters of a populist, anti-Islamic message are well-funded. The Los Angeles-based millionaire couple Aubrey and Joyce Chernick, for example, have funded Robert Spencer's *JihadWatch* website with close to a million dollars (they also donate significant funds to pro-Israel lobby groups in Washington). Geller and Spencer are regularly invited onto the *Fox News* network as 'experts' on Islam and have been backed by senior Republicans

Newt Gingrich and Sarah Palin. Moreover, Spencer has been invited to brief the US military, the FBI and intelligence agencies. This well-resourced US Islamophobia network has been a significant source of ideas, contacts and inspiration for the EDL.

Yet tensions remain. When Roberta Moore resigned from the EDL in June 2011, apparently concerned the organisation was not sufficiently distancing itself from neo-Nazi elements within the movement, Geller and Spencer asked whether the EDL had really broken with the traditional far Right. Tommy Robinson correctly assessed that support for Israel was the litmus test of these new trans-Atlantic alliances and sent a statement to Geller and Spencer hoping to reassure them of the EDL's Zionism: 'In the first public speech I ever gave, I wore the Star of David ... The reason for this is because Israel is a shining star of democracy. If Israel falls, we all fall. This is what our movement has been built on for two years. ... We reject all anti-Semitism. The EDL stands where it always has stood, which is side-by-side with Israel.'

Irrespective of these organisational tensions, the trans-Atlantic networks of the 'counter-jihad' movement have facilitated the circulation of a series of new conspiracy theories to fill the gap left by the Jewish conspiracy theory of the traditional far right, and serving the same purpose of explaining the purported complicity of Western governments with their enemies. One such theory is the Eurabia thesis, outlined in Bat Ye'or's 2005 book *Eurabia: the Euro-Arab Axis*. Her claim is that the Euro-Arab Dialogue – a programme initiated by the European Community's political establishment following the 1973 oil crisis, to forge closer links with Arab nations – was actually a secret plot by European politicians and civil servants to facilitate Muslim immigration, subjugate Europe, and transform the continent into an Arab colony, Eurabia. Like the Jewish conspiracy theory of the *Protocols*, no evidence is offered. Nevertheless, through the mainstream conservative writing of Oriana Fallaci, Niall Ferguson and Melanie Phillips, the term 'Eurabia' has been associated with an image of Europe as cowardly and weak in the face of Islamic intimidation, allowing itself to be 'colonised' by an increasing Muslim presence.

A second conspiracy theory has centred upon the 'infiltration' of radical Islam in the US government, including with President Obama himself. Spencer has stated that:

Barack Obama was a Muslim as a child. He has never explained when or whether he left Islam at all. He identifies himself as a Christian now but it is, I think, perhaps salient to note that a Muslim can identify himself as Christian because Jesus Christ is a Muslim prophet in the Qur'an ... And so it's not out of the realm of possibility that some individual, or possibly Barack Obama, could be a Muslim and identify himself as Christian without even meaning to say that he is a member of the classic Christian tradition at all. ... But certainly his public policies and his behaviour are consistent with his being a committed and convinced Muslim.

Pamela Geller believes that Obama is 'the jihad candidate' who is 'using all branches of government to enforce the Shariah'. His is the 'first Muslim presidency, just eight years after 9/11. ... Everything this president has done so far has helped foster America's submission to Islam.' Like the anti-communist paranoids of the cold war, she believes the US government itself is secretly controlled by Muslim extremists: 'The enemy has infiltrated every department, every division of the federal government and the Obama administration, including the White House. The State Department [is] essentially being run by Islamic supremacists.' For Florida congressman Allen West, 'there is an infiltration of the Sharia practice into all of our operating systems in our country as well as across Western civilisation'. According to a survey for *Time* magazine in August 2010, around a quarter of Americans think Obama is a crypto-Muslim.

For the new conspiracy theorists, Islamist terrorism is just the visible tip of a hidden jihad iceberg. Alongside the use of violence is the strategy of 'stealth jihad' which aims at the infiltration of national institutions and the assertion of Muslim demands through the legal system. Muslims advocating for their civil rights or seeking to win political office are therefore to be regarded not as fellow citizens but as agents of a secret plan to impose totalitarian government on the world. Non-Muslims who stand with Muslims in challenging discrimination are '*dhimmis*', the twenty-first century equivalent of the cold war's 'fellow travellers', who have already internalised the status of second-class citizenship within an Islamo-fascist state. The provision of halal food, sharia-compliant finance or prayer breaks in workplaces is 'creeping sharia', the first steps towards a society ruled by Islam. (Pamela Geller has called for a boycott of Campbell's soup because halal versions of their products are available.) Since the Islamic doctrine of *taqiyya* supposedly sanctions systematic lying to non-Muslims to help advance sharia government, Muslims who say they interpret Islam as a religion of peace and tolerance are not to be trusted. Just as the early cold war produced the 'reds under the bed' fantasy of a vast network of communist agents operating in the US, today there is the notion that almost every American and European mosque is exploiting religious freedom to promote Islamic sedition. According to congressman Peter King, the chair of the House homeland security committee, who in 2011 held hearings on the 'radicalisation' of American Muslims, 80 per cent of American mosques are controlled by extremists. All this adds up to what we might call, with Senator Joseph McCarthy, 'a conspiracy on a scale so immense as to dwarf any previous such venture in the history of man'.

In a sense, this is a return to what Richard Hofstadter diagnosed in 1963 as 'The Paranoid Style in American Politics', now with an equal audience in Europe. But there are also significant differences between today's Islamic conspiracy theories and the right-wing, conspiratorial conception of power of the early cold war. Whereas the anti-communist paranoids saw their enemy as hugely powerful, able to direct world history through secret control of the media and economy, or even through techniques of brainwashing, the new conspiracy theorists do not ascribe to Islam any special abilities or intelligence; on the contrary, Muslims are seen as mired in a regressive, seventh-century culture. Rather, whatever power Muslims have has been granted to them by the West's own leaders, academics and journalists, whose lack of pride in Western culture has led to relativism and appeasement. Hence, the focus is as much on the thorough corruption of Western elites as on radical Islam itself. As Ned May wrote on his *Gates of Vienna* blog in September 2006: 'the Jihad is just a symptom ... the enemy lies within. This war is a civil war within the West, between traditional Western culture and the forces of politically correct multicultural Marxism that have bedevilled it for the last hundred years.'

Terrorism in Oslo

On 22 July 2011, Anders Behring Breivik set off a car bomb outside Norwegian government buildings before disguising himself as a police officer and opening fire on scores of teenagers attending a Labour Party youth camp on the island of Utøya. Seventy-seven people were killed. In his

1,500-page manifesto, 2083 — *A European Declaration of Independence*, published online on the day of the attacks, Breivik describes his ideology. He writes in English, presumably to attract British and American readers. Much of the document consists of advice to fellow far-Right terrorists on weapons, bomb-making, body armour, physical training, rituals to maintain ideological commitment, what music to listen to, political marketing, and the potential use of chemical, biological and nuclear weapons. He claims to be a member of a secret group of new crusaders founded in London in 2002 by representatives from eight European countries, 'for the purpose of serving the interests of the free indigenous peoples of Europe and to fight against the ongoing European Jihad'. One section of 2083 describes the ranks, organisational structure, initiation rites, uniforms, awards and medals to be used by this secret 'Knights Templar' group. These parts of the manifesto — and a section in which he interviews himself, narcissistically listing his favourite music, clothes and drinks — appear to be its only original content. The bulk of the document constitutes a compilation of texts copied from Breivik's favourite websites. Its opening chapters, a long section on 'cultural Marxism' and political correctness, are plagiarised from *Political Correctness: A Short History of an Ideology*, a book published online in 2004 by the Free Congress Foundation — a Washington-based lobby group founded by Paul Weyrich, one of the most influential activists of the US Christian Right. In this section, Breivik has replaced references to 'America' in the original text with 'Western Europe'. The writers Breivik cites most often are Robert Spencer, Ba'et Yor and 'Fjordman', who blogs for *Gates of Vienna* and *Jihad Watch*.

The key argument of the manifesto is that Europe has been taken over by a pro-multiculturalist elite, which is imposing its ideology of 'cultural Marxism' in order to undermine native European culture. Endorsing the Eurabia thesis, Breivik sees multiculturalism as facilitating the 'Islamic colonisation of Europe' through 'demographic warfare'. And the clock is ticking: 'We have only a few decades to consolidate a sufficient level of resistance before our major cities are completely demographically overwhelmed by Muslims.' Through its control of the media, universities and mainstream political parties, the multiculturalist elite has prevented the possibility of democratic opposition, claims Breivik. While individual Muslims do not necessarily follow its precepts, Islam is 'a political ideology that

exists in a fundamental and permanent state of war with non-Islamic civilisations, cultures, and individuals', which means the more Muslims there are
in Europe, the more Islam's inherent violence manifests itself. If this trend
is not reversed, he predicts, a European civil war will break out between
nationalists and Muslims allied with multiculturalists. Finally, Breivik justifies his violence by arguing for 'a pre-emptive war, waged in order to repel,
defeat or weaken an ongoing Islamic invasion/colonisation, to gain a strategic advantage in an unavoidable war before that threat materialises'.

The formal structure of the manifesto's argument corresponds to the
conventional neo-Nazi doctrine of 'race war', in which whites rise up
before it is too late against governments that have tried to dilute their racial
purity. The standard strategy of neo-Nazism has been to actively encourage
such a war by launching attacks on minorities, in order to provoke a violent
reaction that would awaken the white majorities to the necessity of racial
struggle, sending thousands of recruits into the ranks of the nationalist
movement. This was what David Copeland was hoping for when, in 1999,
he planted nail bombs in London's black and Asian neighbourhoods and in
a gay bar, killing three people and injuring over a hundred. There are elements of this provocation strategy in Breivik's manifesto too: he argues for
attacks on Muslim cultural events to incite 'violent riots and various forms
of Jihadi activities'; this, he hopes, will in turn 'radicalise more Europeans'
and spiral until more Europeans 'come to learn the "true face of Islam" and
multiculturalism'. But he singles out the multiculturalist elites as the primary targets for violence, hoping that terrorism will 'penetrate the strict
censorship regime' and damage the multicultural ideology. 'In order to
wake up the masses, the only rational approach will be to make sure the
current system implodes.' Hence the mass murder at Utøya of the next
generation of Labour Party leaders.

While Breivik's narrative formally resembles the 'race war' of neo-
Nazism, he reframes this doctrine by substituting culture for race, Muslims
for blacks, and multiculturalists for Jews. He explicitly rejects the 'race war'
concept and calls instead for a 'cultural war' in which 'absolutely everyone
will have the opportunity to show their loyalty to our cause, including
nationalist European Jews, non-European Christians or Hindu/Buddhist
Asians'. Like the EDL, he uses a culturalist framework to forge new alli-

ances. Yet he also speaks of his 'opposition to race-mixing' and wants 'to prevent the extinction of the Nordic genotypes'. Of Jews, he writes:

So, are the current Jews in Europe and US disloyal? The multiculturalist (nation-wrecking) Jews ARE while the conservative Jews ARE NOT. Aprox. 75% of European/US Jews support multiculturalism while aprox. 50% of Israeli Jews does the same. This shows very clearly that we must embrace the remaining loyal Jews as brothers.

There is no Jewish problem in Western Europe (with the exception of the UK and France) as we only have 1 million in Western Europe, whereas 800 000 out of these 1 million live in France and the UK. The US on the other hand, with more than 6 million Jews (600% more than Europe) actually has a considerable Jewish problem.

Casting Jews as both potential allies (if they join in fighting Islam) and a demographic threat (if there are too many), Breivik is simultaneously anti-Semitic and pro-Zionist. The picture that emerges is far from consistent, with old far-Right ideas of race war being reworked with newer culturalist notions.

The overwhelming majority of Breivik's source material comes from websites of the US far Right, particularly the 'counter-jihad' blogs, which have presented Europe as betrayed by multiculturalism and on the verge of cultural extinction as a result of Muslim immigration. Support for his strategy of violence and provocation cannot be sourced explicitly to these blogs. But 'A European Declaration of Independence', a 2007 blog post by Fjordman, which Breivik reproduces and whose title he borrows, does come close to issuing a call to arms. He writes: 'We are being subject to a foreign invasion, and aiding and abetting a foreign invasion in any way constitutes treason. If non-Europeans have the right to resist colonisation and desire self-determination then Europeans have that right, too. And we intend to exercise it.'

In a section discussing the EDL, Breivik praises the organisation for being the first youth movement to transcend the old-fashioned race hate and authoritarianism of the far Right. He urges 'conservative intellectuals' to help ensure the EDL continues to reject 'criminal, racist and totalitarian doctrines'. But he also considers their faith in democratic change 'dangerously naïve'. Breivik claimed to have hundreds of EDL members as Facebook friends and there has been speculation over his links to senior members of the organisation. Certainly, his manifesto shares much of the EDL's culturalist politics.

Was Breivik 'radicalised' by the EDL's ideology and by bloggers such as Spencer and Fjordman? The relationship between radical beliefs and violent acts is complex. The new crop of 'radicalisation' experts who have sprung up since 2004 are quick to talk of Islamist ideology as a 'conveyor belt' or 'mood music' to jihadist terrorism. But such metaphors usually conceal a lack of knowledge of the actual causal relationship. The question of how precisely ideas inspire actions did not trouble Spencer and his fellow Islamophobes while they were building careers with the simple formula that Islamic ideology causes terrorism. Now a terrorist has adopted their own radical ideology of 'counter-jihadism' and they find themselves in the awkward position of having to explain why their own ideas were not also an 'inspiration' for terrorism.

Breivik's violence may not be reducible to the ideology of the new far Right in any mechanical way but his worldview certainly corresponds to the culturalist politics of the EDL and the US-based Islamophobic bloggers. The extent of his involvement with activists in this milieu remains unclear but his manifesto strongly reflects the themes of the new far Right: the view of Islam as an extremist political ideology; the racialisation of Muslims; the emphasis on multiculturalism as enabling 'Islamification'; the Eurabia conspiracy theory; the rejection of old-style racism and authoritarianism; and support for right-wing Zionism.

These themes were revisited even in the response to the Oslo massacre itself. A *Jerusalem Post* editorial published two days after Breivik's terrorist attack argued that the 'devastating tragedy should not be allowed to be manipulated by those who would cover up the abject failure of multiculturalism'. Similarly, three days after the massacre, in the *Wall Street Journal*, Bruce Bawer, the author of *While Europe Slept: How Radical Islam is Destroying the West from Within*, reflected on the 'chilling' thought that his writing had been cited in Breivik's mainfesto. But, he wrote, the Oslo massacre should not distract from the 'legitimate concern about genuine problems'. Europe, he remarked, was 'in serious trouble' because of the 'millions of European Muslims' mistreating women, creating no-go areas, attacking gays and Jews, and trying to introduce sharia. (On the day of the massacre, the Wall Street Journal had gone to print while the identity of the perpetrator was still unknown. On the presumption that all terrorists are Muslims, the newspaper's editorial argued that Norway had been targeted by jihadists because it is 'a liberal nation committed to freedom of speech and conscience, equality between the sexes, representative democracy and every other freedom that still defines the West'.) A week later, Pamela Geller blogged: 'Breivik was targeting the future leaders of the party responsible for flooding Norway with Muslims who refuse to assimilate, who commit major violence against Norwegian natives, including violent gang rapes, with impunity, and who live on the dole ... all done without the consent of the Norwegians.' The left-wing youth camp on the island of Utøya was, she added, an 'antisemitic indoctrination training center'. She did not think Breivik's actions were justified but: 'There is also no justification for Norway's antisemitism and demonisation of Israel.' In the Netherlands, Geert Wilders blamed the Left for Breivik's violence: 'It is not my words, but your silence about the dangers of Islam which has the negative influences.'

The Liberal Response

The war on terror launched by Western governments enabled the emergence of new forms of racism and far-Right politics, the dangers of which were ignored for a decade, while only Islamist extremism attracted attention. When the US Department of Homeland Security, four months after President Obama took office in 2009, produced an intelligence report on right-wing extremism, the reaction from conservatives was so vitriolic that the unit which produced the report was effectively blocked from doing any further monitoring work. In Germany, the National Socialist Underground terrorist group, which killed nine immigrants and a police officer after being formed in 1998, went undetected for thirteen years, partly because the government had slashed funding for monitoring far-Right extremism. In Holland, analysts at the Office of the National Co-ordinator for Counter-Terrorism and Security told me in the month before the Oslo massacre that they believed there was no danger of far-Right terrorism in the Netherlands. Similarly, when I interviewed officials involved in Britain's Preventing Violent Extremism (PVE) programme in 2009, I was unable to find any examples of work focused on the far Right. The annual budget of £140 million was being spent entirely on tackling Islamist radicalism, with funding allocated in proportion to the number of Muslims resident in a particular local authority area, rather than on the basis of an objective measure of extremism. In 2011, the police's National Co-ordinator for Domestic Extremism told Muslim groups that the EDL was not an extremist, right-wing group and advised them to open a 'line of dialogue' with EDL leaders in order to 'engage them and re-direct their activity'. Reflecting the same mindset, when the EDL marched through Bolton in March 2010, Greater Manchester Police seemed more concerned with Muslim youths and anti-fascist activists protesting against the EDL than about the EDL itself. In the days before the march, the local, multi-agency PVE group, led by the police, distributed leaflets at mosques and schools in Bolton warning people not to attend the counter-demonstration being organised by anti-fascist groups. While EDL supporters were free to rally outside Bolton's town hall, the streets linking Muslim neighbourhoods to the centre of town were blocked by police officers, and coaches were laid on to take local young people out of town.

Finally, over the last year, government officials and the liberal intelligentsia in Europe have begun to recognise the rise of a far-right populist politics, represented by groups like the English Defence League, and discuss how best to respond to it. The earlier focus on Islamist extremism has been replaced by the fear of 'tit-for-tat radicalisation', in which escalating conflict between Islamists and the far right leads to social polarisation and undermines the liberal project. However, it remains to be seen whether policy-makers and pundits are up to the task of finding genuine solutions.

The signs are that they are not. There is an emerging consensus that the root cause of far-right populism is the absence of a positive sense of identity among sections of the white, working class. For many, this suggests the solution lies in new modes of national identification that are not based on exclusive ethnic identities but shared liberal values. Allowing for such US-style 'civic nationalism' to be more strongly recognised in the political process will, it is hoped, win over the softer sections of the European far Right and isolate the more extreme elements. Just as the war on terror officially divides Muslims into moderate and extremist camps, depending on their allegiance to the West, so now nationalists are to be separated into liberals and extremists, the former offered integration into the system, the latter marginalised. On this view, the state positions itself as a neutral mediator between the various forms of extremism that confront it and sees its role as developing forms of identity politics able to draw working-class populations into accepting 'shared values'.

The problem with this is that the proposed cure of a liberal identity politics looks very much like the disease — it does not take seriously enough the new forms of racism that themselves operate in the name of defending liberal values from extremism. And it leaves out of the picture the role of the state's own war on terror ideology in generating the culturalist identity politics of the new far right. In the end, liberalism will be unable to solve its extremism problem unless it can construct forms of political identification that transcend culturalism and speak to the wider social and political context of economic inequality and the collapse of working-class representation. Only if liberalism can be more than just another form of identity politics will it offer a true alternative to the far right.

HINDUTVA'S SACRED COWS

Vinay Lal

The lynching of five dalits – Virender, Dayanand, Kailash, Raju Gupta and Tota Ram – in Jhajjar (Haryana), reportedly by a frenzied mob, for skinning a dead cow is yet another pointer to the criminality that marks mob behaviour, thanks to the communal manipulation of mass religiosity by those who wish to thrive by it. . . . The disturbing truth is that a 5000-strong mob could collect at the drop of a hat to lynch those who skinned a dead cow. But it is doubtful if there would be even five among them willing to mind living cows that need care and protection. . . . We do not know how the cow in the present episode died; whether someone other than the five victims killed it or whether it died of starvation, street accident, old age or sickness. It is almost certain that no one among the murderous mob asked this question. Nor would it have occurred to them that being a friend to cows involves much more than being enemies of the enemies of cows.

Swami Agnivesh and Valson Thampu (2002)

Among contemporary social reformers in India, the Indian monk Swami Agnivesh is a widely recognised figure. Agnivesh gained prominence three decades ago for his efforts in bringing to attention the problems of bonded and child labour in India. The *Bandhua Mukti Morcha*, or Bonded Labour Liberation Front, which he founded in 1981 while he was still serving as Minister of Education in the state of Haryana, became known for carrying out daring rescues of labourers bonded for life, for instance many of those working in the quarries around Delhi. Agnivesh became the public face of India in international forums on the abolition of slavery, but he has also intervened over the years on many other social issues, from female feticide and the Hindu rite of widow immolation to corruption and the Indian state's relation to Maoist revolutionaries.

It is Agnivesh's pronouncements on Hinduism, however, which make him a particularly arresting figure and help illustrate the difficulties in unraveling that strange phenomenon called 'Hindu Fundamentalism'. Though Agnivesh is what would generally be recognised as a Hindu monk in India, he is a member of the Arya Samaj, a Hindu reform movement founded by Dayanand Saraswati in 1875 with the explicit intention of returning Hinduism back to its purportedly Vedic roots. Dayanand held that much of what passed for 'Hinduism' was a later and corrupt accretion, and the Arya Samaj came to reject many of the practices associated with Hinduism but held to be without Vedic sanction, such as idol worship, animal sacrifice, and child marriage. Most controversially, leading members of the Arya Samaj became proponents of the distinctly un-Hindu idea of *shuddhi*, or the conversion of Muslims to Hinduism, arguing that they were only encouraging Muslims to return to the fold (*parivartan*) from which they had departed. Agnivesh himself has been derided by Hindu nationalists as anti-Hindu, and his declaration in 2005 that the famous Jagannath Temple in Puri should be opened to non-Hindus led to his being burnt in effigy. He has been similarly controversial on other phenomena which have a centrality in the cultural imagination of Hinduism, such as the annual and rather arduous pilgrimage to the Amarnath cave in Kashmir where an ice stalagmite is worshipped as a form of the deity Lord Shiva, rubbished by Agnivesh as a piece of ice.

Swami Agnivesh, then, scarcely appears to be a figure that one would lump among the Hindu fundamentalists; indeed, judging from remarks he made at a gathering in 2008 organised by the Jamiat Ulema-e-Hind, where he pronounced the United States 'as the terrorist number one', and stated unequivocally that nothing could be a 'bigger lie' than attributing the wrongdoings of a few Muslims 'to the whole community', Agnivesh would appear to be hostile to Hindu fundamentalists who subscribe to the idea that though not all Muslims are terrorists, most terrorists are certainly Muslims. Yet, as a close perusal of Agnivesh's writings suggest, he often summons arguments or advances ideas in which Hindu nationalists have been trading for many years. There is, for example, a perennial argument from demography: while in India Muslims have retained their share of the population since 1947, doubling in numbers, the Hindu population of Bangladesh has declined from 25 per cent to about 10 per cent, and from 10 per cent to 1 per cent in Pakistan in the same period of time. This decline, Agnivesh argues, has been precipitated both by the 'tolerant philosophical outlook' of the Hindus and the evident intolerance of Muslims. The Hindu is slowly awakening to the fact that the 'basic tenet of this faith [Islam] is to conquer and subdue the whole world in the name of Allah', and Hindus and Buddhists, having seen 'the loss of Hindu influence from Iran to Indonesia to proselytising Islam', are no longer willing to be persuaded that the Quranic injunction of 'You have your religion, I have mine', has ever been taken seriously by Muslims.

Everything in Hinduism, argues Agnivesh, militates against the idea of Hindu fundamentalism, which is in any case 'to a great extent a reaction to national and international Muslim fundamentalism'. What is characterised as Hindu fundamentalism is in fact the everyday ordinariness of a religion such as Islam, and 'even the slightest spiritual movement among the Hindus is immediately branded by the minority communities as Hindu-chauvinism, Hindu backlash or fundamentalism.' For Agnivesh, as for many others, including those who can by no means be viewed as tolerant of religious extremism, the very notion of Hindu fundamentalism is altogether unintelligible: in Agnivesh's words, 'no scripture is absolutely authoritative for all Hindus, not even the Vedas since the highest realisation is always considered above scriptural knowledge.' Agnivesh might well have added what many would concede: even the very idea of a 'Hindu' is relatively recent, for those who today are termed Hindus would never have described themselves as such before the eighteenth century. The influential ideologue of Hindutva (the essence of being Hindu, or Hinduness, more often rendered in English as 'Hindu nationalism'), Vinayak Savarkar, was forthright on this matter, insisting that there is 'no word such as Hindu in Sanskrit, the language in which the texts of "Hinduism" have been written. The Vedas or the Upanishads or even the *Bhagavad Gita* do not mention the Hindus. To the best of our knowledge, none of the *Smritis* [law books] or the *Puranas* [mythological works] talk of Hindu Dharma or the Hindus.'

How is one to speak of Hindu fundamentalism when Hinduism recognises no one single text as supremely authoritative, has multiple centres of priestly authority all of which a practitioner of the faith may however ignore without peril, counts '330 million' gods and goddesses in its pantheon, and is certainly without a historical founder? Some scholars, however sympathetic they may be to such idioms of thought, find this an idle line of reasoning and prefer to argue from the history on the ground. They point to the manner in which the so-called Sangh Parivar, a family of closely knit organisations, has given form to Hindu nationalism, advanced ideological agendas designed to turn India into a Hindu *rashtra* (nation), mobilised Hindus around critical social and political issues, and orchestrated terror against religious minorities. They have in mind the work performed by the Bharatiya Janata Party (BJP), which represents the interests of Hindus in electoral politics; the Rashtriya Swayamsevak Sangh (RSS), often described as a paramilitary organisation that does the ideological, muscle and sometimes public service work of Hinduism; the Vishwa Hindu Parishad (VHP), which is the cultural, quasi-diplomatic, and 'missionary' arm of modern-day Hindus; and an array of other, generally smaller, organisations. Yet, as I shall now argue, there may be other, often less explored, avenues for understanding the contours of 'Hindu fundamentalism'.

Hitler in India

Mein Kampf, which by law cannot be sold in Germany, has what without exaggeration can justly be described as a big market in India. In a country where the sale of 5,000 copies is enough to warrant a title's inclusion in the best-seller list, it is notable that a reprint of *Mein Kampf* by the Indian publisher Jaico had, as of June 2010, sold over 100,000 copies in ten years. When we consider that the book is also sold on the pavement in various pirated editions, the real sales figures are bound to be much higher. London's *Daily Telegraph*, in an article published on 20 April 2009, first drew attention to this phenomenon with a striking headline: 'Indian business students snap up copies of *Mein Kampf.*' Notwithstanding anything that Sir William Jones might have said in the late eighteenth century on the common Aryan links between Indians and Germans, or the Nazi theorist Alfred Rosenberg's views on India as the ancestral home of the Aryans, Indian students appeared to have eschewed the grand historical narratives that have animated so many intellectuals for something seemingly much more pragmatic. The same articles informs its readers that sales of *Mein Kampf* have been soaring in India as Hitler is regarded as a 'management guru', an opinion apparently derived from conversations with several booksellers and students. The owner of Mumbai's Embassy Books, who reprints *Mein Kampf* 'every quarter', explained that Indians read in the book 'a kind of a success story where one man can have a vision, work out a plan on how to implement it and then successfully complete it'. A related BBC article, which appeared a year later, quotes a nineteen-year-old Gujarati student, 'I have idolised Hitler ever since I have had a sense of history. I admire his leadership qualities and his discipline.'

Hitler's popularity in India arises from a conjuncture of circumstances. In India, and in much of the rest of the world, it has become commonplace to view Hitler as the supreme embodiment of evil in the twentieth century, just as Mohandas Gandhi is likely to be seen as the greatest instantiation of good. The cover of a recent issue of *Time* (3 December 2007) sums up this opposition quite well: on the left side of a large sketch of the brain is a hologram showing Gandhi, and on the right side is a hologram featuring Hitler. The cover story is entitled, 'What Makes Us Good/Evil', and the caption accompanying the story states: 'Humans are the planet's most noble creatures — and its most savage. Science is discovering why.' In the land of his own birth, nevertheless, Gandhi appears to have been eclipsed by Hitler, and the comparative sales of *Mein Kampf* and Gandhi's autobiography, *The Story of My Experiments with Truth*, with the former outselling the latter by a margin of nearly two to one at the Crossword chain of bookstores, is only one of the telltale signs of the diminishing place of Gandhi in the country's public life. The young who idolise Hitler's life as a model of 'leadership qualities' and 'discipline' evidently have little knowledge of the manner in which Gandhi left his huge impress upon the anti-colonial struggle, forging a mass movement of nonviolent resistance that at times displayed an extraordinarily high level of discipline, and transforming the principal nationalist organisation, the Indian National Congress, from a party of elites into a body of mass politics. Yet, if there were misgivings about Gandhi in his own lifetime, many of those have become aggravated in an India which views Gandhi as a backward-looking luddite who emasculated India and would have set the country hopelessly adrift in a nation-state system where national interest and violence reign supreme. In such a setting, Hitler's idea of a virile nation set on a course of domination appears as an attractive alternative, even if it left Germany smoldering in ruins.

One might also suppose that it is only natural that Hitler should have a constituency in Mumbai, large chunks of which are under the control of Shiv Sena, a political party comprised in good part of hoodlums who appear to have learned something about both terror tactics and racial ideologies of hate from the Nazis. However, as empirical and anecdotal experience alike suggest, copies of *Mein Kampf* have sold well in other parts of the country, and as the BBC article noted, the more pertinent fact is perhaps that 'the more well-heeled the area, the higher the sales.' The Indian middle class has been strongly inclined to view admirably countries such as Germany and Japan, the success of which, most particularly after the end of World War II left them in ruins, is held up as an example of what discipline, efficiency, and strenuous devotion to work can accomplish. Of Japan's atrocities in the war very little is known in India, and the middle class gaze has seldom travelled beyond what is signified by the names of Sony, Toyota, Honda, Mitsubishi, and the like; as for Hitler, the same middle class Indians marvel at his ability to command millions, forge an extraordinary war machine, and nearly take a country humiliated at the end of World War I to the brink of victory over India's own colonial master.

There is, however, an equal measure of truth and falsity in the *Daily Tele-graph's* assessment of 'the mutual influence of India and Hitler's Nazis on one another. Mahatma Gandhi corresponded with the Fuhrer, pro-Independence leader Subhas Chandra Bose's Indian National Army allied with Hitler's Germany and Japan during the Second World War, and the Nazis drew on Hindu symbolism for their Swastika motif and ideas of Aryan supremacy.' Gandhi addressed two brief letters to Hitler, urging the German leader to renounce war and take advantage of his unparalleled sway over the masses to usher in a new era of nonviolence. But by no means can this be described as a 'correspondence' with the Fuhrer: exercising its wartime prerogatives of censorship, the British Government of India ensured that neither letter reached the addressee. Hitler never wrote to Gandhi. On the other hand, the invocation of Subhas Chandra Bose, who commenced his political career in awe of Gandhi but came to a parting of ways with the Mahatma, may perhaps go some ways in explaining the attraction felt for Hitler among India's youth. Bose is revered nearly as much as Gandhi in India, and certainly has fewer critics; lionised for his relentless opposition to British rule, which eventually led him to an opportunistic alliance with the fascists, Bose is remembered most of all for the creation of the Indian National Army. In a daring escape while he was under house arrest in Calcutta, Bose eventually made his way to Berlin where he founded the Indian Legion, comprised of Indian POWs captured in North Africa and attached initially to the Wehrmacht. Its members, significantly, were bound to an oath of allegiance which clearly establishes the nexus between Hitler and Bose: 'I swear by

God this holy oath that I will obey the leader of the German race and state, Adolf Hitler, as the commander of the German armed forces in the fight for India, whose leader is Subhas Chandra Bose.' It is an equally telling fact that Hitler had little interest in granting Bose an audience, only agreeing to a short meeting more than a year after Bose's arrival in Berlin — a meeting at which Hitler refused to issue a statement in support of India's independence. It was well and good for F. Schlegel, August Wilhelm Schlegel, Goethe, W. von Humboldt, Herder, Schopenhauer, and other exemplars of German enlightenment to celebrate the stupendous intellectual achievements of the ancient Hindus, but it was also not to be forgotten that India was a living testament to the degeneracy to which the eastern branch of the Aryans had fallen when they failed to preserve their purity.

If the troubled relationship of a nationalist hero with the Nazis is insufficient to explain Hitler's privileged place in the middle class Indian imagination, we may turn with greater success to the writings of Hindutva's principal ideologues. At the annual session in 1940 of the Hindu Mahasabha, a political party founded to promote the political interests of the Hindus and advance the idea of a Hindu *rashtra* (nation), Savarkar, in his Presidential Address, described Nazism as 'undeniably the saviour of Germany under the circumstances in which Germany was placed'. Though Savarkar's admirers describe him as a man of great intellectual acumen, it is remarkable that his only riposte to Jawaharlal Nehru, who throughout remained a vigorous critic of both Nazism and fascism, was to argue that 'Hitler knows better than Pandit Nehru what suits Germany best': 'The very fact that Germany or Italy has so wonderfully recovered and grown so powerful as never before at the touch of Nazi or Fascist magical wand is enough to prove that those political "isms" were the most congenial tonics their health demanded.' M. S. Golwalkar, who presided over the RSS from 1940 to 1973 and became the chief spokesperson for the idea of a Hindu nation, was similarly moved to argue that 'the other nation [besides Italy] most in the eye of the world today is Germany. The nation affords a very striking example.' That spirit which had enabled ancient German tribes to overrun Europe was once again alive in modern Germany which, building on the 'traditions left by its depredatory ancestors', had taken possession of the territory that was its by right but had, 'as a result of political disputes', been 'portioned off as different countries under different states.'

Nazism was built, however, on the twin foundations of expansion and contraction: if the idea of *lebensraum* became the pretext for the bold acquisition of territories, Germany itself was to be purified of its noxious elements, principally the Jews but other undesirables as well, among them gypsies, homosexuals, communists, and mental retards. The treatment meted out to Jews was, from the standpoint of those desirous of forging a glorious Hindu nation, an object lesson on how Hindu India might handle its own Muslims. Much ink has been spilled on just who all were the advocates of the two-nation theory in India, though Savarkar is clearly implicated. 'India cannot be assumed today to be a unitarian and homogeneous nation,' he told his audience while delivering the Presidential Address to the Hindu Mahasabha in 1937; rather, 'on the contrary, there are two nations in the main: the Hindus and the Moslems, in India.' These two nations, moreover, did not stand on the same footing, as the Hindu alone recognised Hindusthan as his or her *pitribhu* (fatherland), *matribhu* (motherland), and *punyabhu* (holyland); the Muslim, his eyes always looking beyond Hindusthan, was a rank outsider. The fate of Indian Muslims was sealed: as Golwalkar put it unequivocally, 'the foreign elements in Hindusthan' had but 'two courses' of action open to them, entertaining 'no idea but those of the glorification of the Hindu race and culture, i.e., of the Hindu nation and must lose their separate existence to merge in the Hindu race,' or they were to live 'wholly subordinated to the Hindu nation, claiming nothing, deserving no privileges, far less any preferential treatment not even citizen's rights.' In all this, Golwalkar held up Germany as a country that might usefully be emulated by India: 'Germany has also shown how impossible it is for races and cultures, having differences going to the root, to be assimilated into one united whole, a good lesson for us in Hindusthan to learn and profit by.'

Cartographic Piety

15 November is one of the more significant if less recognised dates in the calendar of some Hindu extremists. Each year since 1950, a strange ceremony has been carried out that day in the city of Pune, recognised as a citadel of Brahmin orthodoxy and Hindu learning. Pune is one of the principal seats of the Chitpavan Brahmins, a highly influential community that, over the course of the nineteenth and early twentieth centuries, saw a precipi-

tous decline in its fortunes. It is in Pune that the first attempt to assassinate Mohandas Gandhi took place in 1934, and it is from the ranks of Pune's Chitpavan community that Gandhi's eventual assassin, Nathuram Godse, arose to put an end to the life of an old man whom he was to designate as the greatest foe of the Hindus. In the early hours of the morning of 15 November 1949, close to two years after the murder of Gandhi, Nathuram and his associate, Narayan Apte, were escorted from death row in Ambala Central Jail and taken to the gallows. As Nathuram took the last few steps of his life, chanting a hymn to the motherland, he clutched a map of undivided India in one hand and a saffron flag in the other.

Nathuram's admirers, and they are legion, gather together every 15 November to recall the martyrdom of the assassin. Gandhi may have been the 'Father of the Nation', but Nathuram was quite certain that he was to be held chiefly responsible both for the vivisection of an ancient land and for making the Hindus vulnerable to the depredations of the Muslims. Though the circumstances of Gandhi's assassination have been probed by numerous government agencies and inquiry commissions, and Gandhi's innumerable biographers have endlessly gone over many of the details of the assassination plot and the outcome of the protracted trial in which Nathuram and several others would be implicated, the cartographic piety in which Nathuram's life is encased has received little scrutiny. Nathuram's last letter from jail, dated 12 November, had ended with the following words: '*Akhand Bharat Amar Rahe! Vande Mataram!*' ('Long Live Undivided India! Hail the Motherland!')

At the 15 November ceremony in Pune each year, the portraits of Nathuram and Apte are inset in a map of 'Akhand Bharat', undivided India, and then garlanded; lamps are lit, one for each year that has passed since their death, and an *aarti* — a Hindu ritual of worship — is performed; and those present take a pledge to work towards the fulfillment of Nathuram's dream of a 'unified India'. Reports published in Indian newspapers and magazines have over the years added some further details: Nathuram's ashes, for instance, are still preserved by his family members, kept in a pot which is placed before the map of 'Akhand Bharat'. Nathuram had left behind instructions that his ashes were to be immersed in the Sindhu river only after the partition of India had been revoked and the river had once again become part of India.

The idea of cartographic war as another mode of conducting politics is familiar to us from large parts of the world. India and Pakistan have long fought a cartographic war, and well-known tourist guides to India, such as Lonely Planet's *India Travel Survival Kit*, are only allowed to be sold in India on the condition that the map of India reproduced in the guide is accompanied by a special stamp stating that the borders shown in the map do not reflect the view of the Government of India regarding its own territorial borders. The Survey of India, which was established in 1767 and is charged with giving accurate topographic expression to India's borders, states that 'publication of maps depicting inaccurate external boundaries and coastlines of India [is] tantamount to questioning the territorial integrity of India and is a cognisable offence under the Criminal Law Amendment Act, 1961.' Cartographic espionage falls under the rubric of the Official Secrets Act (1923), and the government's extreme reticence in allowing the sale of topographic maps even to Indian citizens became more pronounced in the wake of China's cartographic offensive, followed by a swift blitzkrieg in 1962 that sent India's armed forces into a tailspin, over the north east Indian state of Arunachal Pradesh which China claims as part of its territory.

We might say that a related kind of cartographic anxiety has been at the heart of Hindutva, well before the partition of India was announced by the colonial regime as the logical culmination of Indian history. By the late nineteenth century, there was some awareness among the educated elite of the idea of a 'Greater India'. The Bengali intelligentsia might have imagined itself as the vanguard of a new Indian cosmopolitanism, but for centuries before the advent of the European presence in India the vast Indian Ocean trading system had drawn into its fold an impressive array of players, among them Gujaratis, Konkanese, Sumatrans, Malays, Chinese, Arabs and many others. There was perhaps only a dim recollection, which nationalists would attempt to energise, of India's sway over much of Southeast Asia and the Indianisation, over many centuries, of the Malay archipelago, Java, Kampuchea, and Indochina. However anomalous it might have appeared to suppose that a subject people could once have presided over a large empire, it was a marvel that India had brought its weight to bear upon others not by dint of arms but rather by the force of its cultural, spiritual, and intellectual legacies. Perhaps the real task of Hindu nationalism would be to reclaim the world it had lost — not so much to the British, as to the Muslim, invader?

The 'political testament' of Har Dayal, published in 1925, makes for arresting reading in this respect. He does not figure prominently in most intellectual histories of Hindutva; to the contrary, he is more warmly remembered as the founder of the Ghadr party, a political organisation that, from its multiple locations in the Indian diaspora and beyond, sought to liberate India from colonial rule. Writing in the Lahore-based Urdu newspaper the *Pratap*, Har Dayal declared that 'the future of the Hindu race, of Hindustan and of the Punjab, rests on these four pillars: (1) Hindu Sangathan [organisation], (2) Hindu Raj [rule]; (3) Shuddhi [reconversion] of Muslims, and (4) Conquest and Shuddhi of Afghanistan and the frontiers. So long as the Hindu nation does not accomplish these four things, the safety of our children and great-grandchildren will be ever in danger, and the safety of the Hindu race will be impossible.' It is remarkable that, at a time when even the independence of India was far from becoming a political reality, Har Dayal should have been thinking of the Hindu 'conquest' of Afghanistan — 'formerly part of India' but 'at present under the domination of Islam' — and the reconversion of its Muslims to Hinduism. Har Dayal would go on to argue that, unless Hindus secured the frontiers for themselves, it would be 'useless to win Swaraj': 'mountain tribes are always warlike and hungry', and there would be nothing to prevent the emergence of Muslim tyrants at India's borders. Har Dayal draws the lesson home with an explicit agenda: 'If Hindus want to protect themselves, they must conquer Afghanistan and the frontiers and convert all the mountain tribes.'

For all his ambition, Har Dayal's conception of 'Greater India' was rather modest, animated by a concern to secure India's borders and perhaps restore a Hindu empire that might once have stretched to Afghanistan. The question of an 'Asian civilisation' was very much in the air, prompted by Japan's triumph over Russia in 1905, enhanced exchanges between Asian intellectuals, a profound disenchantment with the idea of Europe after the brutalities of the 'Great War', and the rise of anti-colonial movements. Hindutva's ideologues had something else in mind when they thought of 'Greater India', 'Asia', or the notion of empires. Savarkar had advanced his own definition of a Hindu as one who looked upon the land that extended from the Indus to the seas as his fatherland (*pitribhu*) and motherland (*matribhu*), and further considered Sindusthan as his holyland (*punyabhu*) besides claiming inheritance from his Aryan forefathers, but in practice there were sometimes a complicated set of considerations that determined one's fitness to be a Hindu. He permitted Parsis the privilege of being considered Hindus, or at least akin to them, presumably because of the shared Aryan ancestry, even though they did not view India as *punyabhu*, or holy territory. Hindus who had moved overseas need not fear being considered anything less than the Hindus at home, and he even urged 'our colonists' to 'continue unabated their labours of founding a Greater India, a Mahabharat, to the best of their capacities' — and why not, for 'the only geographical limits to Hindutva are the limits of our earth!' Golwalkar, expounding on the same theme, thought it unnecessary to test the limits of imagination; it would suffice if the Hindu were acquainted with his history. Once the Hindu was made aware of his glorious past, it would dawn on him that 'our arms stretched as far as America on the one side — that was long before Columbus "discovered" America — and on the other side to China, Japan, Cambodia, Malaya, Siam, Indonesia, and all the South-East Asian countries and right up to Mongolia and Siberia in the North. Our powerful political empire too spread over these South-East areas and continued for 1400 years.' This would be the true realisation of Akhand Bharat, the reunification of Indians in America with their brethren in the primordial Aryan homeland of India.

Diasporic Aggression

There is now a 'Greater India' that exceeds even the fertile imagination of Savarkar, Golwalkar, and Godse's followers. One of the questions discussed on Hindutva websites, initially spurred by the extravagant claims of the writer P. N. Oak, who was of the view that nothing worthwhile in India had been achieved which did not have the stamp of Hindu origin, is whether Denmark might not be considered yet another outpost of the adventurous and bovine-loving Hindus. On this reasoning, Denmark is derived from the two Sanskrit words 'Dhenu' and 'marg', or the way of the cow; and since Denmark is particularly rich in dairy products, the claim has appeared to some Hindus of fecund mind as not lacking credibility. Oak and his followers have also given it as their opinion that Argentina may have been one of the many places visited by the Pandava prince Arjuna — hence Arjuna Town, or Argentina — as he traveled incognito during his period of exile, just as the word Vatican is derived from the Sanskrit *vatika*, meaning hermitage. The Hindus seem to have been prolific travelers, and the intent partly seems to be to respond with vengeance to colonial representations of Indian society as parochial and stagnant.

A different conception, and one that merits serious attention, of a 'Greater India' has begun to emerge in more recent years, one that sees especially North American Hindus as the vanguard of a resuscitated and resurgent Hinduism. There are many chapters in this narrative, indeed far too many to be recounted here, but the broad contours of how Hindu fundamentalism — and here fundamentalism may not be a misplaced word, considering the fact that Christian fundamentalism in the US presents itself as a tacit template for Hindus struggling with the idea of how they might serve their own faith — has acquired a force and presence in the 'land of the free and home of the brave' may be understood by gesturing briefly at some discrete but related phenomena. What is called 'Hinduism' has effectively only been present on American shores since the immigration reforms of 1965 made it possible for Indians to migrate to the US in large numbers, even if, as is widely known, Hindu sages and yogis had been visiting the US since at least the time of Swami Vivekananda. It would take another genera-tion before Hindus in the US, whose increase in numbers can be gauged by, as an illustration, the growth of temples, felt sufficiently emboldened to interest themselves in American politics, lobby Congress to adopt policies favourable to India, or take firm positions on matters of some political, economic or social urgency in India itself.

In December 1992, the Babri Masjid, a sixteenth-century mosque sup-posedly built on the site of a Hindu temple marking the exact birth spot (Janmasthan) of the revered deity king, Lord Ram, was destroyed. Extrem-ist Hindus had argued that the mosque was an eternal reminder of the humiliation they had been forced to bear at the hands of Muslim invaders. This agitation furnished one of the first instances in which Hindus in the US had made themselves heard. From the late 1980s onwards, Indian American Hindus lent emotional, spiritual and material support to Hindu extremists, even bringing out newspaper ads in support of the argument that the Mus-lim usurpation of Indian history would no longer be tolerated. The Chicago chapter of the VHP would go so far as to release a statement, in the wake of the mosque's destruction on 6 December 1992, celebrating the 'thunderous successful culmination' of attempts to liberate Ayodhya from the yoke of Muslim tyranny and usher in a golden dawn of *azaadi* (freedom).

Though far removed from India, and fully aware of their own position as an ethnic, cultural and religious minority in the US, Indian American Hindus would also show themselves adept at deploying discourses of multiculturalism to simultaneously stake their rights in a pluralistic America and interrogate the loyalty of Indian Muslims to the Indian nation-state. It is significant that, through the institution of an award for the 'Hindu of the Year' in 1994, two years after the wanton destruction of the Babri Masjid brought shame to India and left a long trail of arson, murder, and rioting, the Los Angeles-based Federation of Hindu Associations (FHA) would seek to honour in the first two years these three public figures in India: Bal Thackeray, Sadhvi Rithambara, and Uma Bharati, whose entire political careers have been built, among other shenanigans, on mocking the circumcised Muslim as a metaphor for the Muslim community that, in constant emulation of the partition, always seeks to further cut up or circumcise India. Thackeray's goons have mastered the art of bringing terror to the streets, though, in all fairness, it may be added that they are somewhat ecumenical in spreading around their hatred and contempt, targeting not only Muslims but, in recent years, working class immigrants from Bihar, Uttar Pradesh, and elsewhere.

The Temple Hinduism of Swaminarayan Gujaratis in the US furnishes perhaps one of the more unusual guides to Hindu fundamentalism. Both students of Hinduism and of recent Hindu political movements might wonder at this choice — the former because the Swaminarayan movement appears to be an entirely legitimate development within the Hindu faith with a large following, and the latter because so much scholarly work has been riveted on the history and organisation of the RSS, VHP, and BJP, on the electoral strategies of the BJP and the Shiv Sena, the terror tactics of the Bajrang Dal and the Shiv Sena, the ideological work performed by the RSS, the worldwide efforts of the VHP at diffusion of 'Hindu culture', and so on. However, the September 2002 terrorist attack on Akshardham, a huge temple complex in Gujarat's capital city of Gandhinagar, which serves as the world headquarters of the Swaminarayan faith, suggests that those who perpetrated the atrocity, which took the lives of twenty-nine people and left three times as many wounded, were extremely careful in choosing their target. In late February 2002, let us recall, many ordinary Hindu residents of Gujarat, apparently inflamed by the news that nearly sixty Hindus had been killed when two coaches of a train were set on fire at the train station in Godhra, carried out a chilling pogrom against their Muslim neighbours in Ahmedabad, Baroda, indeed across large parts of the state. The violence lasted over many days, even stretching out to weeks in some parts of Gujarat, and is estimated to have led to the deaths of over 2,000 Muslims and displaced well over 100,000 people, some of whom, ten years after the killings, continue to languish in relief camps. There is ample evidence that some of the state's highest functionaries, charged with the maintenance of law and order, did not merely permit the violence to take place under their very noses, but often goaded the arsonists and killers to be more efficient in the execution of their tasks.

When terrorists struck Akshardham six months after the pogrom in Gujarat, they would not have been unaware of the fact that the leaders of the Swaminarayan faith maintained a spectacular even sinister silence during the whole course of the pogrom. We should not be surprised that adherents of the Swaminarayan faith claim that they steer clear of politics and were bound to observe neutrality, and it is entirely germane, to a consideration of this point, that Gujarat's Chief Minister Narendra Modi, under whose regime the pogrom took place and who was returned to power shortly thereafter with a thumping majority at the polls, has cleverly sought to position Gujarat as the ultimate 'developmental' state where Muslims and Hindus alike are benefitting from a clean, efficient government. It is the same clean-shaven looks of the Gujarat government, behind which lurks a state machinery that has been assiduously studying and even improving manuals on ethnic cleansing, that have endeared it to overseas Indians and moved them to become among Modi's most ardent supporters. The Swaminarayan faith, though originating in India, similarly receives the bulk of its sustenance from diasporic Gujaratis in east Africa, Britain, and mainly the United States; moreover, owing to the disproportionate influence of Gujaratis among Indian ethnic and linguistic groups in the US, the adherents of the Swaminarayan faith have come into the position of being able to shape the contours of Hinduism in the US and even the course of politics in the state of Gujarat. Pramukh Swami Maharaj, the current leader of the Bochasanwasi Shri Akshar Purushottam Swaminarayan Sanstha (BAPS), the organisation through which the faith came to be institutionalised in 1907, has been actively courting overseas Gujaratis since the 1970s.

What is most distinct about the Swaminarayan faith is that its leaders and adherents are determined to usher Hinduism into a new era of monumental architecture and modernist achievement. Nowhere is this more evident than in the BAPS temples which have sprung up not only in Gujarat but even more spectacularly so in the diasporic setting of north America. When the BAPS Shri Swaminarayan temple was inaugurated in Neasden, just out- side London, in 1995, it was described as the world's largest Hindu temple outside India — barring Angkor Wat, which, however, is an archaeological site. The temple website proudly states that '2,820 tonnes of Bulgarian limestone and 2,000 tonnes of Italian Carrara marble were shipped to India, carved by over 1,500 craftsmen and reshipped to London. In all, 236,300 carved pieces were assembled like a giant jigsaw puzzle in less than 3 years. It is a miracle of modern times worked by over a thousand volun- teers.' BAPS then broke its own record when, in quick succession, it opened, on each occasion, the world's largest temple — in Houston (2004), Chicago (2004), Toronto (2007), and Atlanta (2007). The temple in Bartlett, some 40 miles from downtown Chicago, is described on its web- site as a place of 'wonder': 'This masterpiece of ancient design and work- manship, which was put up in only 16 months, is testimony to the sheer dedication and devotion of over 1,700 volunteers.' The Atlanta temple's introduction begins on a more innocuous note: 'A Mandir is a Hindu place of worship — a haven for spirituality and a place of paramount peace.' Apparently, to rehearse an old belief, places of worship should reflect the greatness of God; and so, effortlessly, the site goes on to rehearse nearly the same facts about yet another temple: 'The BAPS Shri Swaminarayan Mandir was inaugurated in August of 2007 after only seventeen months of construc- tion time utilising 1.3 million volunteer hours. The Mandir is comprised of three types of stone (Turkish limestone, Italian marble, and Indian pink sandstone.) More than 34,000 individual pieces were carved by hand in India, shipped to the USA and assembled in Lilburn [Georgia] like a giant 3-D puzzle.'

Nearly all the major BAPS temples in the US have been entered into tourist guidebooks. This has fulfilled one ambition of the Indian American community, namely to render Hinduism more visible. There is an anxiety of influence that pervades adherents of Hinduism in the US, none more so than the affluent Gujaratis who are followers of the Swaminarayan sect. We notice how the sheer enumeration of large numbers marks the description of each achievement; but, as if this were not enough, like many middle class Indians the BAPS members appear to think that certification from the Guinness Book of Records is the ultimate in human achievement. In 2000 alone, the BAPS spiritual leader, Swami Pramukh, received a Guinness certificate for the largest Hindu temple outside India, and another one for performing a world record 355 temple consecration ceremonies between 1971 and 2000. These certificates are proudly displayed in the foyer of the Neasden (London) temple. Hinduism need not just be the 'oldest' religion in the world, it must also display some of the energising and self-aggrandising features that many middle-class Hindus otherwise associate with Islam.

Coda: Bovine Science

There is much else that is remarkable about the BAPS temples. Though in the diasporic setting Hindus initially made do with makeshift temples, converting an abandoned church or unused storefront into a temple, with growing affluence members of the Hindu community have become more particular that temples should conform to the norms stipulated in the *shilpa-sastras*, ancient temple construction manuals. BAPS temples are, as I have suggested, immensely ornate affairs, but what is extraordinarily striking is how monumental BAPS temples have been transformed into museums of ancient Indian culture and Hinduism. The exhibition, 'Understanding Hinduism', unveiled at the opening of the Neasden BAPS Shri Swaminarayan Mandir in 1995, is a case in point. The viewer is introduced to the auspicious sound 'OM', and more elaborate panels advert to the history and beliefs of Hinduism. The section called 'Glory' sets the tone for what is to follow, even if one should believe that the nationalism on display is by no means unusual. As the exhibition catalog states, 'Hinduism existed before the sun rose on the kingdoms of Egypt or set on the Roman Empire; even before it sparkled upon the Chinese civilisation. Well before the Renaissance in Europe, Hindu astronomers were mapping the skies, doctors were performing surgery, and seers were composing scriptures.'

It is understandable, of course, that there may be no room for subtlety or scholarly finesse in an exhibition aimed at the general audience. Many scholars have spoken of Hinduism as an invented tradition, and the fact is that neither the word 'Hindu' is encountered in the ancient texts nor did those described as Hindus think of themselves as such. These observations will appear to 'observant Hindus' as unnecessary quibbles or as arguments designed to malign the faith. Whether the Hindus thought of themselves as Vaishnavas, Shaivites, Shaktos, or Tantrics, they had — as a section called 'Hinduism for Society' announces in grander detail — established a university at Takshashila (Taxila) in 2700 BCE, or were in the know, as the *Surya Siddhanta* of the astronomer Bhaskaracharya (c.600–680) shows, about the law of gravity 1,200 years before Newton. The Gupta era astronomer Aryabhata (c.476–550) had similarly argued a thousand years before Copernicus that the earth revolves around the sun. Indian science has, not surprisingly, claimed Aryabhata for itself — India's first satellite is named after him. The question remains why he or Bhaskaracharya should be on display in a section purporting to show how Hinduism has worked to produce a better society. The more alert viewer at the exhibition would have noticed two further peculiarities. First, the Hindu nationalist still seeks approbation from the West: thus all the quotations — from the Australian Indologist A. L. Basham, the first century CE Greek traveller Apollonius Tyaneaus, Romain Rolland, Mark Twain, and Arnold Toynbee, among others — pointing to the wisdom of the ancient Hindus are from Euro-American sources. Secondly, there is a constant endeavor to suggest that the findings of Hinduism and modern science are compatible: if the modern Hindu had a modicum of knowledge of the historical past and the rich spiritual legacies of the faith, he or she would show some awareness of being uniquely armed with spiritual insight and material well-being alike.

The Bartlett BAPS Mandir, in the western suburbs of Chicago, has a similar permanent exhibition with exactly the same title, 'Understanding Hinduism'. The museum-in-the-temple is already a nod to Western science and to the supreme importance of the museum modality in modernity; and, yet, it is the eternal persistence of modernity on which the Gallery of Hindu Achievements rides its success. The Guinness Book modality is gloriously on display here, as India is projected as the land of firsts. Whatever the domain of knowledge, the ancient Hindus were there first — they excelled in aviation, in the production of atomic energy, and in aeronautic espionage, anticipating the very scientific developments for which the West takes credit. The law of gravity was first discovered in India, but now the credit is given to 'Maharshi Kanad, an Indian physicist' rather than Bhaskaracharya. The viewer is told that the concept of 'zero' was introduced to the world by India; and since this claim is undisputed, the viewer may be lulled into believing much else: thus 'the first history book, the first university, the first Hospital – all [were] founded in India, hundreds of years before any thought of [these arose] in countries across the world.' It will not do to argue that some claims are fraudulent, while others are plausible or even clearly established. The more substantive question is what relationship such achievements of Indian science have to Hinduism, and equally why a religion which claims to be the world's oldest has to validate itself in the language of science.

Hindu science has a lighter side to it, which brings me, in closing, to the subject of cows. These bovine and overwhelmingly benign animals are as good a place as any to commence any number of histories, whether of Hindu communalism, colonial writings on India, Hindu-Muslim riots, cow protection in India, and so on. There are a nearly endless number of communal riot narratives where a fracas between the two 'communities' is said to have commenced when a cow's head was thrown into a temple or a mosque was desecrated by a pig's head. Colonial writers sought to represent the gap between Hindus and Muslims as unbridgeable: the former burn their dead, the latter bury them; the former have millions of gods and goddesses, the latter believe only in Allah and in Muhammad as his Prophet. But perhaps the more lively way to get across this difference was to suggest that the Muslim loves to eat the cow, while the Hindu loves to worship this animal. One should not be surprised that Gandhi, the great votary of *ahimsa* (non-violence), was himself a staunch advocate of *gau raksha* (cow protection), likening the cow to both Mother Earth and the divine figure of the mother. However, though there is little relation of his Hinduism, however that might be characterised (a no easy task considering his declared view that 'a man may not believe even in God and still call himself a Hindu'), similarly Gandhi would have looked askance at many of the claims made on behalf of the cow.

To consider what Hindutva bovine science has reaped, a small booklet published by the Rashtriya Swayamsevak Sangh, *The Protection of Cow-Clan* (2000), furnishes a delightful guide. Drawing on some of the shastric [scriptural] texts, which delineate the benefits to be derived from the consumption and use of the five products (*panchgavya*) of the cow — milk, curd, ghee, urine, and dung — the RSS's modern experts, who might claim to be animated by the spirit of scientific experimentation, improve upon the recommendations of the Hindu seers. 'Ghee made from cow's milk saves environment from atomic radiation', and similarly 'cow dung and urine is best for stomach diseases, heart diseases, kidney ailments and TB.' Since what is called 'Delhi Belly' afflicts a huge number of Indians, and cows are also to be found in marvelous abundance in India, one wonders why the RSS cadres have not subjected more of their fellow Hindus to some of the remedies put on offer. Virgins have most likely been considered desirable in every culture, and the urban folklore about sex with a virgin being a cure for AIDS has had many adherents, but RSS's own experts clearly have unique insights into this delicate matter: thus 'the urine of virgin cow is the best', and since the cows of foreigners 'lack the properties which our cows do have', it stands to reason that the urine of virgin Hindu cows is without comparison. Given the entrepreneurship for which India is justly known, and the culture of *jugar* or homegrown innovation on which much of the country seems to run, it may be a puzzle why this potent beverage has not been patented so far. Or could it be that the Indian, who is never very far from a cow in the motherland, has only to go within the earshot of the cow to achieve that bliss for which we all crave: 'Sound of cow's mowing [sic] automatically cures many mental disabilities and diseases.' A hundred million cows mooing together may yet cure India of that disease called Hindu fundamentalism!

TAKING LIBERTY

Gordon Blaine Steffey

'When liberty is mentioned, we must always be careful to observe whether it is
not really the assertion of private interests which is thereby designated.'
GWF Hegel

Recently I took a Muslim friend to study the buffet of print laid into the
Liberty University bookstore. The university and its bookstore sit on Liberty Mountain in Lynchburg, Virginia, where an SUV trimmed with stickers
reading 'Not I, but Christ' and 'Socialism isn't cool' abridges the local tem-
per. Liberty University is the latest iteration of the institution founded as
Liberty Baptist College in 1971 by the late Jerry Lamon Falwell, Sr. Americans remember Falwell as skipper of the Moral Majority, a political action
group born in 1979 as a consequence of the political realignment of conservative Christians in the wake of the excesses of the 1960s and the
increasingly secularist drift of the Democratic Party since the presidential
campaign of George McGovern. Dissolved by Falwell in 1989 and succeeded by the Christian Coalition of America, the inter-denominational
Moral Majority lobbied politicians and solicited voters to reverse a regnant
acceleration into decadence, hallmarks of which included *Roe v. Wade* and the
broad media assault on 'family values'. The British may recall an incongru-
ously sober philippic on the sexual politics of the BBC programme *Teletub-
bies*. Falwell's *National Liberty Journal* insisted that the purple, purse-toting
Teletubby topped with a triangular aerial was the fifth column in a 'subtle'
re-education of straight children worldwide. Muslims will recall Falwell less
for outing Tinky Winky than for his incendiary twaddle about Islam and the
Prophet Muhammad, twaddle no more forgivable for being de rigueur
among demagogues on the Christian Right in the aftermath of 9/11. This
followed Falwell's daft attempt on 9/13 to blame 9/11 on 'the pagans, and

85

the abortionists, and the feminists, and the gays and lesbians . . . who have tried to secularise America'. None of these inanities were commemorated on the artless exhibits cluttering the Jerry Falwell museum, whence my friend and I launched an informal tour of this Christian evangelical madrasa.

The earnest young man tending the museum armed us straightaway with a courtesy copy of *Falwell: An Autobiography*, the mood of which appears in exhortation form near the book's terminus: 'Let your vision become an obsessive reality.' Falwell presently confesses his 'burning obsession,' to wit, 'I truly believe the only way I can evangelise the world in my generation is to train Young Champions for Christ at Liberty University.' Now forty years on from its inception, Liberty enrolls 12,560 residential Champions for Christ with another 61,000 Champions enrolled online. Neither Falwell's prodigious and profuse gaffes nor his 2007 translation into celestial bliss have dimmed the flames of Liberty or dammed its emanation of Champions. Clamorous efforts by pillars of the so-called New Atheism to replace 'delusion' with 'renewed Enlightenment' have not discernibly abated the achieving of his vision. Infrequent stopovers by Richard Dawkins nourish the lean tribe of Nay-saying lions who prowl the periphery of Lynchburg but fail to constitute the 'great noon' whereof Nietzsche's Zarathustra speaks. Every inch as imperious and frothy as the late Falwell, Dawkins speaks a language native to Liberty Mountain. While both malcontents court the attentions of Nemesis, Dawkins' diatribes find no refuge in the Liberty University bookstore, where my friend cocked his head at a book titled *Stuff Christians Like*, an intramural raillery with a dulled edge. He mused aloud about members of the set stuff: 'Shopping?'

Summoned to realise and practice citizenship in the joy of unrelieved desire, Americans are relentlessly being formed in what Vincent Jude Miller in his *Consuming Religion* terms 'consumerist habits of use and interpretation' that disfigure their religious beliefs and practices. Theological counter-narratives are met by a 'system' that 'welcomes the most radical denunciations of the shallowness of our civilisation and its global excesses in the same way the sated gourmand welcomes the tartness of a sorbet between courses of a heavy meal.' It is therefore imperative to engage the system 'on the level of practices and structures rather than meanings and beliefs,' which, in a post-traditional society that converts parishioners into consumers of services and thus germinates niche ecclesiology, are fluently commodified as themed wristbands, auto decals, and mobile or Facebook apps. Christian identities have never been cheaper. Where Miller scents trouble, others embrace opportunity. On the threshold of the 2007 opening of the new Thomas Road Baptist Church complex (another face of Falwell's empire), which boasts a 6,000 seat sanctuary, indoor playground, wired café, and restaurant, Jerry's son Jonathan, now senior pastor of Thomas Road, gushed: 'It's like a Christian Starbucks. We built this for people who live in the community and we want to reach with the gospel. We believe it is all part of God's plan.' Christianity no longer moderates excess but manifests it. Shadowboxing Darwin but in bed with Mammon, Liberty strains gnats but swallows camels (Mt. 23:24).

Thrown ultimately onto the seemingly familiar sands of a university bookstore (a Barnes & Noble's affiliate), my friend and I nevertheless encountered some alien trimmings. Tall shelves brimmed with books filed beneath exotic headings, e.g., 'Global Missions' and 'Apologetics.' The embrace of these headings proves to be broader than the house classification scheme suggests. The sorely limited range of titles available for the study of Islam include George W. Braswell, Jr.'s *Islam: Its Prophet, Peoples, Politics and Power*, 'written from a western Christian viewpoint' and described by its publisher as a 'valuable reference' for 'ministers' and 'missionaries'. Available too are Mark A. Gabriel's *Culture Clash: Islam's War on America*, Bat Ye'or's *The Dhimmi: Jews and Christians Under Islam*, and Keith Swartley's *Encountering the World of Islam*. The latter promises to reveal the 'frustrations and desires of Muslims' and thereby equip the reader to 'pray for and befriend them' or 'reach out to them in Christ's love'. Even a shallow acquaintance with such texts should suffice to forewarn readers that Islam is not likely to feature among stuff these Christians like. A Pew survey of nearly 2200 evangelical VIPs who met at Cape Town in October 2010 for the Third Lausanne Conference on World Evangelisation found that 67 per cent held an 'unfavourable overall opinion' of Muslims and 59 per cent identified Muslims as a 'top priority' for evangelisation. Ranking fourth behind secularism, consumerism, and popular culture, the 'influence of Islam' was reckoned to be a 'major threat' to evangelical Christianity by 47 per cent of responders. Such data tends to support the view that the best Muslim is an ex-Muslim.

Until quite recently Liberty University had its very own 'best Muslim,' to wit, Ergun Mehmet Caner. Brio and martial rhetoric seethed on the

occasion of his 2005 appointment by Jerry Falwell to pilot Liberty Baptist
Theological Seminary. The ex-Muslim and new Dean pledged to produce
'special forces' for the 'frontlines', 'specially trained generals, not just soldiers'. Caner explained that 'a general understands the mind of the adversary, as well as the rules of engagement. Christ has called us to nothing less.'
One cannot help thinking that this 'Christ' who summons 'us' to technically
competent warfare, theological or otherwise, is surely not the son of Mary
from Nazareth. To borrow from *According to John*, a text that often comes to
mind when I land in evangelical company, 'Sir, if you are the one who carried him off, tell me where you have laid him and I will bear him away'
(20:15). Perhaps this cheery militarism is a residue of Caner's multinational
training as a jihadi. In speaking engagements across the country, Caner
condensed his Muslim rearing into an unambiguous confirmation of his
audiences' fears and insecurities in the terrible aftermath of 9/11. 'I hated
you,' Caner insisted, where 'you' means American and/or Christian. He
tracked that sentiment home to the culture of 'Islamic jihad' in his native
Turkey and to the Beirut madrasa where he trained in anticipation of
answering the Ayatollah Khomeini's summons to islamise the United States.
In 1982 and as a consequence of a school mate's tenacity, it dawned on
Caner that, as he framed it for Floridian undergraduates attending the 2008
State Baptist Collegiate Conference, 'Jesus strapped a cross to his back so I
wouldn't have to strap a bomb on myself.' It is on the back of this near miss
or this archetypal American rags-to-riches chronicle that Caner secured his
celebrity in evangelical society.

As many Americans floundered in the tempestuous wake of 2001, casting
here and there in efforts to fathom the disembodied Muslim mind, Caner
and his brother Emir co-authored the exposé *Unveiling Islam: An Insider's Look
at Muslim Life and Beliefs*, described by Caner as an 'act of love' and deplored
by critics as an act of 'hate' and 'profiteering'. Therein the Insider-turned-
outsider 'summed up' the life and legacy of the Prophet Muhammad in three
words: 'complexity, expediency, and depravity'. At a 2002 conference where
he cited *Unveiling Islam* as a resource, erstwhile Southern Baptist Convention
president Jerry Vines infamously described the Prophet Muhammad as a
'demon-possessed paedophile'. Soon defended by that other blustery Jerry
(from Lynchburg), Vines' howler quickened the media spectacle of pundits
competing to define Islam and/or the Prophet Muhammad as essentially

peace-loving or bloodthirsty, decent or decadent, good or bad, in the several minutes running up to adverts for exquisitely soft bath tissue.

Once steeped in the dark counsels of the 'adversary,' now bleached by the cross-strapped 'Son,' Caner leaped eagerly into the role of guide for the perplexed. His improbable journey from jihad to Jesus, energetically narrated, rhetorically frank, and seasoned with cheek, was a story that delighted many audiences precisely because it aggrandised so many. America is the 'city on a hill,' Jesus is the Right Answer. Caner sang his song from sea to shining sea, from California to Florida. In 2005, he provided pre-deployment training to Marines from Marine Corps Air Station in New River, North Carolina, entreating them not to swallow the milquetoast Islam peddled by talking heads with letters after their names. In contrast to this smiling mask of 'American Islam,' Caner invited Marines 'to look very carefully at my face' and to see there 'the face of a declared enemy'. Caner would surely characterise cultural training at New River as he characterised his *Unveiling Islam*: an 'act of love'. In this and in much, he runs afoul of the state motto of North Carolina: *esse quam videri*. To be rather than to seem.

Unlike Tinky Winky, Ergun Mehmet Caner was not what he seemed to be. His extraordinary biography, including that apparently eleventh-hour rescue from the vivid death-dealing Islam of distant madrasas, was more fable than fact. In 2010, an international, interfaith alliance of bloggers detected yawning discrepancies between the narrative Caner thundered from pulpits and podiums and the humbler narrative he consigned to print. Born in Sweden, Ergun Michael Caner (or so his name appears on local government proceedings) settled in Ohio as a toddler. Tutored in Islam by his father, Caner was reared principally by his non-Muslim mother after his parents' divorce. He converted to evangelical Christianity as a teenager and matriculated at several average institutions before accepting consecutive posts at Criswell College and Liberty University. What of madrasas in Turkey and Lebanon and Egypt? What of the hatred he learned there and bore here? In February 2010, Caner posted a formal reply to his increasingly strident hecklers: 'I would be surprised if no discrepancies were discovered.' He termed these discrepancies 'pulpit mistakes,' insisting that they differed from lies to the extent that he 'never intentionally misled anyone'. When Caner told Marines in 2005 that 'I knew nothing about America until I came here when I was fourteen years old,' this is presumably a 'pulpit mistake' or an effect of undue zeal. Winding up his reply, Caner observed that 'the misguided attempt by Muslim apologists to discredit converts to Christianity is not limited to me; in fact it seems to be standard operating procedure.' Unsurprisingly, this explanation failed to disperse the gathering storm clouds. As bloggers' findings migrated to mainstream media outlets, Liberty University sluggishly launched a 'review', which confirmed 'discrepancies related to matters such as dates, names and places of residence' and ultimately concluded that 'Dr. Caner has made factual statements that are self-contradictory.' The self-appointed unveiler was unveiled. What became of Ergun M. Caner now that his robust record of toxic misrepresentation stood open to view? Sacked as Dean in 2010, Caner was retained on faculty at Liberty Baptist Theological Seminary for the 2010–11 academic year, at the terminus of which he accepted a post as Provost and Vice President for Academic Affairs at Arlington Baptist College in Arlington, Texas, where President D. L. Moody described Caner as sharing 'the values that I have for biblical authority, evangelistic fervour and godly example'. It was surely 'evangelistic fervour' (akin perhaps to a 'pulpit mistake') that induced Moody to extol his 'godly example'.

The Unlikely Disciple: A Sinner's Semester at America's Holiest University by Kevin Roose, is a chummier exposé than *Unveiling Islam*. It chronicles Roose's 'study abroad' at Liberty University, where he encounters a 'culture more foreign to me than any European capital, and these foreigners vote in my elections!' A self-described secular liberal, Roose invites readers to join his undercover infiltration of this distant society. Its residents are, remarkably, 'not a group of angry zealots,' by which he seems to mean not bloated demagogues cut from the pattern of Falwell and Caner. Not yet, I might add, and not on that account salutary or toothless. Roose struggles with this, perhaps because of a merry spirit. No angry zealots here, he assures us, and yet he laments his failure 'to understand how well-intentioned Christian kids — some of the nicest people I've met all semester — can end up on streetcorners in Florida, shouting hellfire and damnation to the masses.' He rightly observes that these same kids 'are convinced that their actions are compassionate and altruistic' (acts of love?), convinced in part by what Roose misidentifies as 'pep talks', wherein rhetoric transforms haranguing passersby with the prospect of posthumous torture into the dispensing of 'cures' to the 'terminally ill'. By what route, though, have we arrived on street corners in Florida? Roose gamely joined a Liberty-sponsored mission to Daytona Beach, Florida, a popular destination for students on holiday and thus a fertile field for 'battleground evangelism'. Initially puzzled by an overhead disproportionate to its miserable harvest, Roose later comes to view low-yield mission as a 'tool for self-anaesthetisation, a way to get used to the feeling of being an outcast in the secular world'. If unrelieved rejection 'feels awful,' in due course 'you get the point – you are going to be mocked and scorned for your faith and this is the way it's supposed to be.' Indeed, battleground evangelism is a practice calculated to modify its practitioner, specifically, to constitute its practitioner as an outsider and through repetition to reconcile the practitioner to the outside. One becomes a 'Champion for Christ' by physically, rhetorically, and repeatedly invading a space predisposed as 'Satan's home turf,' e.g., a nightclub or public beach. While the differential formation of social identity is not intrinsically problematic, it becomes so when it is 'naturalised'. Surrounded by and engaged with mechanisms that convert relations of difference into relations of otherness and shielded in part from them by his cloak and experimental attitude, Roose cannot fathom the relationship between the normal, nice kids of his acquaintance and the angry zealots in the offing (the same kids viewed anew in Daytona Beach). Angry zealots are not born that way, but 'born again', and these 'seemingly normal' kids have not yet been brought to term. *The Unlikely Disciple* opens a window onto the second gestation.

The Creation Hall Museum in the Arthur S. Demoss Learning Center on Liberty Mountain is windowless and a rude shade of the higher profile Creation Museum in Petersburg, Kentucky. Opened in 2007 at a cost of 27 million dollars, the Creation Museum fatuously objectifies legendary material in Genesis, occasionally and feebly letting fly at Darwin in fidelity to its mission to 'counter evolutionary natural history museums that turn minds against Scripture'. In staggering contrast to this 70,000 square foot facility set on 49 acres, Liberty's Creation Hall Museum is a broad but shabby corridor housing several wooden cabinets stocking insipid exhibits that espouse a 'biblical view of origins'. I submit that patient study of these cabinets yields neither decisions against Darwin nor 'decisions for Christ'. My Muslim friend and I departed unconverted and somewhat dimmed by the crude aesthetic and cruder science of the 'museum', deficits compensated for in Kentucky by camel rides and Cincinnati-style chilli at 'Noah's Café'. The museum is an accessory of the Center for Creation Studies, the engine behind 'History of Life', a course required of all Liberty students and promising to 'provide a thorough understanding of the creation-evolution controversy,' though not at the expense of a 'consistent biblical view of origins,' meaning that God made the cosmos 'in the time and manner specified in Genesis'. Yes, 'in six normal, solar days'. Yes, 'from the dust of the ground and not through an evolutionary process'. Dinosaurs? Snuffed by Noah's flood several thousand years ago. I was reminded of James Thurber's *The Macbeth Murder Mystery*, wherein an unnamed Englishman is engaged in conversation by an American lady who, mistaking that play for a whodunit, exonerates the Macbeths and fingers Macduff as the killer because 'it would spoil everything if you could figure out right away who did it.' Sadly, this is no genre confusion. In creationism, a fetish and an affirmation concealed as an antithesis, we encounter the total degeneration of Christianity into a purely bourgeois religion serving its own interests. This ism is devoid of the virtues prerequisite to negotiating what my fellow tourist in the Falwell empire terms 'postnormal times'. In a recently published essay, James Davison Hunter, American sociologist and author of the famous 1991 book, *Culture Wars*, argues that what fundamentalisms 'share in common is a reassertion of certainties in meaning and moral order in a context in which those certainties are rendered implausible or denied altogether'. In short, when the ground trembles and expectations misfire, some take refuge in the hypocrisies of the past, in a diverting *ressentiment* that seeks to 'save America' and yet 'offers no constructive proposals for the everyday problems that trouble most people . . . no vital solutions to the problems of pluralism and change'. Is it fitting or ironic or tragic that a symbol of their fidelity should take the shape of museums filled with bones? 'Leave the dead to bury their own dead; you must go . . .' (Lk. 9:60).

Neither my friend nor I danced in the deserted burial garden of Jerry Lamon Falwell, Sr., which offers a lovely panorama of the Blue Ridge mountains and overlooks Lynchburg to the west. It was breezy, the meagre heat of the day had given way to a chilly evening. The 'eternal flame' guttered atop a white cross standing in the rectangular fountain before his tomb. We did not linger; there was nothing there. In the days following his father's death, Jonathan, heir apparent to his dad's air-conditioned pulpit at Thomas Road, discovered a balm for his grief in Joshua 1:1-2: 'After the death of Moses the servant of the Lord, the Lord spoke to Joshua son of Nun, Moses' assistant, saying, "My servant Moses is dead. Now proceed to cross the Jordan, you and all this people, into the land that I am giving to them, to the Israelites."' In Joshua, Jonathan detected the cheering message that 'God still had great things in store for those of us left behind to continue the ministry he began.' Does God indeed? A 2011 Pew survey found that 53 per cent of evangelical VIPs in America see the current state of evangelical Christianity in America as worse than it was five years ago and 48 per cent foresee that state worsening in the next five years. Standing in the burial garden, we could not share their gloom. We heard a campus humming with optimism, saw projects nearing completion, other projects beginning, and the grounds thronging with Champions for Christ. 'Moses' (the elder Falwell) conceived Liberty as a tool whereby 'to change the world'. At the September 2008 Values Voter Summit in Washington, D.C., 'Joshua' (Jonathan, the son), corrected the premature obituary of the Christian right: 'There are lots of people in the media who say that the religious right is dead. The rumours of death are greatly exaggerated. We are very much alive. We are very much moving forward into the future to continue to change our nation [and] to lead our nation back to where it began.'

The Falwell dynasty aims to remake the world in the image of Liberty Mountain. Among evangelicals, politics is the preferred mechanism of change. The Constantinian politics of conquest wherein the Champions of Liberty Mountain are tutored is a method of engagement incompatible with the logic of the postnormal times. James Davison Hunter proposes a post-Constantinian method of engaging the world 'that neither seeks domination nor defines identity and witness over against domination. For most, this will mean coming to terms with the past'. Hunter enjoins Christians to recognise that America was never a Christian nation 'in a theologically serious way,' nor was the so-called West a Christian civilisation 'in a theologically serious way'. There is therefore no returning to or leading back to or rescuing from, etc. The pluralistic maturity of the world is irreversible and attempts by Christian fundamentalists to reverse it are pointless, ignoble, and unchristian – not to say highly dangerous. To shape open futures characterised by justice, decency and play, persons of faith and no faith, motivated by neither resentment nor indiscrimination, must take new risks and new departures, cultivating practices that permit us to walk together into a 'new age of normalcy'.

As my friend rocketed through the several rooms of the Jerry Falwell museum, I explained to the Young Champion for Christ that he was a visitor from London. He confessed to having heard that England was not especially stout in 'faith'. To this I hmm-ed noncommittally. What the sparkle in his eye portended, I cannot say, but you should not be surprised to see him shouting hellfire and damnation in Enfield and Croydon, Hillingdon and Havering, Sunderland and Plymouth, Birmingham and Liverpool . . .

LOT'S LEGACY

Shanon Shah

On 9 January 2012, the Kuala Lumpur High Court acquitted and discharged Anwar Ibrahim, the Malaysian federal opposition leader and former deputy premier, on charges of sodomising his former political aide. This was the second time Anwar had been tried for homosexual sodomy, and the second time he had been acquitted. Back in 1999 the High Court sentenced Anwar to six years in prison on fabricated charges for corruption, and the next year he was sentenced to another nine years in prison for sodomy. In 2004, however, after spending six years in prison, the Federal Court acquitted and freed Anwar of the sodomy charge. In June 2008, months after the opposition had made historic inroads in the general election, the second round of sodomy allegations against Anwar emerged.

When Anwar was first accused of homosexuality I was twenty. For the past thirteen years, I have had to grow up and live with the psychological consequences of that charge. There is no denying the visceral impact of the Malaysian state charging a charismatic leader of a grassroots opposition movement, who almost became prime minister, for sodomy. The accusations were designed specifically to appeal to Malays who were presented with a simple argument. Namely, that homosexuality is a Western, infidel disease, and that a Muslim could not by definition be homosexual. Ergo, if ever there was such a thing as a Muslim homosexual, this person was as good as a diseased Western infidel. Therefore Anwar could not possibly be a viable leader for Malays. This is powerful logic in Malaysia, where Malays form the numeric ethnic majority and are constitutionally defined as Muslim. Thus, if Malaysian Malay-Muslims professed Islamic faith, we had to automatically reject Anwar on the grounds that he could be gay. This became the dominant framework of Malaysian politics which we had either to accept or work against at our own risk.

By summoning the spectre of homosexuality into public consciousness, the state created a dominant discourse obsessed and haunted by sexuality. The year 2011 alone was bookended by responses that were extremely hostile to homosexuality. In January, threats – some of them violent and murderous – continued against Azwan Ismail, a Malaysian Muslim man who 'came out' as gay via a YouTube video. In December, some Malaysian Muslim groups were up in arms at news that Ariff Alfian Rosli, a Malaysian Muslim, had entered a same-sex partnership with a white Irish man in Ireland. Just before, in November, state ministers, parliamentarians, religious scholars, the government-controlled media and several Muslim groups had condemned, intimidated and threatened Seksualiti Merdeka, a recent annual event promoting the rights of 'lesbians, gays, bisexuals and transsexuals' (LGBTs).

Why am I using these recent Malaysian examples to address an issue as huge and complex as homosexuality in Islam? Firstly, as a Malaysian Muslim, these are developments that are the nearest to me. Secondly, these are issues I have also grappled with in a professional capacity, initially as a human rights advocate, and then as a playwright and journalist. Thirdly, Malaysia occupies a unique, albeit often overlooked, position in the politics of Islam.

This last point needs some elaboration. The global South, specifically Muslim-majority countries, have often looked to us as a role model for development. Many Southern countries also saw one of our previous prime ministers, Dr Mahathir Mohamad (Anwar's mentor turned nemesis) as someone who could be counted on to stand up against 'Western hegemony'. The global North, on the other hand, often sees us as allies: exemplary 'moderate' Muslims, especially in a post-September 11 context.

Although Malaysia can be considered a Muslim-majority country, it has a sizeable non-Muslim minority, estimated at around 40 per cent of the population and consisting of Buddhists, Christians of various Eastern and Western denominations, Hindus, Sikhs, and folk religionists. Islam is the religion of the federation which practices a Westminster style of government akin to the UK's constitutional monarchy and established Church. Unlike the UK, however, Islam in Malaysia plays a direct and overt role in politics and government. The second largest political party is the Malaysian Islamic Party (PAS) which is currently part of the federal opposition coalition. The largest political party, the United Malays National Organisation (Umno), leads the ruling coalition, and while it is a race-based party, it constantly uses Islam for political leverage.

Islam is thus constantly and heavily discussed in public and in private, via the media, in Parliament and in coffee shops. Islam also influences state policies and is regulated by state policies. Thus, 'Islam' in Malaysia's case is whatever emerges as the product of political, bureaucratic, popular, learned and private expressions.

In other words, the Malaysian experience is complex, rich, and can contribute a great deal toward critical new discussions on Islam. Specifically, it is an ideal starting point to ask deep and searching questions about Islam and homosexuality. After all, we've given the world its first and perhaps only Muslim deputy prime minister-turned-opposition leader to have been twice charged and twice acquitted of homosexual sodomy.

I am not suggesting that Anwar is gay. We know that he is not. But this is not what this reflection is about. Neither am I writing to support or condemn Anwar — in my work as a journalist with an independent online Malaysian newspaper, I have written and edited my share of critical pieces about him.

Rather, my purpose is to point out how the two sodomy charges against him have introduced painful and complex questions about homosexuality and Islam. This is especially so when, in contemporary global discourses, the word 'Islam' is emotively connected to issues such as terrorism, violence, lack of human rights, and lack of democracy. In the western perception, homophobia and Islam go hand in hand.

The first question most Muslims and non-Muslims instinctively ask is, 'What does Islam say about homosexuality?' As though 'Islam' were a singular, monolithic entity capable of speaking independently of human mediation and interpretation. And as though 'homosexuality' were an untroubled, eternal category, devoid of historical circumstances and cultural assumptions. Many in fact do not even bother asking the question. They simply know that Islam condemns homosexuality and offers nothing but the severest penalties to those who engage in homosexual acts. In other words, Islamic theology is simplistic and barbaric. Those who are unconvinced are referred to the oft-rehearsed arguments condemning homosexuality in Islam.

The first stop in this argumentative journey is usually the handful of Qur'anic references to the people of the prophet Lot, the equivalent of the Lot of the Hebrew Scriptures. A particular verse from the Qur'an is fre-

quently quoted: 'We sent Lot and he said to his people. "How can you practice this outrage? No one in the world has outdone you in this. You lust after
men rather than women! You transgress all bounds"' (7:80-81). The next
stop is usually the far more numerous traditions (hadith) of the Prophet
Muhammad, such as: The Prophet (peace be upon him) said, 'If you find
anyone doing as Lot's people did, kill the one who does it, and the one to
whom it is done.' Then the conversation stops. A thick line is drawn and a
wall is built on it. You're a believing Muslim? Then you stand and stay on this
side of the wall where you must accept what the Qur'an and traditions say.
Oh, and you must condemn homosexuality and homosexuals unreservedly.

But this mentality often works in the opposite direction too. You have no
problem with gay people? Why, then you must condemn the barbaric religion of Islam and its adherents, because you, too, understand that 'Islam' is
reducible to a list of misogynistic and homophobic pronouncements. Stand
and stay on the other side of the wall, please.

On both sides of the wall is a dynamic that seeks to address and explain
homosexuality and Islam in 'basic' terms. Yet it sets us up for some very
painful and complex political, social, cultural, psychological and legal effects.
How does this work?

Let's start with the fact that there is a growing body of Muslim scholars,
leaders and activists challenging these 'basic' assumptions about Islam. For
brevity, let's call these assumptions 'Islamic homophobia'. Some of the more
prominent individuals who come to mind are the openly-gay imams Daayiee
Abdullah from the US and Muhsin Hendricks from South Africa, scholars
such as Scott Siraj Al-Haqq Kugle from the US, and LGBT Muslim groups
such as Al-Fatiha in the US, Salaam in Canada and Imaan in the UK.

These believing and practising Muslims return to what they see as the core
message of Islam which upholds justice and embraces diversity. They challenge and complicate the idea that Islam is inherently and inflexibly homophobic. Pro-LGBT Islamic scholars and imams use a variety of hermeneutical
and exegetical tools to uphold inclusive approaches in Islam. This is very
similar to the approach taken by Islamic feminists to uphold gender equality
in the spirit of Islam.

These approaches are grounded within traditional Islamic methods of
interpretation and analysis. For example, in challenging homophobic readings
of the story of Lot, pro-LGBT Islamic scholars recover commentaries from

the classical age that interpret the Qur'anic account without hostility towards those we now label 'homosexuals'. They reclaim the story of Lot and point out that it is not about God punishing people for being gay, but for arrogantly committing criminal acts of violence and coercion with impunity. Pro-LGBT Muslims also highlight numerous other Qur'anic verses exhorting a celebration of diversity, individual liberties, and a respect for dissenting views.

Besides, the Qur'an does not prescribe earthly punishments for homosexuality – these are found in the hadith and later jurisprudence. This is also where pro-LGBT Muslims challenge prevailing anti-homosexual interpretations by using, again, classical Islamic methods of exegesis and analysis. For example, even hadith scholars of the classical era of Islam found the call for execution of homosexuals, attributed to the Prophet Muhammad (S), to be unsound and unreliable.

The work of pro-LGBT Muslims, therefore, is impressively Islamic in the spirit and practice of their critiques. In fact, what is interesting about their work is that they do not need to find 'modern' interpretations of Islam   it was later human interpretations that developed a distorted view of Islam regarding homosexuality.

Now we come to the complicated part of the argument. While these advocates are Muslim, a vast proportion of them also operate from 'Western' or 'secular' contexts. It is ludicrous to use this against them, especially since there are many Muslims all over the world working overtime to prove that Muslim minorities in 'the West' are neither traitors nor represent a threat to the state they now call 'home'. Nevertheless, this is an argument that serves to strengthen the prejudices of both anti-homosexual Muslims and anti-Muslim pro-homosexual advocates. In other words, the only good Muslim is a truly Westernised Muslim.

To appreciate the explosive nature of this argument we need to see it in the context of the current geopolitics of Islam. The majority of Muslim states experienced colonisation by Western powers ranging from the directly brutal, such as Algeria, to apparently benign condescension, as in Malaysia. This business of colonialism is far from finished. It is evident in the nervous commentaries coming out of the West in response to the ongoing Arab uprisings: 'What about the Islamists?'; 'Will free elections benefit the Muslim Brotherhood?'; 'Do they want to impose the shariah?'; 'Will this be bad for business?'. In sum, 'Muslims are backward because they don't have democracy, but now that they have a shot at trying it out we're pretty sure they can't handle it.' These attitudes play an integral important part in the overall argument about Islam and homosexuality.

Imagine, for example, what happens when Western LGBT-identified Muslims ally themselves with the broader Western LGBT movement, which now has the power to effectively lobby Western governments on an array of sexuality-related policies. From the point of view of a traditional, conservative Muslim, it would look very much as though LGBT Muslims are synonymous with Western LGBTs, who are then synonymous with 'secular-liberal' values, which are synonymous with hostility to Islam. These cognitive leaps might seem bizarre or illogical to some. But at the same time, think about how easily and confidently so many Americans joined the dots between 'Osama bin Laden' and 'Taliban' and 'terrorism' and 'Islam', and then proceeded to use these labels interchangeably with great ideological force.

Perhaps I can rephrase my question: imagine what happens when someone like David Cameron, Conservative Prime Minister of the UK, threatens to restrict foreign aid to countries that continue to criminalise homosexuality? Cameron announced this in October 2011 at a meeting of Commonwealth heads of government. To be certain, many African governments bristled at Cameron's threat, but there are also several Muslim member states of the Commonwealth that would be similarly affected. This is significant because Cameron is the same person who, earlier in February, told the Munich Security Conference how afraid he is of 'radicalised' young British Muslim men and wants to cut funding for numerous Muslim groups in Britain.

Cameron is not alone. In her December 2011 speech at the United Nations in Geneva, US Secretary of State Hilary Clinton also said the US would fight discrimination against gays and lesbians worldwide by using foreign aid and diplomacy. Imagine how this news would be received by the vast majority of Muslims who, also in December, found out that President Barack Obama had legislated to allow terror suspects – those pesky Muslims again – to be held indefinitely without trial. The dynamics this time are similar to when President George W Bush said in 2001 that he would invade Afghanistan to save poor, defenceless, burqa-clad Muslim women from horrible Muslim men. 'We like Muslims, but only when they're women or gay, because then we get to save them and make them like us.'

Given the sensitivity of this issue, let me make it clear that I am not excusing anti-homosexual tendencies justified in the name of Islam. Neither is it my intention to discredit or dismiss LGBT-identified Muslims residing in the West who do important and sincere work to reclaim inclusive expressions of Islam. Nevertheless, I insist on recognising and analysing how issues are interconnected. The messier or more complicated these interconnections, the more urgent the requirement for analysis. As Joseph Massad noted in an article in *Public Culture*, 'it is not the Gay International or its upper-class supporters in the Arab diaspora who will be persecuted but rather the poor and nonurban men who practise same-sex contact and who do not identify as homosexual or gays.' The reality is, we need to think about those sexually marginalised Muslims who are not cultural or financial elites and who do not benefit from Western-style LGBT advocacy.

The queer theorist Jasbir Puar has pointed out how power relations within the global LGBT movement have marginalised LGBT groups opposed to the Israeli occupation of Palestine. Her analysis has been met with exasperation and ridicule from LGBT advocates who hold Israel up as a beacon of LGBT rights in the homophobic wasteland that is the (Muslim) Middle East. These criticisms miss the point, however. Puar does not deny the hostilities that sexual minorities in Muslim societies face. In fact, she carefully points out the existence of several LGBT or queer Palestinian organisations doing important work against both homophobia and the Israeli occupation. In the same spirit, let me suggest a possible framework for discussing homosexuality in Islam.

But first a caveat. You may have noticed a lack of consistency in my use of language. I have used the terms 'homosexual', 'LGBT' and 'sexual minorities' quite interchangeably. Surely there must be consistent, politically correct terminology I could use? I'm really not so sure. I appreciate those LGBT movements that connect their struggles against homophobia to other issues such as Islamophobia, anti-Semitism, racism, misogyny, xenophobia and the continued marginalisation of the working class.

Yet I increasingly find the term 'LGBT' unwieldy and conceptually difficult. As Ziauddin Sardar has observed, 'these acronyms are not only cumbersome and rather unattractive but also dehumanising. To have one's identity truncated to acronyms or worse merely initials (Ls, Gs, Bs and so on) is to be reduced as a human being.' I prefer the terms 'sexual diversity' or 'sexual minorities', but I also recognise the need to address what happens when we insert 'homosexuality' into Islamic discourses.

The main problem is how does one read modern, culturally-specific concepts such as 'homosexuality' into the sacred texts of Islam? Or into any pre-modern text for that matter? Thoughtful Christians have the same difficulty figuring out where or how 'homosexuality' is addressed in the Bible in ways comparable to modern usage. The issue with any text is that it needs to be interpreted. When it is a religious text, interpretations can shift or develop over the course of history, or in fact in different cultural and political contexts. For instance, the majority religion in Iran and Turkey is recognisably Islam. Yet Islam is articulated rather differently in both countries on a range of issues, from justifying the type of political state in existence to day-to-day gender relations.

The situation is similar when it comes to homosexuality. There are uncompromisingly hostile interpretations of Islam which some will argue are 'correct', and then there are the inclusive interpretations, frequently labelled 'deviant'. Laying aside the question of who exactly has the earthly power to declare one interpretation 'correct' and another 'deviant', I am more curious about other interpretations or opinions. Surely 1.6 billion Muslims cannot be cleanly divided into the uncompromisingly 'correct' and the irredeemably 'deviant'. And surely Muslims all over the world do not share homogenous assumptions about 'homosexuality', even Muslims with same-sex desires.

I am therefore interested in opinions such as those of Tariq Ramadan. On the surface, it would appear that Ramadan errs on the normative or 'correct' side of Islamic interpretation. In other words, he considers homosexuality to be sinful and wrong. This has provoked European LGBT advocates to dismiss him as yet another Muslim homophobe. But let us examine Ramadan's position more closely. He says:

For more than twenty years I have been insisting — and drawing sharp criticism from some Muslim groups — that homosexuality is forbidden in Islam, but that we must avoid condemning or rejecting individuals. It is quite possible to disagree with a person's behaviour (public or private), while respecting that person as an individual. This I have continued to affirm, and gone further still: a person who pronounces the attestation of Islamic faith becomes a Muslim; if that person engages in homosexual practices, no one has the right to drive him or her out of Islam.

So Ramadan thinks homosexuality is forbidden on religious grounds but also insists that homosexuals – even Muslims – should not suffer discrimination or persecution. How is this a dangerous position? How does this make Ramadan any worse than, say, European Christians or Jews (or perchance atheists) who disapprove of homosexuality? In fact, some might wish that more 'Muslim homophobes' thought like Ramadan.

Ramadan's position is touching on two counts. Firstly, he makes his point about Islam and homosexuality succinctly and painlessly. The bit that he takes great pains to elaborate is how the acceptance of homosexuality has now become a burden disproportionately placed on Muslims in Europe. Why do European Muslims have to prove that they embrace and delight in homosexuality in order to assert their citizenship credentials? Is it not enough that they can separate their own personal opinions from their respect for each individual's basic dignity and rights, especially those who are different from them? Ramadan seems almost heartbroken that sexuality is now the preferred method of Muslim-baiting in the West.

Yet there are more Muslims like Ramadan in Europe. A 2011 poll by thinktank Demos found that British Muslims are more likely to strongly agree with the statement 'I am proud of how Britain treats gay people' than even people of no religion. In fact, fewer than 25 per cent of British Muslims polled disagreed with the statement.

I am tempted to call these signs of hope, but the fact is that even doing this might be condescending. It would be as though we are waiting for Muslims elsewhere to 'catch up' with British Muslims. The point is, this is reality. Muslims, like any other group of people, hold diverse views on homosexuality. This fact alone should not be surprising. What should be surprising is that so many people find it surprising.

It should therefore be equally unsurprising that there are diverse views about sexuality in Islam, and that it has always been so. Western LGBT Muslims are not alone in upholding gay-affirming interpretations of Islam. In 2008, the Indonesian Islamic scholar Siti Musdah Mulia said Islam 'recognised' homosexuality. She — yes, this Islamic scholar is a woman — justified her opinion from the verses of the Qur'an, partly basing her reasoning on 49: 13 ('People, we created you all from a single man and a single woman...). Almost immediately, several other Indonesian Islamic groups condemned her opinion, but that's not something completely dissimilar to, say, the Anglican Communion's current global crisis on sexuality.

We cannot, under any circumstances, justify state-driven violence and intimidation of sexual minorities. But at the same time, we have to acknowledge that issues of sexuality are complex, intimately connected to political context, and thus generate a wide variety of opinions and positions. It is not simply a question of being for or against homosexuality. It is interesting to note that Anwar took a nuanced position when the Malaysian state demonised and threatened the organisers of LGBT rights festival Seksualiti Merdeka. On one level, he was emphatic that his party endorsed neither the festival nor LGBT rights. However, he went on to say: 'The issue here is not whether to support or not to support. The issue is you attack them. That's something else. Can't we talk about things in this country?'

Indeed, can't we just talk about things before jumping to conclusions? I would love to hear a conversation on Islam and homosexuality between Siti Musdah Mulia, Tariq Ramadan, Scott Siraj Al-Haqq Kugle and Sheikh Yusuf al-Qaradawi, the Egyptian theologian best known for his Al-Jazeera programme, 'Shariah and Life'. One can imagine the heat if such a public dialogue was moderated by someone like Amina Wadud, the controversial Muslim-American feminist. I wouldn't want them to agree with each other or to shout each other down. I'd hope for them to keep the integrity of their positions, but also listen to each other thoughtfully and respectfully, and to engage meaningfully.

It is not easy to do this as Muslims in the contemporary world, especially given the geopolitical minefield we have to tiptoe through and the constant spotlight on our every move. Yet this makes it all the more important for us to walk this path with integrity and courage. We don't become lesser Muslims just by having nuanced ideas about human diversity or by locating them within larger critiques of global politics.

But for those who would quote a hadith to shout me down, here's one whose simplicity and forthrightness I adore: 'A man was with the Prophet (peace be upon him) and a man passed by him and said: Apostle of Allah! I love this man. The Apostle of Allah (peace be upon him) then asked: Have you informed him? He replied: No. He said: Inform him. He then went to him and said: I love you for Allah's sake. He replied: May He for Whose sake you love me love you!'

SECTARIAN GULF

Fanar Haddad

As I was writing, the Internet was flooded with reports of Gaddafi's death. In the age of video-sharing websites and mobile phone cameras, we were also inundated with footage of Gaddafi's last moments and of his lifeless corpse. I was immediately reminded of Saddam Hussein's demise back in 2006. It seems the two tyrants do have one thing in common: they were both subjects of the modern day public execution; their final moments broadcast to millions across the world through mobile phone cameras and the Internet. However, the Arab public reaction to the two events has been very different. The indignation expressed at Saddam's execution led to protests in several Arab cities and, rather ironically, to a public day of mourning being announced in Gaddafi's Libya. Fast forward five years to Gaddafi's demise, and yes there was much public indignation in the Arab world at the manner of his execution, but the dynamics were so different that whatever indignation was being expressed was likely to be fleeting and was ultimately overshadowed by the fact that Libya's rebels enjoyed a considerable measure of admiration, sympathy and legitimacy in Arab public opinion (Gaddafi's downfall led to only one demonstration, in Syria, and it called for Bashar al Assad to share the same fate as his deceased Libyan counterpart). The differing reactions to the downfall of the two tyrants are indicative of the broader reality: Libya is not another Iraq and Iraq will never be another Libya.

Throughout the anti-Gaddafi rebellion that began in February 2011, much analysis and commentary focused on the question of how to avoid a repeat of Iraq: a political vacuum that descends into civil war and widespread anarchy. Whilst the epic proportions of Iraq's civil strife and violence since 2003, and the accompanying social and political conditions, are (thankfully) near impossible to replicate in Libya, there is still some way to go before Libyans can breathe a final sigh of relief. Libya has yet to establish a viable, cohesive and functioning government that can project its authority over the country. Emboldened and highly fragmented rebels have yet to put down their weapons and accept a political process that mandates winners and losers. There have been sporadic outbreaks of violence linked to competing militias and tribal disputes. In short there are serious questions concerning the maintenance of law and order, the provision of services, and the rejuvenation of the hydrocarbons sector that underpins the Libyan economy.

Justified as these concerns might be (and I am by no means the first to raise them), they are not necessarily veiled predictions of doom. In fact the early signs are leading many towards a cautious optimism. The widespread looting, chaos and bloodshed that heralded the birth of the new Iraq have not been seen in Libya. Whilst abuses have taken place, and in likelihood will continue, there is nothing to suggest that the cycle of vengeance that devoured post-2003 Iraq will descend upon Libya. Perhaps the most important difference is the legitimacy that the new Libya enjoys within its borders and beyond. This sense of legitimacy is underlined by three crucial factors that were/are glaringly absent from Iraq: for good or ill, Libya's regime-change had domestic and organic roots; regionally, Arab public opinion has been overwhelmingly sympathetic to the Libyan rebels; finally, Libya is blessed with the benevolent absence of a sectarian divide.

Regime change in Iraq, again regardless of pros and cons, was an external imposition; it was alien and bore little relation to political realities and actors within Iraq. The Iraqi exiles who championed regime change and who led the new Iraq were as detached from Iraqi social and political realities as the invading Americans and the British. Coupled with the greed, incompetence and criminality they have exhibited since 2003, their near-utopian pre-war fantasies about an Iraq they had no recent experience of recall Octavio Paz's reflections on the birth of modern Mexico where a detached elite 'sacrificed reality to words and delivered us up to the ravenous appetites of the strong'. In their defence, even if the Iraqi exiles had not proven so inept, their reintegration into an Iraq they had not seen for decades was inevitably hindered by the fact that they were associated with a foreign invasion and occupation.

In retrospect, given these factors and so many more, it seems unsurprising that Iraq quickly, almost instantly, descended into chaos. Why not loot? Why not be selfish? After all – and here is where the difference with Libya begins to border on the tragic – there was no sense of purpose, no sense of being part of a historical moment, no sense of being part of something bigger and better on the streets of Iraq in April 2003. In Libya, there was a sense that 'we the people' are part of something noble, something that occupies a near irreproachable morality; there is a sense of ownership and duty that was completely absent from Iraq. Again in retrospect, how could it have been any different? In Iraq, 'we the people' had no say and took no part in the historical moment. There was no public sense of ownership of events in 2003; even those within Iraq who may have welcomed the invasion (and make no mistake they did exist) could not feel part of the event for the simple reason that they did not and could not play a part in a process that was dictated from above by foreign actors (Iraqi or otherwise).

This whole dynamic was encapsulated in the pulling down of Saddam's statue in Firdos Square; the tragic symbolism was not so much of the passing of one regime and the birth of a new one as of the irrelevance of the Iraqi people in the events of 2003. The small crowd of Iraqis that gathered in Firdos Square tried to assume ownership of the event by attempting to tear down their tyrant's statue by themselves; however, try as they might, they could not bring it down and, in what could serve as a parody of the Iraq war, the task was left to an American armoured vehicle. This pattern of exclusion and impotence continued, and perhaps accounts for the proliferation of armed groups: after all, the space for participation and ownership between 2003–08 was far more generous for those who chose violent rejection. This is not meant to be a moral judgment on April 2003; rather, it is an attempt to understand why the new Iraq has been the catastrophe that most people agree it is. For many Iraqis (within Iraq of course), April 2003 was an embodiment of destruction – war, invasion, occupation, the collapse of the old regime and its institutions; for many Libyans, 2011 was an embodiment of construction – rebellion, sacrifice, success, building a new Libya.

There are other, more tangible reasons for Iraq's troubles: foreign invasion and a criminally incompetent occupation; an equally inept Iraqi political elite; the poverty and rampant criminality of the sanctions era; and the decimation of society and the contraction of the state since 1990. Violence was perhaps inevitable in a post-Saddam security vacuum; there were too many scores to settle in a country awash with weapons and a society brutalised by three wars and decades of dictatorship. But one wonders if the violence would have been so vicious and so prolonged were it not for the sectarian dimension – the most damaging factor and the most illustrative difference between Iraq and Libya.

In post-2003 Iraq, sectarian identity was intertwined with geopolitics, the legitimacy of the Iraqi government, relations with the Arab world and popular perceptions regarding the new Iraq – in short sectarian identity was politicised. So much so that before long everything was viewed through the prism of the sectarian divide; and here it needs to be said that, intentionally or otherwise, a range of actors (the occupation, the new Iraqi elite, militants, regional powers, the media and the Iraqi people themselves) were instrumental in the politicisation of sectarian identity. Libya, homogenous in sectarian terms, will escape such a fate.

Doubters will correctly point to the possibility, in any society, of other, non-sectarian, societal cleavages being politicised. However, what societal cleavage is capable of intertwining itself so profoundly with politics and society? What societal cleavage is capable of influencing foreign policy and the geopolitical outlook of a region?

Let us reframe the issue by examining the differences between Saddam and Gaddafi. Was the sympathy Saddam received from the Arab world in the post-2003 era and the absence of Arab solidarity with Gaddafi in 2011 the result of the successes and failures of the two tyrants' PR campaigns? Did Saddam's rash attack on Israel in 1991 buy him enough credit to last him into the twenty-first century? Or are the divergent Arab perceptions of the two related to the fact that Saddam had been toppled by an American invasion that empowered out-groups (Kurds and, even more alarmingly, Shias) in a region that remains allergic to the organised assertion of out-group identities? How else do we account for the Arab public's acceptance of NATO's involvement in Libya? I, for one, am not convinced that the absence of foreign boots on the ground and the mandate NATO received from the all but defunct Arab League played as large a role in shaping public perceptions as some believe. Let us for a moment imagine that foreign airpower was used to support rebels in pre-2003 Iraq and that these rebels were labelled 'Shia'; would Arab publics have sympathised with them? Or would the 'Shia' label have conjured the spectre of the anti-Arab, Iranian bogeyman, as is usually the case when Shia activists (benign or nefarious) make their voices heard?

The answer is perhaps obvious when one considers the reactions of Arab public opinion and Arab media to Iraq 2003, Libya 2011 and Bahrain 2011. Societal cleavages in Libya may have the potential to threaten short-term stability but their ability to draw in regional players and animate regional passions is limited. Iraq's or Bahrain's sectarian cleavages however, particularly given Iran's proximity to and undeniable involvement in both countries, command a magnetic pull on public, state and media attention across the Arab world (particularly in the *Mashreq*) for the simple reason that Sunni-Shia identities (when activated) are politicised transnational identities based on religion and, equally if not more profoundly, based on the widespread conflation of sectarian identity with ethnic identity in the Middle East. As a result, Libyan rebels humiliating and killing Gaddafi may elicit disapproval in the Arab world without generating a sense of involvement in what is after all a Libyan affair. Saddam's execution in 2006, however, inflamed sectarian identity across the Arab world and activated feelings of triumph or encirclement: the execution was an assertion of Shia identity and had the very predictable consequence that sectarian identities were bolstered across the region amongst both Shias and Sunnis, particularly in countries that are home to competing sectarian groups.

'Sectarianism'

Seldom does one come across a term as overused and as useless as 'sectarianism'. I myself prefer using the term 'sectarian' coupled with a relevant suffix (sectarian relations, sectarian hate, sectarian harmony and so forth). Even then, the mere mention of sects raises a set of linguistically inescapable terms that have become so emotionally charged as to make rational debate a rarity. With that in mind, I should clarify my usage of the terminology in this article.

I tend to use the terms 'sectarian group' and 'communal group' interchangeably, for the simple reason that there is little differentiating the two; at heart, sectarian identity is a form of communal identity. The sectarian divide I am referring to is the Sunni-Shia divide amongst Muslims. This does not reflect a definitional stance and there are indeed many sectarian divides besides the Sunni-Shia one; however, it is the Sunni-Shia divide that is the strongest in the Middle East in terms of historical legacy, demographics and, most importantly, political relevance. In the current climate, it intertwines itself with nationalism as Shias and Sunnis in any one country seek to prove their national authenticity and support their competing senses of entitlement. It is played out in religious discourse, as both Shiism and Sunnism seek the mantle of legitimate embodiments of Islam. In the Arab *Mashreq* and to a lesser extent in the Maghreb, the Sunni-Shia divide is conflated with ethnic divisions as Iranian claims to ownership of Shiism are validated by Arab Sunnis' equating of all things Shia to all things Iranian. Finally, the Iran factor lends the Arab world's Sunni-Shia divide an inescapable politicisation due to Arab-Iranian rivalry and the (often justified) political antagonisms between Iran and several Arab states. Whilst I will be arguing that ethnic and/or religious 'out-group' identities are unusually problematic in the Middle East, the Sunni-Shia divide is particularly contentious due to the 'Iran-factor'.

The second qualifier I feel is necessary in any discussion of Sunnis and Shias is a very obvious one and one I will never tire of repeating: nothing can be said about all Shias or all Sunnis as both groups are far from monolithic; consequently any mention of Sunnis and Shias will necessarily contain an element of generalisation by identifying and focusing on dominant trends and lines of discourse. Indeed similar qualifiers are needed when discussing any mass-group identity, and at heart the Sunni-Shia divide is an issue of competing mass-group identities regardless of whether these identities come with religious, theological or philosophical props. As I see it, Sunnism and Shi'ism are largely incidental to Sunni-Shia competition. Religion provides the backdrop for the animosities, it provides the assurance of the righteousness of the group and indeed of the group's animosities, but beyond that I would argue that the vast majority of people imagine their sectarian identity in very temporal and secular terms. To illustrate: how important was religion to 2011's events in Bahrain? Yet how profound was the effect of those same events on sectarian identity in Bahrain and beyond?

The third qualifier is made with those critics in mind who will point to the numerous examples of sectarian harmony as proof that sectarian identity is barely relevant in Arab popular conceptions of self. As I have argued elsewhere, the first step to understanding sectarian relations is to recognise their fluidity. Rather than focusing on episodes of sectarian discord or romanticising examples of sectarian harmony, our understanding of the issue would be better served if we recognised that the salience of sectarian identity is subject to erratic fluctuations, and whilst sectarian identity can lose political relevance and lie dormant for many decades it can be awoken by a number of drivers leading people to lend it a hitherto absent centrality in their conceptions of self, before eventually losing salience again and being relegated under other forms of self-definition. The 'we are all brothers' mantra is as flawed as the notion that Sunnis and Shias are locked in perennial existential struggle. No group identity can remain mobilised indefinitely and sectarian identity competes with other group identities in our multi-layered definitions of self and reacts to social, political and economic stimuli. Therefore if I mention current sectarian dynamics they need to be understood as reflective of a particular context and a particular time period.

It is unfortunate that the salience of sectarian identity is currently elevated to unprecedented levels in many parts of the Middle East, and Iraq must take much of the dubious credit for this. The relevance of sectarian identity in the post-2003 Middle East, particularly in the *Mashreq*, is difficult to exaggerate. The empowerment of Iraqi Shias in 2003 and the carnage that followed has bred competing sectarian identities far beyond Iraq that are rooted in self-righteous claims to victimhood, feelings of encirclement and uncompromising claims to legitimate representation of faith and nation. Since 2003, events in Iraq itself have been framed in sectarian terms, starting with views towards Saddam and regime change – pity the Shia who supported Saddam and the Sunni who supported regime change, for these two political stances were almost immediately commandeered by sectarian discourse. Whilst much has changed in Iraq since the civil war of 2006–07, it is still viewed in much of the Arab world as a 'sectarian issue'. Furthermore, we are still periodically reminded of the impact of 2003 on sectarian identity in the Middle East, particularly in the reactions to the tentative attempts to spread the Arab Spring in the *Mashreq*.

Celebrating the Arab Spring

The Arab Spring: that most unexpected and most overdue of upheavals. Regardless of how events turn out in the countries that it has visited (and there is no reason to presume that the short term effects will be benevolent), recent events constitute an organic chapter in Arab political development driven from below that comes after decades of political stagnation. Indeed, I can think of no other event in the history of the modern Arab nation-state that has enjoyed this level of popular participation. As expected, alongside the customary conspiracy theories, Arab public opinion has been largely supportive and proud of the fact that the previously unthinkable has happened in several Arab states. However, this support has not been extended to all countries experiencing popular protest and there have been some grimly predictable exceptions.

Whether in the form of face paint, flags, illustrations or political cartoons, the countries depicted in celebrations of the Arab Spring are Tunisia, Egypt, Syria, Yemen and Libya. Why is Bahrain not included? After all, like Syria, Yemen and Libya, Bahraini protestors tried to emulate the Tunisian and Egyptian examples with tragic consequences. The scale of the upheaval in Bahrain places it in a different category to say Iraq or Saudi Arabia where the scale and tempo of the protests was somewhat sporadic; surely the demonstrations in Bahrain and the dramatic clampdown that followed should qualify Bahrain for membership in the Arab Spring. The reality however is that Bahrain did not and never will qualify for the same reason that Hezbollah's Hassan Nasrallah, the Iraqi government and Iran quite correctly highlighted the plight of Bahraini protesters and yet failed to show the same solidarity with embattled protesters in Syria. On the contrary: they condemned the protests there. The answer to this discrepancy in views regarding the Arab Spring lies in the post-2003 sectarian climate that pervades not just state policy but public perception as well.

The stark contradictions in how different protests in the Arab world are viewed by Arab public opinion illustrate how Arabs conceive of themselves – it illustrates who 'we the people' are both in a national and transnational sense. A comparison of reactions to Libya, Iraq and Bahrain serves not only to illustrate the workings of sectarian relations but also reveals the broader problem of ethnic and/or religious out-group identities and their expression in the Middle East.

The modern Middle Eastern state, and to a significant extent modern Middle Eastern society, is unhealthily attracted to the myth of ethno-religious uniformity. This is why communal identities and communal rights and representation have been such taboo subjects in the Arab world. When it comes to discussing communal identity, one often glimpses a self-enforced hegemonic public imagination in Arab public opinion and media that makes little allowance for ethnic and/or religious out-group identities. This hegemony is partially the result of the fluid relationship between national identity (Syrian, Omani, Egyptian and so forth) and transnational Arab identity. The Middle East is imagined as an Arab and Sunni Muslim space and, indeed, Arab Sunnis form the overwhelming majority of the people of the Middle East. However, this is not necessarily the case in the individual nation-state – to say nothing of non-Arab Middle Eastern nation-states. Yet the dominant Arab discourse – as propagated by transnational media and as reproduced by Arabs themselves – blurs the distinction between the national and the transnational and consequently views non-Arab and/or non-Sunni groups as 'minority groups' regardless of their numerical weight in their own particular country; hence my preference for 'out-group' as opposed to other terms that I use interchangeably – sub-national, minority, communal. The Shia in Bahrain or Iraq are not minority groups; yet due to the transnational element that places Arab Sunni identity at the heart of what it means to be part of the Arab world, there is a distinctive 'otherness' in their portrayal: they are an aberration from what is normally considered 'we the people'. It is this 'otherness', rigorously enforced in both the hegemonic discourse and in the discourse of out-groups themselves, that places Arab Sunni identity at the heart of transnational Arabism and creates and reinforces the 'out-group' or those that are not naturally a part of 'us'. The existence of out-groups is not unique to the Middle East, nor is it necessarily a problem in and of itself – indeed every country has such groups. However, what makes ethnic and religious out-group identities problematic in the Middle East is the restriction of their expression in the public sphere. It is almost as if such identities are a dirty secret to be hidden away alongside other skeletons in the national closet.

Perhaps the roots of this phenomenon lie in the anti-colonial rejectionism that marked the birth of the Arab nation-state and that mandated a clearly defined and distilled 'us' against the coloniser. Or is the answer to be found in the form in which Arab-nationalism manifested itself in the early to mid twentieth century and made 'Arab' credentials a central criterion for inclusion in the nation-state? Or maybe the problem is with the authoritarianism that characterises much of the Arab nation-state's political history and which saw communal identity being used by regimes to divide people by presenting out-group identities as a threat to the otherwise blissful unity that Middle Eastern regimes have been so keen on portraying?

Whatever the explanation, we can safely accuse the Arab nation-state of (to varying degrees) failing to provide mechanisms for the legitimate expression of sub-national out-group identities and of failing to create a relative cultural homogeneity that can subsume communal identities. Instead, the myths of purity and unity are propagated from above and reproduced from below as a soothing alternative to the difficult question of how to accept difference under a strengthened citizenship that caters for all. In other words the 'unity' and the 'purity' that define 'we the people' are myths enforced by dominant groups (whether in terms of cultural, political or numerical weight) as it resonates with their sense of self. As described by Egyptian scholar Moustapha Safouan, this illusory unity is little more than, 'a mere desire, or a libidinal aspiration, which has no more reality than the petty songs with which the regime tries to drug people'. Hence we see the continued and pervasive censorship of sub-national ethnic and/or religious identities that are condemned to remain private and silent by both the state and popular discourse.

The reality is that communal groups exist, within religions and within nation-states, and, when salient, these compete with each other and with dominant groups to define the myths and symbols – the narrative – of a mutually-claimed cultural and political space. As such, Shias and Sunnis will both claim to have the answer to the unanswerable question of what 'true' or 'correct' Islam is and, in the context of the nation-state, they will both champion their respective claims of belonging, ownership and entitlement based on their antagonistic narratives of who and what 'we the people' of a particular country are. These competing narratives have the potential to dictate how contemporary events are understood and remembered. This antagonism and these overlapping claims to a singular mass-identity (nation, religion), coupled with the shortcomings of Middle Eastern nation building, have left religious and ethnic out-group identities in the Arab world particularly prone to politicisation and have enabled them to inhere on the formation of popular memories.

Bahrain

That the Bahraini regime and other regimes in the Arab world tried to discredit the protesters in Bahrain is hardly surprising; what is far more remarkable is the roaring success that these efforts have achieved in Arab public opinion. Even the emotional tide generated by the Arab Spring was unable to challenge the state's discourse when it came to Bahrain, according to which the protests were part of a pernicious plot hatched, planned, incited and executed by Iran; a plot designed to serve none other than Iran's interests. Accordingly, the protestors themselves were, wittingly or not, treacherously serving the Iranian enemy. This line has been warmly received and reproduced by Arab media and Arab public opinion despite the fact that similar state efforts to discredit protestors in Egypt, Libya, Syria and Iraq (all of whom described their protestors as terrorists and/or foreigners serving foreign agendas) fell on deaf ears. The reason Arab public opinion accepted the official narrative of Bahraini events was due less to the popularity of the Bahraini regime than to the unpopularity of the Bahraini protestors. The basic reason why the state's attempts to discredit the protestors were so successful was that they chimed with public perceptions that view organised assertions of out-group identity, in this case Shia, with fear.

Arab media painted the Bahraini protests in a distinctively negative light, with some networks going to great lengths to convince viewers of the difference between what was happening in Bahrain and the wider Arab Spring. Sunni religious leaders (from the most humble to the celebrity televangelists), analysts, television presenters, writers and commentators condemned the protests in Bahrain in unequivocal terms: this was a sectarian movement driven by Iran that targets Bahrain, the Gulf and Sunnis generally. One sentiment prevalent in commentary on Bahrain is that the protestors should be ejected from Bahrain: 'let them go to Iran', 'strip them of their nationality', or in the words of one Kuwaiti pundit, 'may death take you and those that rule you in Iran'. Yet if we look at the protestors' discourse we find absolutely no mention, in any way shape or form, of Iran – and let us not forget that whatever our views of the protestors they are Bahraini citizens. Despite that, Arab public opinion immediately, predictably and uncompromisingly held the Bahraini protests, Iran and sectarianism as near synonymous terms. It is regrettable that the Arab reaction to the events in Bahrain so lucidly illustrates my point: that the divide between dominant groups and ethnic/religious out-groups becomes unbridgeable if and when the latter seek to assert their identities simply because such out-groups are not considered equally legitimate citizens in the popular imagination. As a result, sympathy and solidarity are reserved for 'us the people' and overwhelmingly withheld from 'the other' even if that 'other' is a constituent part of the nation-state – a citizen. Doubters need only look at the scarcity of compassion in the Arab world with any issues relating to Western Sahara, Copts, Kurds, Shias and other out-groups.

Sensationalism and fear-mongering were standard fare in the Arab media's treatment of events in Bahrain. To give but one example, in late September 2011, protestors marched through a Bahraini shopping mall shouting anti-regime slogans. *Al Arabiya* reported the incident under the following headline: 'An hour of horror and people falling unconscious in a shopping mall in Bahrain ahead of the elections', with the sub-heading: 'Carried out by a group described by the Ministry of the Interior as saboteurs'. The report went on to describe the details of the incident:

Visitors to one of central Manama's shopping malls experienced an hour of horror and fear on Friday after a group described by the Ministry of the Interior as saboteurs stormed the mall whilst chanting for the overthrow of the government and against the [Bahraini] King, the [Bahraini] Prime Minister and Saudi Arabia.

In addition to the 'hour of horror and fear', the group did not merely enter the mall, rather, they stormed or broke into it [*iqtaham*]. The report continues:

Al Arabiya was touring the shopping mall on Friday afternoon; it was calm and visitors were shopping and quietly going about their lives without racket until, suddenly, the situation was entirely transformed into screams, fear and people falling unconscious as a result of that group's storming of the mall.

The report goes on to say that a Bahraini family was attacked by the group leading to the injury of an old woman, 'as one of her sons tried to protect her', and that the *Al Arabiya* crew were attacked by the same group. However the same *Al Arabiya* report is clumsily accompanied by video footage that paints a very different picture. For one thing the group of protestors is overwhelmingly composed of women; more importantly the protestors marched through the mall without physically attacking anyone or anything and restricting themselves to chanting the familiar slogans of Bahrain's recent protests: 'Down with [King] Hamad'; 'The people want the over-throw of the regime'; and 'With blood and spirit we sacrifice ourselves to the martyr.' At no point in the footage was there any sign of anything that could realistically induce fear or horror, let alone unconsciousness, nor was there any evidence of violence – even when towards the end of the footage a rival group formed and shouted pro-regime slogans.

It may seem trivial to outline the details of this article – in truth I chose it more for its absurdity than its virulence. Nevertheless it is symptomatic of a broader trend in Arab media regarding recent events in Bahrain and that reflects Arab public opinion's allergy to the assertion of out-group identi-ties. A cursory look at Arab media coverage and user-generated commen-tary (social network sites, chatrooms and so forth) on the Bahraini protests reveals an alarming polarisation of views along sectarian lines: generally, Shias are sympathetic to the protestors and Sunnis are against them. This worrying politicisation of sectarian identity, whereby political stances are shaped by one's sectarian identity, is a phenomenon that is as visible in Bahrain as it is in the wider Arab world. No evidence has thus far been produced to prove Iran's alleged role in the Bahraini protests besides the Iranian media's praise for and sympathy towards the protestors after the fact; nor has there been any evidence presented for the protestors' alleged incitement to sectarian hate. In fact, what footage has emerged of the pro-tests on YouTube and elsewhere shows a remarkably 'Bahraini' discourse with a near-ubiquitous presence of the Bahraini flag in Pearl Square and chants and slogans against the regime rather than against Sunnis – indeed there is evidence to suggest a limited Sunni presence amongst the protes-tors. Nevertheless Arab public opinion across the Middle East remains overwhelmingly convinced that what happened in Bahrain has nothing to do with the Arab Spring or legitimate political demands and everything to do with Iran. It seems that, as far as Arab public opinion is concerned, it is simply inconceivable that Shia Bahrainis can possibly make political demands independently of Iran. The *Al Arabiy*a article elicited an impressive 522 com-ments and, whilst I am in no way treating what Stephen Fry correctly described as 'the most unbearable creature that inhabits the floor of the Internet' as an accurate scientific survey, it is nevertheless instructive that out of 522 comments only fifty expressed sympathy with the protestors or scepticism towards the sensationalist tone of the article.

Given the pervasiveness of a mindset that views out-groups with such deeply rooted suspicion, reform relating to communal groups in the Middle East can only be achieved in the unlikely event that it is championed by members of the dominant group: legitimate Shia activism in Bahrain will always be attacked as an 'Iranian plot' just as legitimate Sunni activism in the new Iraq has been attacked as a 'Baathi plot'. It is difficult to see how this dynamic can change given its broad resonance with public opinion. What chance do the 'doves' in the Bahraini royal family have against their 'hawk' relatives? A hawkish position not only serves the interests of the royal family, but is also genuinely popular with significant sections of society. It is patently obvious that Bahrain's rulers reacted to domestic unrest in the same way that autocrats have always reacted in countries that are home to a sectarian divide: by ensuring the sectarianisation of the unrest in the public imagination so as to garner support and discredit the opposition. Facilitating this policy are the suspicions and inflated perceptions of 'otherness' in Arab views towards ethnic and religious out-groups.

In the current climate, the public's suspicions and prejudices and the narrow interests of autocratic elites act in a mutually reinforcing way that may well preclude meaningful reforms in the near future. In Bahrain, Syria, Iraq and elsewhere we see the employment of communal identities for political ends with the inevitable result that communal identities are sharpened and more people come to view a shared public space through the exclusionist prism of their own communal group identity. In all three countries history is contested between communal groups, each wielding an impressive sense of victimhood and/or entitlement and a narcissistic historical narrative that places them at the centre of the nation-state. All three countries are home to pluralistic societies and hence cannot accommodate such charged and contradictory narratives of a mutually shared space.

The imperative therefore is to find a way of depoliticising group identities and fostering acceptance of difference in the national mix. Only then can an historical narrative of 'we the people' be constructed in a way that is truly inclusive and that would not shy away from incorporating aspects of the other's popular memory. As things stand, all three countries refuse even to admit let alone face the problem of communal identities. This is illustrated by the fact that censuses are such problematic issues, and by the fact that the nation-state's history (meaning the scientific and objective study of the nation-state's past) remains so contentious even amongst academics. Regarding Shia-Sunni relations, Arab-Iranian rivalry makes resolution all the more difficult as it lends an ethnic dimension to what would otherwise be an issue of religious group identity and an international dimension to what would otherwise be an internal affair. Hence the callous positions taken by Iran, Iraq and Hezbollah towards Syrian protests and the equally callous position taken by most Arab states and Arab public opinion against Bahraini protests, or indeed with regards to Iraq since 2003. The ease with which sectarian passions are aroused and the toxic salience of sectarian identity in the post 2003 *Mashreq* present formidable challenges to would-be reformers, and may end up validating Patrick Cockburn's grim prediction that sectarian animosities will prevent the Arab Spring from spreading east of the Sinai.

TOTTENHAM RIOTS

Gary McFarlane

There is something in the air and everyone can smell it, even if they don't know where it comes from or even why it exists. The Victorians had a word for it: Miasma — and it brought disease in its wake. Our contemporary Miasma — in Egypt, in Tunisia, in Greece and in the UK, too, has, I would argue, a more positive aspect. Whatever it is that's mysteriously hanging in the air, it seems to be driving wider and wider circles of people to distraction. Of course, it isn't actually 'bad air' that is at the root of our current social malaise. It is, instead, the very real dislocation afflicting the world economic and social order in the perhaps equally mysterious, to some, workings of the capitalist market. You know the fanciful tale of interconnectedness — supposedly based on chaos theory — where the butterfly beats its wings in one place and hurricanes arise in response in another? Let's transform the butterfly into a banker and the hurricane into a protester or 'rioter' in Cairo or London. This is the interconnectedness that dare not speak its name.

Just days before the Tottenham fire that set alight petrol lakes of the inequality and hopelessness that exists right across the UK, a meticulously coiffured tour guide in Cairo (even his eyelashes appeared sculpted), surely from a respectable middle class family, told me that the poor people of Egypt were generally happy with their lot, and, ignoring the contradiction, in the same breath explained how Mubarak lost his way by not spreading the wealth that the rich were harvesting as a direct result of his neo-liberal economic reforms. Despite my guide's faulty reasoning he had exposed the connection between economic and social injustice and the revolt against tyranny — the self-same inequality and lack of control experienced by large numbers of people in Britain.

Granted, we do not have a one-party police state as constituted in Mubarak's Egypt, although it should be noted, that much of that state unfortunately remains intact. But there must be increasing doubts that the British citizen really does live in a thorough-going democracy. For example, an adamant and large majority were against the Iraq war yet the war was still prosecuted. Similarly, a large majority are against bailed-out bankers being paid outsized bonuses yet the largesse shamelessly continues. So it's not just the global economy that's dysfunctional. Clearly, the body politic is equally at sea, and the point is that everyone can see it, even poor unemployed and disaffected young people in Tottenham, north London. Forget the Miasma — it is rebellion against social injustice that's in the air, and there is no wall between that and the wider political challenge it presents to our global ruling elite.

A few days after my conversation with the Cairo tour guide I flew back to London, finally getting to my home in Tottenham at around five in the morning. When I eventually arose from my slumbers, all hell had broken loose. I had flown into the eye of the storm.

As it happened I had heard about the killing of Mark Duggan, from the text messages on my phone from friends back home and the news websites I accessed, at exorbitant cost, on the same mobile device. Don't get me wrong, holidays can be fun, but the downside for social activist news junkies like myself is the frightening prospect of missing something, such as a strike, student protest and the like. Consequently, I was unaware that there was to be a protest march to Tottenham police station on the Saturday of my return. There have been lots of marches over the years to that police station and I have been involved in organising a few of them, notably in the case of the death of Joy Gardner at the hands of police and immigration officers and more recently Roger Sylvester. As the horse-racing enthusiast might put it, the police have form in Tottenham, and as in the case of those two deaths, the police had not forgotten the 'golden hour' rule: get your version of events out first to shape the story. I still bump into Joy's mother Myrna Simpson from time to time. She's a god-fearing woman and as such knows in her mind that there is a higher justice awaiting the killers of her daughter, but the bitterness is still palpable; a bitterness made all the harder to bear because of the self-justifying aspersions that were thrown around by the authorities to muddy her daughter's character. In Joy's case, she was an 'illegal immigrant', Roger Sylvester was 'mad' and Mark Duggan a 'gun-toting gangster'. The unsaid inference of this calculated storytelling, or at best selective and one-sided briefings to the press, is that all these named victims were in some way responsible for their own demise, not the people who did the killing. Of course the obvious point should be explicitly restated by way of rebuttal: even if Mark Duggan was a 'gangster', which he wasn't, it didn't justify what many in the local community came to see as his execution at the hands of racist police officers. And of course there was one case of death at the hands of the police that many more people are likely to have heard of — that of Cynthia Jarrett. Cynthia died when police officers stormed her house in 1985, sparking the Broadwater Farm riots. As with recent events, 'riots' doesn't adequately relate the meaning of what happened on that sprawling 1970s housing estate — where all the blocks are handily named after World War Two RAF bases just so that you know you are entering a potential war zone, although I'm sure the Le Corbusier inspired town planners had higher ideals of courage and valour in mind. Many locals prefer the word uprising.

Soon, for many people around the world, Tottenham would, again, become associated in their minds with more than just a famous football club — a club, incidentally, that was in a hurry to get out of the area but now might be staying after the government made noises about throwing them some financial sweeteners to hang around a bit longer. However, before we assess the riot itself we need to assess Tottenham; what it was and what it has become.

It's hard to believe now but once upon a time it was quite hard not to have a job in Tottenham. The Lea river runs past Tottenham to the east and since the days of the industrial revolution has fulfilled the role of major north-south arterial thoroughfare for the transport of goods into and out of London along a canal cut for that express purpose. In the 1950s, when African Caribbean immigrants first came to the area, engineering factories could be found all along the 'Valley' — in pre-canal times it was more of a marshy plain than a valley — from MK Electric to Metal Box. Today there is a Coca-Cola bottling plant (in nearby and equally deprived Edmonton, where, on the border with Tottenham, an IKEA store was opened in February 2005 leading to a near-riot at its well advertised grand opening when fighting broke out in a desperate surge by poor people to get their hands on what seemed like once-in-a-lifetime bargain offers) and that's about it, unless you count storage warehouses and retail/leisure parks as productive industry.

Tottenham's population was on the decline until the early nineties when a renewed influx of migrants added to the African Caribbeans that arrived in the fifties and sixties and the Turkish and Kurdish communities who came in the eighties. Eastern Europeans and Africans have all been added to the mix, while all the while the old white working class community shrank as many moved north to Enfield, Palmers Green and beyond, increasingly joined by African-Caribbeans too — all in search of 'better' neighbour-hoods. Suffice to say Haringey, the borough of up to 300,000 souls in which Tottenham is situated, on its eastern side, is the most unequal in London. Of its nineteen wards, four are in London's richest 10 per cent while five are in the poorest 10 per cent. The borough stretches westwards as far as leafy Highgate, taking in Muswell Hill and Crouch End where the respect-able working class nestles amid the thespian types that reside in the area, along with others of London's trendy middle classes. Yes, and you guessed it: there wasn't any rioting in Muswell Hill, Crouch End or Highgate, although the looting did spread to Wood Green and Turnpike Lane, inter-mediate destinations in our tale of two cities. The social stats for Tottenham are truly shocking but little spoken of in the days before or after the riots. According to the Campaign to end Child Poverty 48 per cent of the chil-dren in Tottenham live in poverty. Life expectancy in Muswell Hill is 78.3 years. The same figure for Tottenham is a miserable 70.8 years. Around 6,000 people, 8 per cent of the adult population, claim Jobseekers Allow-ance. The Northumberland Park ward has the highest unemployment rate of any ward in London, standing at 13.7 per cent. For young people — those under tewnty-four — the unemployment figure, disguised by various training schemes and such, is around 50 per cent, about the same as for Spain's under tewnty-fours. The demographics are typical for inner city London with some 65 per cent of the population coming from the black and minority ethnic communities. Of those around 10 per cent are from the African Caribbean community and it was the youths from this community that constituted the backbone of the shock troops behind the Tottenham disturbances. Mark Duggan was also of this heritage – his mother is white – as were the other three people killed by the police in earlier years and cited above.

Those social metrics are all fairly horrendous in themselves. But add to that the cuts recently announced and/or imposed by both central and local government and the picture darkens further. Earlier in the year (March 2011) Haringey Council, run by the Labour Party, announced cuts of £84 million. The total budget is £273 million, so that gives you some idea of the scale of the retrenchment. Indeed, the word 'cuts' is something of a misnomer. The austerity being imposed on Britain and places like Tottenham, threatens to destroy the essence of the welfare state. The council went for the soft targets first. The budget for youth services has been decimated by a 75 per cent cut that has seen eight youth centres closed. There were only thirteen to start with. Young people used to complain during the economic boom years — a boom that passed by those at the bottom of the pile — that there was nothing for them to do; that's even more true today. And if the same young people want to get some advice on how to get a job, forget about it: the Connexions career advice service aimed at the young has also been hit with a 75 per cent cut. In short, if you're looking for social deprivation in the UK, look no further than Tottenham.

And wherever you get poverty you get crime and Tottenham is no different in that regard. It is what's known in the lingo as a 'rough' area. Having said that, as with most crime, the perception is worse than the reality. Street robbery is perhaps the most prevalent crime. It's easy to commit and the rewards can be relatively high given the abundance of mobile gadgetry we stuff our bags and pockets with, even in poorer neighbourhoods. But contrary to the imaginings of well-heeled readers of London's *Evening Standard* newspaper, for example, the biggest victims of such crimes are in fact the very same young people routinely demonised in the media. Unfortunately for said young persons, they are of a demographic that is either feared or despised, or both. Not surprisingly then, the police rarely respond in a serious fashion if a young person reports that they have been a victim of a street robbery despite being the most likely victims. The sad truth is that in the stereotype stakes the police are the worst culprits, especially where black kids are concerned, although their behaviour, motivated as it is by racial and social profiling with black people thirty times more likely to be stopped by police than white people, is by no means confined to that ethnic group — white working class kids on the housing estates also fall within the orbit of suspicion. So to do Muslim youth in east London many of whose number were imprisoned for the flimsiest of misdemeanours following the protests against the war unleashed on Gaza by Israel in 2008/09.

The dominant response by the authorities to the riots, as far as social policy goes, has been guided by a law and order agenda. Outrageous sentences have been handed down for what can only be described as trivial cases of theft, even more so when considered alongside the white-collar crimes of our esteemed bankers who continue to loot the public finances. Some of the sentences sound like they came straight out of a Dickens novel: six months for stealing £3.50 worth of water, sixteen months dished out to twenty-two-year-old Anderson Fernandes, for stealing two scoops of ice cream, of which he took a lick, decided he didn't like it, and then gave the rest away to a passer-by. Two others were jailed for four years for supposedly 'inciting' riots through posting on Facebook. The overtly political and anti-working class nature of the courts' response to the riots laid bare the lack of independence of the UK's supposedly impartial judiciary – the bedrock of democracy and the hallmark of a 'civilised' country. Leaked documents made this abundantly clear, as a *Guardian* report at the time explained: 'Magistrates were urged to abandon sentencing guidelines when dealing with rioters last month because "nothing like this was envisaged"… The text of two controversial emails circulated to justices' clerks immediately after August's disturbances raises questions about judicial independence and the use of blanket guidance irrespective of individual cases… The documents [were] written by a senior justices' clerk in the London regional office of Her Majesty's Courts and Tribunals Service.' Unfortunately for the powers that be, it is a response that will not only fail to deter 'rioters' but in all probability make matters worse.

The Tottenham riot was different to those that followed in its wake, given the clear motivation of rage at police racism and violence that lay behind the killing of Mark Duggan, the subsequent march to the police station and the police lies and indifference that culminated in an explosion by 7.30-8.00pm that evening.

Nevertheless, only a fool or the wilfully ignorant could fail to notice that the scenes of anti-police violence, destruction and looting that followed on two subsequent nights, took place among groups of people and areas of the country that held in common many of the economic and social attributes of Tottenham. The riots elsewhere were different but the same. None of this was made apparent to a shocked nation as shops were emptied and burned and police driven off streets, but in the weeks that followed, despite the politicians and the mainstream media, some of that truth has emerged. Martin Luther King captured the meaning of those summer riots, even though he was not alive to witness them, when he surveyed the urban insurrections that rocked the US in 1967, a year before his death: 'Riots are the voices of the unheard.'

The Unheard Speak

So what really happened in Tottenham on the night of 6 August 2011?

I arrived home from my Egyptian family holiday at about 5am on Saturday morning and didn't rise until early afternoon. Unbeknownst to me a march was about to take place from Broadwater Farm Estate heading to Tottenham police station on the High Road that follows the route of the old Roman road, Ermine Way, running due north out of London. At the police station the group of around 200 or so protesters made up of Mark Duggan's family and friends and concerned residents, waited for a senior officer to make an appearance. Up until this point (Mark was killed on the Thursday of that week) no one from London's Metropolitan police force had bothered to contact any member of the family, not even to say that Mark was dead. What information the community had was gleaned from the media, a media that the recent Murdoch press phone-hacking scandal has shown to be hand-in-glove with the police, allegedly paying officers money for stories, and even employing past employees of News International to front their public relations and press operation. Far from ameliorating the crowd, the police, in their unfathomable cleverness, decided to conform to type — lots of black people in one place must mean trouble, even though over 2,000 mostly black people had marched peacefully to New Scotland Yard to protest at the killing, allegedly by the police, of another black man, 1980s reggae star Smiley Culture, a few months earlier. The police response to the peaceful but angry march was to line the front of the station with a handful of police officers in riot dress, a move that of course did nothing to either encourage the crowd to disperse, or to lead anyone to think any attempt at serious and respectful engagement with the community was likely to be forthcoming. Stafford Scott, who I now work with in the Tottenham

Defence Campaign (tottenhamdefencecampaign.co.uk), summed up what happened next and the attitude of many in the community:

Up until now they haven't come and helped them or advised them. They haven't met with any family liaison officers at all. We were absolutely disgusted by that, so we decided that we needed to come to Tottenham Police Station, because they may not be aware that a murder has been committed… We came to the station to have a peaceful demonstration, and it was largely peaceful. [We explained] that we wanted someone senior from the police service to come and explain to us what was happening. They kept on prevaricating. The most senior person they gave us was a chief inspector. We said that person wasn't senior enough — we wanted a senior ranking officer of superintendent or above. Eventually they sent for a superintendent, but by then it was too late.

It was the Prussian general Carl von Clauswitz who famously suggested to the leader of any military force that wanted to listen, that it was always a bad idea to attack unless you had a pretty good chance of winning. It sounds obvious but no one at Tottenham police station was listening that early summer evening. The motley crew of police officers assembled at the front entrance to the 'cop shop' was neither enough to defend or attack. Nevertheless, the dozen or so officers were in belligerent mood. To be honest, they are not exactly trained to be any other mood.

Eyewitnesses have said that the escalation that turned protest into riot happened when the police lashed out at a young woman who approached their ranks to remonstrate. They beat her to the ground with their shields and truncheons: 'the violence started after a 16-year-old girl "threw something, maybe a stone, at the original riot police line".' He added that this was met with a furious response, with around fifteen riot officers pounding her with shields. This description of events was corroborated by another local who spoke to BBC News. He said that 'the girl was "set upon" by police and that the crowd surged forward in anger.'

That's true in the sense of violence against the person — it was the police that started it. But in reality the torching of the police patrol cars, which upped the ante and signified the tipping point, took place a little earlier. For reasons again only known to the police commanders, two patrol cars were left unmanned near the crowd as the family decided they'd had enough of being humiliated and were urging protesters to disperse. It was when people were beginning to break up that some young people took out their frustration on those vehicles, left abandoned like a red rag to a bull. Within minutes they were both in flames and full-frontal attacks on the police station ensued. The uprising had begun.

There's something about riots you might not be aware of. Certainly, intrepid, poorly disguised journalists from national newspapers probably weren't. It's sometimes referred to as 'mob rule' and it fills the High Court judges of the land with fear and loathing. It was remarked upon at a meeting I spoke at alongside the *Guardian's* special projects editor, Paul Lewis (one of the notable exceptions to the otherwise one-sided and inaccurate media reporting), and the *Times* football editor, Tony Evans, on the matter of the misreporting of the riots. Evans told how he was once a 'rioter' in the early 1980s when the Tories brought mass unemployment to Britain, much as they are today, and of how the riots then provided an outlet for working class kids, normally subject to the unyielding authority of the state in the shape of the police, who are able to hit back and in so doing to feel empowered, often for the first time in their lives. Frank Murray from the RMT trade union and a member of its committee at Finsbury Park underground station, a couple of miles down the road from Tottenham, told a similar story, this time when we were out together delivering flyers imparting legal rights information on behalf of the newly formed Tottenham Defence Campaign to the residents of some of the toughest housing estates in north London, a couple of weeks after the riots ended: 'You know Gary,' he said, 'it makes the youth feel good when they fight with the police. I remember what it's like.' I replied, 'Yeah, it's a festival of the oppressed.'

And so it was that night in Tottenham.

Much has been made of the people burned out of their homes, the shopkeepers deprived of their livelihoods as they watched their shops go up in flames. The bird's-eye shots from Murdoch's Sky TV News helicopter the following morning showed those fires still burning and buildings smouldering, seeming to confirm the narrative. It wasn't quite like that though. Indeed, as the fires spread that night the police were not interested in getting firefighters through to put out the flames. Many of those who were burnt out have directed their rage at the police. That was certainly the mood at a meeting organised by the government at the Bernie Grant Arts Centre on 3 November 2011 to take evidence from the community into the causes of the riot. 'I kept calling the police and they weren't interested. Even when they were on the streets and there were no rioters in the area, still no one came to put out fires,' explained one exasperated householder. A popular belief, borne out by events, is that the police let Tottenham burn that night, as we shall see.

I live a five-minute walk from the epicentre of the uprising, as many of us in Tottenham prefer to call it — an uprising that only came to my attention when I saw the first report on the TV news at about 8.00pm. By the time I got to the action the police had thrown two lines across Tottenham High Road, one immediately south of the police station, not far from the Chances club at which, coincidentally, a Love Music Hate Racism gig was taking place, and one immediately to the north of it. They had successfully repulsed attacks on their station but seemed to be having a lot of difficulty bringing in reinforcements. The best they could do was to hold their ground. Traffic travelling north had been stopped by a police roadblock of sorts, made up of a lone traffic police car and a couple of officers in yellow high-visible jackets. By now, hundreds if not thousands of people were on the streets. Time and time again I heard people exclaiming: 'it was bound to happen', 'it's about time', 'the feds [the police] had it coming to them' — many were expressing surprise that this explosion hadn't happened earlier. There was a cross-section of the community on the streets. Where I was initially standing (near the junction of Phillip Lane and the High Road) and observing, there were Turkish people, Eastern Europeans, Africans, African-Caribbeans and Hasidic Jewish people. Every now and again the police would make a half-hearted charge towards us but would then just as quickly retreat. People from among the Hasidic Jewish community, distinctively dressed in their black hats and coats, handed out bread as it slowly dawned on us that the police were not about to retake the streets. On the contrary they were progressively losing control.

I wandered around to the other police line, the one that held the road on the northern side of the station. I had decided to take a circuitous route a little distance to the east of the station. As it turned out there was no need to be so cautious about making contact with vengeful groups of riot cops or to fear being 'kettled' in one of the containment operations that in recent times had become the primary tactic for dealing with public order threats, that the police usually believed demonstrations by students and others to be.

On this side of the police station it became clearer that the forces of law and order had no intention, at this stage, of trying to drive back their adversaries. The best they could do was to hold their position. Defence of the police station seemed to be the only objective. Time stamp circa 10pm and no looting had yet broken out. Instead, youths were more concerned with the 'war on the feds'. I was now positioned directly adjacent to the fighting but standing on the pavement, not in the middle of the road with the infantry. All manner of projectiles rained down on the police and it wasn't too long before petrol bombs began to come within a more threatening range, although this artillery was fairly ineffectual, tending to ignite harmlessly in front of the static police line. The Molotov cocktails didn't appear to be armed with enough fuel. Nevertheless, every time one impacted on the road a cheer went up. This wasn't 'mindless violence' — it was targeted, at the police. In the road sat the wreckage of the two burnt-out police cars attacked at the protest earlier in the day, as youths milled about planning their next move, improvising further assaults on the thin blue line ahead of them. There was something vaguely medieval about the next tactic to be adopted. The large steel dumpsters used by retailers to discard waste had their contents set alight and were then sent trundling towards the police like modern-day siege weapons. Again, they provided theatre more than military effectiveness. The police line wasn't driven back but neither did it advance.

A half-hearted attempt to build a barricade was begun with an awning being ripped from a shop front. It wasn't long before the first window was smashed. Shouts of 'leave the shops alone' could be heard but it didn't stop the small music equipment and instrument shop being the first to be looted — a shop I buy my guitar picks from. Youths could be heard complaining that he was 'too expensive' by way of self-justification. The police made no effort to intervene. They were too scared. Next it was the turn of the solicitor — no ordinary solicitor, this was the office of the lawyer favoured by the police. You would be given the number of the 'police solicitor' if you were being held at the station and didn't have a better one to call. The firm was seen as being an adjunct of the police and not a true representative of a defendant. The firm's office wasn't a target for looting but for burning. It was the first premises of any kind to be torched. Seeing the flames beginning to spread to the shops adjoined to it and the flats above, several of us hurried to the car park behind the properties to alert occupants, if they weren't already aware of it, of impending danger. Even though people's lives were now being endangered the police didn't budge from their positions. Soon flames enveloped the nearby betting shop, the first of at least six that were to be attacked.

Interestingly, there are two competing theories as to why bookmakers were targeted, both of which were probably true. The obvious one from the standpoint of the usual motive for looting, is that those doing the raiding assumed, wrongly, there was money in the tills — perhaps because many of those involved in the uprising stood at a distance from the world of work they were not aware of the practice of removing all monies from retail premises at the end of the day's trading for safe deposit at the bank. A more compelling motive for taking down the betting shops, however, was because they were in the business of leeching on the blood of poor people — after all it was the black revolutionary and Muslim Malcolm X who remarked that 'wherever you find a capitalist you find a bloodsucker' — and was why the betting shops were hated as parasites preying on the hopes and poverty of the poor. Again, not picked up and linked by the media, local or otherwise, there had been a recent and successful campaign to stop the Paddy Power chain of bookmakers from taking over the premises of a much-loved record shop of some thirty years standing — Every Bodies Music — that had just seen its rent hiked by £10,000 a year and was considering selling out. The council had not raised any objection to changing the use of the premises and adding to the veritable plague of betting shops that infested Tottenham. Another aspect of the west/east divide that scarred the borough was the non-existence of such businesses in the affluent west, where, by contrast, in Tottenham there were thirty-eight of them. The campaign waged by local activists was successful and Paddy Power were not able to move in to the prime location opposite Seven Sisters tube station, and an iconic cultural landmark was saved.

It was around 11pm when the police at last started to push north, but they were in no hurry and their numbers were still thin. Strangely, the police made no effort to block retreating northerly moving crowds from behind, so all that their efforts achieved was to push the rioting into new areas. Is this all the manpower the police could muster from across London? That's what I, and no doubt many others, were thinking.

Motorists found themselves driving merrily into the riot zone, forced into a u-turn when the extent of their mistake became apparent. It wasn't long before the driver of a red double-decker London bus found himself making a similar mistake. There was no one on the bus as it was out of service. For a moment the driver stayed in his seat. He didn't look so much scared as bemused. It's not every day you find yourself in the middle of a riot. I suggested to the driver it might be an idea if he abandoned the bus before it went up in flames. With a smile, he took my advice while the young people around me discussed whether to commandeer the vehicle. 'You know they got video on them buses', one of the kids usefully reminded those assembled. Any plan to drive the bus at police lines quickly evaporated when it was discovered no one could drive, another indication, perhaps, of the lowly social-class profile of participants. The media quickly latched onto the news that a bus — often referring to buses when there was only one — had been hijacked and set alight, also failing to mention the fact that it was out of service so there were no passengers and no one was put in danger (I was being kept in touch with the mainstream news coverage through the timely text messages sent by my partner watching the TV at home).

Barclays bank took a hit next, but young people had better sense than to try and loot it. The post office on the other side of the road near the junction with Bruce Grove was not so fortunate. A shout went up, 'they're in'. A phenomena not dissimilar to air rushing in to fill a vacuum unfolded as what must have been around one hundred youths stormed the building through its breached doorway in the hope of being able to break open the safes they hoped still contained plenty of cash.

The smoke was thickening all the time as people scampered about, smiling as they went or with fixed earnest expressions, gathering up what to some might seem the most ridiculous items of booty, such as bags of frozen chips, bottles of beer, toilet rolls and other mundane household items. But that such commodities were being taken was a testament to the fact, already highlighted, that Tottenham was one of the poorest places in London. Aldi, the German-owned supermarket filled with food brands no one had heard of but at prices as affordable to the poor as the sub-standard food on sale at the Iceland frozen food store also to be found on the High Road, was being emptied.

The acrid smoke was making it harder to breathe. I couldn't see much either. A little later the carpet outlet just north of Aldi would be inciner-ated, including the flats and belongings of those that lived above it, forced to flee in the clothes they were sleeping in. This is the scene that found its way on to the front pages and the news bulletins of the world's media the following morning. The German Luftwaffe's bombing of London during the Second World War was invoked: the Victorian-era building had survived the Blitz but not the feral marauding and lawless black youth of Tottenham wreaking their wanton destruction, was the none-too-subtle unwritten subtext. I had decided to venture back to the south side of the police station where my observations started, before the Victorian landmark was turned to charcoal and rendered too dangerous to be inhabited or rebuilt. It would be levelled before the end of the following week, just like the post office that was looted and torched earlier.

The time was approaching midnight and the streets were still filled with people and the police were still struggling to bring in reinforcements, although they had started to block off some of the side roads that ran off from the High Road, mostly on the eastern side.

A young man near me said: 'Let's stop fighting the police and go to JDs'.' JD Sports sells sporting apparel and is a favourite among the young and fashion-conscious of 'urban' Britain. In deeply unequal societies superficial things such as fashion matter even more: clothes become a way of project-ing a certain status. People started to make their way to the large retail park near Tottenham Hale tube and rail station about a quarter of a mile or so from the High Road. The police were now bringing up more infantry and as they zoomed up the High Road from the south they were pelted with bricks. Walls had been knocked down near a disused public toilet building. Many of the bricks found their mark with a dull thud registering the hits. The traffic cops that had thrown up a road block of sorts had long since gone, leaving behind an abandoned police car that was now in flames. You could tell it had been burning for a while as the paint had long since melted making it unrecognisable as a police car. It was other police vehicles in simi-lar states to this one that the TV news would infer were the cars of residents that had been randomly torched. Wrong again.

Before I take a look at what was happening up at the retail park, a word on looting because so much nonsense has been said of it. Every large-scale riot by working class people in every country has involved looting to a greater or lesser degree. It happened in Britain in the riots of the early 80s, it happened in the riots of the 1930s, it happened in the US in the Los Angeles riots of 1992 following the beating of Rodney King by racist cops, it happened in the urban insurrection that stretched across the same country in the 60s as poor black communities fought back against social and economic injustice. Looting is a very immediate way of poor people evening-up the score — taking those things they normally were not able to have, as in the case of unaffordable iPads, or the everyday necessities they would usually have to spend their meagre resources on but could, for now, get for free. Even the most liberal of the British newspapers couldn't get their collective heads round this. The middle classes really need to get out more. Here's Zoe Williams pontificating in the *Guardian*: 'I think it's just about possible that you could see your actions refashioned into a noble cause if you were stealing the staples: bread, milk. But it can't be done while you're nicking trainers, let alone laptops.'

There wasn't much worth looting on Tottenham High Road. There was much talk of the heart being ripped out of the community by the riots, not least by our ineffectual local MP David Lammy who the following morning was to disgrace himself playing to the gallery of a media-massaged public opinion that had already decided there was 'no excuse' for rioting and that it was all the work of 'criminals'. But the 'heart of the community' he and they spoke of had expired long ago. And since when is the 'heart' of a community judged by how many big retailers have outlets in the area? It was precisely this kind of thinking — Thatcherism, market madness, rampant consumerism, call it what you will — that partly underlies the rationale for the very looting the authorities, politicians, and media so despised and condemned.

I walked along the path alongside the major gyratory one-way system that led to the retail park. Behind me I saw the flashing blue lights of what seemed like a large police convoy. Gosh, now they've had it I thought as the retail park started to come into view. As it happens, it was a stone's throw from here, so to speak, on Ferry Lane, that Mark Duggan had been gunned down by police. But to my amazement the police convoy turned down Park Road and away from the retail park. The police seemed to be doing everything they could to avoid confrontation. Now perhaps they had absorbed the meaning of von Clauswitz's dictum referred to earlier: they couldn't be sure to win so they didn't attack. They ran away. I stood across the road from the stores. 'It's shopping time,' laughed a young Hasidic Jewish man who, like me, watched in amazement as large boxes, presumably containing hundreds of phones, came out the back of Carphone Warehouse, one of the UK's premier mobile phone retailers. These particular looters hadn't bothered going through the front door, at least initially, instead astutely choosing to target the stock room at the back of the premises. The complete lack of police anywhere to be seen further encouraged looters to 'expropriate the expropriators' as Marx had injuncted, although he had in mind taking the factories into common ownership to get back the fruits of our labour. But if you are unemployed and marginalised there are other ways to hit back. It's a phenomenon that always takes place in street-level rebellions. Let's hear from Naomi Klein on the mass rioting, known as El Saqueo — 'The Sacking' — that accompanied the economic crisis visited on Argentina by the structural adjustment programme of the International Monetary Fund: 'The economy was in freefall and thousands of people living in rough neighbourhoods (which had been thriving manufacturing zones before the neoliberal era) stormed foreign-owned superstores. They came out pushing shopping carts overflowing with the goods they could no longer afford — clothes, electronics, meat. The government called a "state of siege" to restore order; the people didn't like that and overthrew the government.'

And so it was in the land of austerity in Britain 2011. Although a state of emergency wasn't declared, many a pundit spoke of bringing in the army, equipping the police with rubber bullets, water cannon and other 'non-lethal' weapons, as the rioting spread across London the following night and to the big cities of the rest of England the night after that.

Back where it started the looting had spread not just to the retail park at the Hale but also two miles west, to Wood Green one of north London's major shopping malls.

I looked at my watch as I reached the Tesco supermarket near Seven Sisters tube and at my trusty iPhone showing a nearly empty battery — videoing the historic scenes of mayhem had its price in computing-hardware terms. To the north there was a screen of smoke, perhaps reminiscent of the London fog of Dickens's day. Fitting perhaps, considering the Dickensian repression that was to follow. To date over 5,000 people have been arrested in relation to the country-wide rioting. It was 5.00am, time to go home.

Behind the Headlines

In the following days we are subjected to headlines proclaiming the rioters to be 'scum', bemoaning the breakdown of 'normal society' and respect for authority and property, and laying the blame at the feet of 'a feral under-class' in the words of the misnamed justice secretary Ken Clarke. Rioters were all dismissed as gang members organising copy-cat outings using their Blackberrys. This wasn't about protesting, it was about thieving. It unleashed vile overt racism too. Historian David Starkey spoke out on the BBC's flag-ship current affairs programme 'Newsnight', complaining that: 'What has happened is that a substantial section of the chavs...have become black... The whites have become black.' We even had the laughable spectacle of the white middle classes of Hackney and elsewhere organising riot clean-ups. There were not many black or white working-class people out with their brooms. They had better things to do.

In truth, the riots of the summer of 2011 were a cry of rage and despair but also defiance. Many of the kids that had been on the streets that night had been on them the year before in the great student uprising in Novem-ber 2010 when 50,000 students marched against the hiking of tuition fees and the move to abolish the Educational Maintenance Allowance (EMA). There were literally thousands of students and their families in Tottenham in receipt of EMA, a £30 a week payment to help students get to college, pay for lunch and so on. For ex Eton public school boy prime minister Cameron, the money was peanuts, but to many working class families up and down the country it represented a sizeable chunk of the family budget. The students occupied and then destroyed Millbank Tower, the headquar-ters of the ruling Conservative party. Other demonstrations, all of which ended in fighting with the police were to follow. The students marched on Parliament on 9 December. It culminated in pitch battles with riot police. The student movement was seeing something different going on: middle class university student had made common cause with overwhelmingly working class further education college kids (sixteen to eighteen-year-olds) to create one big fist. The kids from the estates didn't run from police charges. They dealt with police brutality on a daily basis and didn't scare easily. Together the students fought back. The government is shutting down hope for millions of young people, especially those at the bottom of society:

'We're from the slums of London, yeah. How do they expect us to pay £9,000 for uni fees? And EMA is the only thing keeping us in college. What's stopping us from doing drug deals on the street any more? Nothing!' Unfortunately no one was listening. Maybe some more stats will help to concentrate their minds.

There are now over a million young people unemployed in the UK, and that figure is rising by the day. In Haringey half of all unemployed people are aged between sixteen and twenty-four. Some 40 per cent of young people in the borough live in poverty. In January 2010 the Institute for Public Policy Research found that 'mixed ethnic groups had seen the biggest increases in youth unemployment since the recession began, rising from 21 per cent to 35 per cent in the period.'

It goes on. Far from being an all-black affair, 42 per cent of those brought before the courts were white; 35 per cent of adults were claiming out-of-work benefits; two-thirds of the young people appearing in court had some form of educational need, more than a third of that number had been excluded from school, one in ten of those had been permanently excluded; 26 per cent were juveniles, that is aged between ten and seventeen and 42 per cent were in receipt of free school meals, in other words they were very poor people.

A young person interviewed in a film posted on the *Guardian* newspaper's website looking at the decimation of services witnessed in the shutting down of youth centres as part of Haringey council's cuts, and before the riots took place, was prescient: 'They were something for us to do. Now we're just out here, getting up to no good.' Another youth says, 'there will be riots.'

Before these riots broke out the campaign group Black Activists Rising Against Cuts had been holding public meetings up and down the country highlighting the disproportionate impact of the cuts on the black community — pointing out that people would not take it lying down. I don't want to blow my own trumpet, but I predicted on the steps of Haringey Civic Centre late last year when the cuts were set in motion, that the riots of the early eighties in Britain would look like a tea party in comparison with what would inevitably come to pass.

Nearly a year since Mark Duggan's death at the hands of the police the family are no nearer in their search for justice. Two thousand attended his funeral. At the reception that took place on Broadwater Farm Estate, among the crowds rival gang members met in peace and contemplated the future. That truce, no matter how brief, between the 'postcode' gangs is of massive significance. Although the gangs played a minority role in the uprising, the fact that they declared a truce for four days spoke to the underlying political motivation behind the disturbances — the gangs were joining forces to confront the police. We should also not forget another important characteristic of this rebellion when compared to those of the early eighties — this time the riots were much more offensive. Whereas those of the 1980s had fought battles to keep police out of Brixton, Toxteth, Handsworth, and St Pauls and elsewhere in inner city Britain, this time the battle was taken beyond those locales and into some of the country's more prosperous neighbourhoods and even into the city centres.

Even if nothing else had been achieved, at least people around the world had heard of Mark Duggan, and the youth of Tottenham were of necessity realising the urgency of a political response. The Tottenham Defence Campaign was launched in the days following the uprising to fight for justice for Mark and to defend those caught up in a night of rage against police racism and social inequality. At the time of writing, at least 5,000 people have been brought before the courts, with many of those sent to prison. But out of such fires weapons of struggle are forged. That's what happened in the US after the sixties riots: it culminated in the formation of the revolutionary Marxist Black Panther Party. We can only hope for similar developments in the UK, developments that will reach across communal lines to unite ordinary people regardless of background in the battle against the 1 per cent at the top, so eloquently and powerfully brought into view and confronted by the worldwide actions of the anti-capitalist Occupy movement.

Race and class were at the root of this rebellion. I suspect that, one way or another the ruling elite of Britain will be hearing from the unheard again in the not too distant future.

I HATED MYSELF

Farouk Peru

For most of my life I have hated myself for being a Muslim. Of course, Muslims aren't allowed to have feelings of contempt for themselves as Muslims or for the *Ummah*, the worldwide fraternity of Muslims. It goes against our cultural make up. We are to stand loyally with the *Ummah*, no matter what it says or does. It is almost as if the *Ummah* was an independent entity producing its own thoughts, like a beehive with a brain. These thoughts are of course invariably objective and infallible. Therefore, whatever feelings of self-loathing we experience must be an aberration, a mere abnormality brought about by secret sympathies for the West (the arch enemy of the *Ummah*!) or by a passing moment of a lapse of faith. No, Muslims aren't allowed to self-loathe at all. We are to suppress that feeling deep down where it would not threaten the façade of the singular, united *Ummah*.

My own experience with self-loathing came as a nagging feeling which initially I could not name. The lack of a name to that feeling translated into the lack of a definition and lack of recognition. It simply became 'that' feeling, whose voice should be silenced at all costs before it grew louder and threatened the integrity of my faith.

I grew up in Malaysia during the 1980s and 1990s. Malaysia was then ruled by Mahatir Muhammad, or more appropriately Tun Dr Mahathir, the grand old man of Malaysian politics with twenty-two years experience as the Prime Minister. For myself and millions of Malaysians of my generation, he was all there was to Malaysian public life. So ubiquitous was he that when he retired from office, he became simply known as 'Tun', the highest honour bestowed by Malaysian royalty on an individual, despite the dozens of 'Tun's who received their tunships before him. Sort of how Shakespeare simply become 'The Bard'.

Mahathir was behind the Islamisation of Malaysia. Islamisation is normally associated with the ratification of Sharia law. However, for Mahathir, Islamisation was something else: an expression of one's Muslim identity. As an overt sign of this, Malaysian women started to use the headscarf. However the cases of 'moral depravity' caught by the moral police hardly changed despite this process, except now the morally depraved included the hijabis! Perhaps one could say it was an Islamisation of form rather than actual substance.

In Malaysia, the religious identity of a Muslim is a done deal. If one is born a Muslim, one shall die a Muslim, officially speaking anyway. Whether or not you actually believe is another matter entirely. It is after all written on one's identity card! A Muslim is usually a Malay and a Malay is always a Muslim; and ethnic Malays are not allowed to have 'Islam' deleted from their identity cards. As Muslims, all Malays are required to attend classes in Islamic education for the duration of their primary and secondary schooling, a total of eleven years — half-hour lessons five times a week.

This is where my self-loathing began. I can remember my very first classes in Islamic education. We started by learning about Abd Al-Mutalib, the grandfather of the Prophet. I remember being baffled. I was baffled by these classes and did not know how to accept the information I was being fed. So I made the conscious decision — at the age of seven no less — to simply memorise this information even though I didn't quite know what to do with it. I had an exam to pass, get an 'A', as my religious teacher kept reminding me.

Religion became a burden when my grandmother died in 1985. Up to now, my family had been less than religious. The sudden shock of seeing a death up close brought about a sense of repentance and piety. Overnight we became practising Muslims and started praying five times a day. With the new found fervour of the 'born again Muslim', naturally we had to do these prayers in congregation, and I was inevitably dragged in. I found that I was no longer free to watch my five o'clock cartoons as it coincided with the 'Asr prayers. So religion became a burden at home as well as school.

The religious fervour also brought a sense of religious responsibility on the part of my family. Despite the fact that I was already learning Traditional Islam in school, a Qur'an-reading instructor, an *ustad*, was engaged from one of the nearby villages to teach me proper recitation and enunciation. The *ustad*, who I later discovered did not understand a word of Arabic, would come on hot Malaysian afternoons to listen to my recitation and corrected my pronounciuation whenever he wasn't reading his newspaper. Unsurprisingly, I did not come to adore the man too much. Harmless as he was, I still found his presence in my life terribly inconvenient. He was not punctual and less than regular in his visits. There would be times when he simply did not turn up without even as much as a call. I had a rule: if he didn't turn up by 4pm, I was off the hook. That rule meant that close to 4pm, if he hadn't turned up, I'd be praying that he wouldn't at all. I'd be counting the minutes till 4pm, even the seconds! Isn't it ironic that my most heartfelt prayer was to be let off from an ostensibly religious duty? I did not understand a word of the Qur'an I read so carefully. It was simply pages and pages of unintelligible writing. Beautiful calligraphy no doubt, but simply unintelligible. Not just to me but my *ustad* as well. He knew the exact nasal quality needed to execute a particular elocution but he didn't know a word of what he was carefully enunciating.

I was glad when I finally completed the Qur'an. There was a lavish ceremony to mark the occasion. We had a huge dinner attended by people from the local mosque who said prayers for our well-being. My *ustad's* parting message to me was to read the Qur'an daily and if I couldn't manage it, to read it weekly or monthly. If I couldn't even do that, I was to open its pages and kiss it as the pages contained a special *baraka* (blessing) which would be orally transmitted to me.

I didn't open the Qur'an again for years.

I lived in a predominantly Chinese neighbourhood. The Chinese had their own religions, a mixture of Taoism, Buddhism and Confucianism. Some older folks were kind enough to explain their religious beliefs to me. They had delved into the philosophical side of their religion and had much deep wisdom to share. They asked questions about the nature of reality, the nature of the soul, who was God and how man should live. The profundity of the questions appealed to me. The old uncles, as I came to call them, never again appeared in my life so vividly and today I can barely track them down. But they did leave me with a passing message: that I should also look for these issues within the Islamic Tradition

To my great surprise, I found that Islam was also rich in wisdom and philosophy. The surprise was not because I had a low opinion of Islam but simply because I had not been exposed to this aspect of Islam. Coincidentally, in our school's Islamic classes, we began to read about (as opposed to actually study) Sufism and Islamic Philosophy. It had only taken us eight years of Islamic education, learning the minutiae of rituals, to finally arrive at something substantial. Philosophy and spirituality. *Falsafah* and *tasawwuf*. The language of spirituality offered by *tasawwuf*, the Sufi way, gave me the connection I needed to connect with Islam. Suddenly, Islam became meaningful and, for a while, I thought it was perfect. The undercurrent of boredom, bafflement and confusion I felt evaporated.

But this brief period of blissful self-loathing-free life was shaken from its blissful slumber only a few years later. By that time, I had acquired some knowledge about Sufism and I identified myself as a Sufi. I had become very partial to the Sufism of Shaykh Abd Al-Qadir a Sufi whose book *The Way of Muhammad* I really liked, though didn't quite understand. Shaykh Abd Al-Qadir was the leader of the Murabitoon, a UK and European-based Sufi outfit. The Murabitoon were not simply about the *tariqah*, the way of Sufi-sim, they had a deep grounding in Sharia as well as *Falsafah*. They had the most complete system of Islam I had seen and I was convinced that their system was the answer to all Muslim problems. I defended the Murabitoon from attacks. It was like defending your football team. I would defend my team no matter what. Indeed, I planned to start the Malaysian branch of the Murabitoon as soon as I reached twenty-one. But then the extremism of the Murabitoon raised some doubts.

In the midst of all this, I faced an ethical dilemma; and self-loathing returned with a vengeance. It began with Asif, my best friend. We basically grew up together. We loved the same geeky things. In the days when having 640K memory PC was considered advanced, we used to trade computer games and tips. In our early adolescence, we discovered the world of Dungeons and Dragons and role-playing games and they filled our imaginations. But now Asif wanted to leave Islam.

He was by no means unique. There had been cases before where individuals and even families wanted to leave Islam. As Islam was an official entity in Malaysia, the act of removing oneself from it therefore becomes an official matter. One's innermost personal and theological conviction is a matter of state arbitration. Not just the arbitration of any state, mind, but a state which enshrines very draconian laws about a Muslim's religious identity.

Asif had a Muslim grandfather whom he never knew. His grandfather married a Hindu, who converted to Islam for the sake of marriage. They had Asif's mother who eventually married Asif's father, another convert from Hinduism. One can see at this point that Islam was simply an inconvenient official matter for their family. They did not practice Islam or had any affinity with it. But Asif and his sister had to attend school registered as Muslims. They had to attend Islamic classes, and learn by rote the minutiae of Islam. These classes were already tedious to children from traditionally Muslim households. For children who did not identify with Islam, these classes were far worse. In the case of Asif, his lack of background knowledge in Islam became an issue. The *ustads* were relentless in trying to 'bring Asif and his entire family to Islam'. Constant jibes were hurled directly at him.

The full extent of Asif's dilemma became apparent when we left school. We were both in college and were done with Islamic studies forever. Asif and I discussed spirituality a lot. While he did not identify with Islam, he had a profound knowledge of other spiritualities. He delved into new age spiritualities, the human potential movement and various other techniques and philosophies of human development. We spent many hours talking about these things.

When Asif said to me he wanted to leave Islam I knew this would have no effect on how he lived his life. All it would mean is that he would not have to go through the usual official procedures for how Muslims run their lives. His future spouse would not have to convert to Islam as his own father had to. His children would not have to attend Islamic classes with a potentially demeaning *ustad*. It was simply a move to free him of being what he never was.

Yet I felt a sense of deep betrayal. One night, I blurted out that that in a true Islamic state, what he said would be construed as apostasy and liable for the death penalty. I reproached him loudly for his bad intentions against Islam. Asif, with his usual amiable manner, tried to calm me down on the pretext that he was musing. The deep betrayal I felt was very pronounced. The clear cut decision of Sharia law as far as I knew was the apostate had to be given a chance to repent for three days and if he failed to do so, he was to be put to death. Apostates were traitors and Asif was a traitor to my faith. There can no be reason to think otherwise.

Except that I did.

That night, when my emotional storm had passed, I felt a deep sense of regret at my outburst. I felt there was something wrong deep inside me. My inner voice was asking: 'where is the compassion in Islam we talk about?'

I looked for alternative views but found none. The relatively homogenous Islam indigenous to Malaysia simply does not allow a multiplicity of views. I knew about the Sufis, a little about the Shia. But other varieties of Sunni Islam, or lesser known sects as Ismailis or Ahmadis, were simply unknown to me. This was 1994 after all and internet hadn't reached our shores. As for reading and interpreting Islam on my own, I had been scared off the notion long before. Only with sheer arrogance can one hope to challenge the accomplishments of the scholars of the early generations who spent their lives codifying Islamic knowledge and I did not want to be an arrogant upstart. And my flirtation with the Murabitoon made me even more cautious. So I was stuck — there was only the death penalty for those who leave Islam.

But I cried out for justice. How could we punish people who were saddled with Islam through no fault of their own? They were forced to convert to Islam for the sake of love and marriage and now, their own children were stuck with all the restrictions which came with being a Malaysian Muslim. Shouldn't faith be a personal matter? What if one born to a traditional Muslim family and raised a practising Muslim felt he did not want to be Muslim anymore? Are we Muslims for the sake of God or are we Muslims for the sake of making Malaysia a Muslim majority state? I hated being a Muslim.

My self-loathing only increased when I was told that my inner conscience was totally contradicted by sacred law. Someone told me that an authentic hadith in Sahih al-Bukhari shows that the Prophet himself had made a clear pronouncement — whoever leaves Islam, kill him. I was therefore harbouring an opposition to the Prophet himself. For a young person who wished to dedicate his life to what he considered the Islamic Resurgence, this lead to a severe emotional upheaval. I could not silence my gut feelings yet the law is perfectly clear and I was opposing it.

I now entered a period of profound self-loathing as a Muslim. I felt a deep sense of discomfort in standing with this apostasy law but also a deep sense of guilt for questioning it, let alone daring to contemplate rejecting it. And worse still, Asif's family were good people. No, they were the best of all the people I knew – including Muslims. I had known them for over twelve years and they treated me with great care and love. Yet I considered them traitors to my faith. I ignored their basic goodness because they wanted to abandon the faith which had been inflicted on them.

I began to wonder how Islam could preach this inhumane doctrine. We claim no compulsion in religion but that is only in conversion. Once you're in there is no way out. It does not matter if you lost your faith or were tricked into converting or forced into it because of marriage. You were a Muslim. Full stop. Somehow your departure would cause great strife in the *Ummah,* as if the *Ummah* based its integrity on forced acquiescence and state legislated faith.

Over the years, I have met several Muslims who have also experienced similar self-loathing due to problems within Islam — and there are many! They had other reasons for self-loathing. However I did detect a common element — the sheer inability to negotiate one's faith. Islam as we know it was simply 'take it or leave it'. Either you accepted Traditional Islam in full or you rejected it. The human element in the articulation of Islam is ignored completely.

Is there a solution to this problem? I believe the problem arises due to sacralisation of what is human. For the most part, Islam is a human endeavour. I believe only the revelation, the Qur'an, is Divine. The rest, including the life of the Prophet, is interpretation. When the human is elevated to the level of the Divine, serious problems and conflicts ensue.

I was indoctrinated from an early age to regard everything Islamic as not only sacred but divine. What this meant was that Islam came to have an aura of un-touchability which scares away any potential questions one might have. The problem is we are human, emotive beings. We feel things and these feelings if left unattended would simply manifest as a detachment or worse, as in my case, self-loathing.

Was Islam always like this? Was it always untouchable and beyond scrutiny? More serious study at graduate level led me to believe the case is actually the opposite. In the early years of Islam, free thinking was the norm. Muslims negotiated their religion with their current situations and absorbed whatever wisdom they encountered. If we read early Muslim philosophers, such as ibn al-Rawandi or Abu Bakr al-Razi, before orthodoxy reared its head and ossification took place, we would find that their notion of Islam was very different from what we perceive as Islamic today. They routinely questioned even the very notion of revelation and this was not a problem. Better to completely reject Islam than to lead a double life where one's outward persona is Muslim but one's internal state is elsewhere.

As for me, I no longer loathe myself for being a Muslim. I came to the UK for my tertiary education soon after that period and discovered the mind-boggling multiplicity of Islam. It took me a while but eventually I freed myself from the hold of obscurantist dogma. I began to study the Qur'an and found that it resonates with my inner conscience. There is simply no compulsion to belief. At all. Unconditionally. Belief or *iman* is something one attains if one interacts with the signs of God. Everyone experiences those signs differently and to think we can legislate faith is not only impossible but arrogant.

Muslim self-loathing is not a pleasant experience. It eats at one's soul and manifests as erosion of one's commitment to one's identity as a Muslim. You feel a distaste or dislike for some aspects of Islam or maybe even for Islam as a whole. This is not something you can or should hide or push deep inside. You have to deal with it by acknowledging it. Then you have to question, investigate, critique, and ask if your self-loathing really has roots in Islam. And you have to have the courage to reject what you inwardly feel is wrong.

ART AND LETTERS

Crescent Films is an award-winning independent production company with a record of producing high quality, original and entertaining television programmes for, amongst others, the BBC and Channel 4.

Based in London, Crescent films specialises in documentaries on South Asia and the Muslim World. Our recent productions include 'The Life of Muhammad' a three part documentary series for the BBC, 'Seven Wonders of the Muslim World', 'Muslim and looking for Love' and 'Women only Jihad' for Channel 4.

www.crescentfilms.co.uk
crescentfilms@btinternet.com

SIX POEMS

Stéphane Chaumet

Paris-based poet, novelist and editor, Stéphane Chaumet casts an apocalyptic eye on the contemporary to produce these poems, crowded with disease, migration, the inhumanity of urban space, time, mystery and death. He discovers the spiritual in the sensuous and a beauty inextricably connected to horror.

Standing on the shoulders of the symbolist and surrealist traditions, this is poetry of savage contrasts, visceral revelations, dark epiphanies. Much of its meaning is found in its powerful sound effects. Chaumet reads each poem aloud in one urgent breath, like a vehicle plunging brakeless down a slope.

to the mitochondrian Eve

the archaeology of slowness
the cult of instantaneity
the dream of abolishing waiting
of sliding over the great limpid arborescent flow toward infinity
our maps of trajectories on computer screens
the abandoning of entire territories for urban moors
around air-conditioned cities pedestrian-free conurbations
the recovery of territories
urban fringes gnawing at coastlines
deserted in favour of floating nomadic cities
where luxury refugees scare themselves
watching pirate populations
the human flood
rivers of hopes panic
flowing over borders directionless scrambling the radar

climatic deportation
the lethal beauty of viruses
mankind snarled in its own technical progress
not knowing how to shed its skin
the mental revolution aborted
the electric discharge of the artificial neuron
the identikit picture of our souls
memories governed by law
and cemeteries changed to garbage dumps

translated by Hugh Hazelton

along the road of return
tension sharpens your senses
as you search for splits
to get lost in
and see one more moment
of splendour emerge

along the road of return
dead birds are raining

translated by Madeleine Stratford

A little girl takes a bite out of death
devilishly
mocking death with delight.
Her laugh says Life is vanity
and of the highest worth.
A little girl says
Death must be simpler than life
but come the day I won't say a word.
A little girl takes a bite out of death
and praises life in a song

more painful than our apocalyptic litanies.
She says Behind the fear of death
hides a fear of life.
A little girl takes a bite out of death
says Your death will but mirror your life.
In death there are no more mirrors.

translated by Madeleine Stratford

gipsy gestures
sultry steps
serious sacred
games
fearfully fire
intensely earth
joy dances within your dance
a joy blazing in your body's fire
a joy bursting inside my mouth
juice overflowing the fruit
your legs hips fingers dancing
your wrists neck dancing your pelvis knees ass
dancing your heart dancing your feet and ankles dancing
your shoulders eyelashes blood
your skirt opening up the sky
everything in you
vibrates
from mind to nipples
everything instantly touches penetrates me
and I can't find the source of the thirst
you bring to my lips and muscles and feverish head
of all that dances within you and is you
your eyes your sweat
your smell your hair your wetness
your smile overflowing my face
giving me the unspeakable transient

certainty that I understand a little better
why we live on this earth

translated by Madeleine Stratford

for Li Qingzhao

We too drink
clinking eyes
and I suddenly think of her
the pin slipping from her hair in the embrace
the light sweat moistening her dress
the silk stretching around her feet
that fragile voice in the water of time
and warlike rumblings
the ever vulnerable force of spring we await
struggling with the snow
the sobbing of wheels tracing the crack in the road that leads
to exodus to mourning the gaze that jolts along hanging from bitter
nostalgia
a flower that loses the sharpness of its red
like the red rubbed off lips in the violence of a kiss
remember
the loss the glory of hours stolen
for the intensity the gift of an instant
of an inebriety on the wine she loved so much
and on much more than the wine
give me your eyes
we'll dive together as she sings into this glass
this reversal slowing down the patient gulf.

translated by Hugh Hazelton

Hay caminos que no tienen regreso
I read at the Mexican immigration office.
Roads
how many have I taken, abandoned
how many delighted, deceived me
how many where I've gotten lost
lost and open, lost and found
where I've found another.
What have my soles mapped out? What have I brought back?
Roads that are always the same? Mine?
There are roads that have no return
others that don't lead anywhere.
But the return is a lure
and nowhere is called the quest.
Your road is only the web
woven by and weaving your life.

translated by Hugh Hazelton

Poetry of the Taliban

Alex Strick van Linschoten
& Felix Kuehn (Editors)

Preface by Faisal Devji

'Afghanistan has a rich and ancient tradition of epic poetry celebrating resistance to foreign invasion and occupation. This extraordinary collection is remarkable as a literary project — uncovering a seam of war poetry few will know ever existed, and presenting to us for the first time the black turbanned Wilfred Owens of Wardak. But it is also an important political project: humanising and giving voice to the aspirations, aesthetics, emotions and dreams of the fighters of a much-caricatured and still little-understood resistance movement that is about to defeat yet another foreign occupation.' — **William Dalrymple**

9781849041119 / May 2012
£14.99 hardback / 248pp

Overlooked by many as mere propaganda, poetry offers an unfettered insight into the wider worldview of the Afghan Taliban. This collection of over two hundred poems draws upon Afghan tradition and the recent past as much as upon a long history of Persian, Urdu and Pashto verse. The contrast between the severity of their ideology and the Taliban's long-standing poetic tradition is nothing short of remarkable. Unrequited love, vengeance, the thrill of battle, religion and nationalism — even a yearning for non-violence — are expressed through images of wine, powerful women and pastoral beauty, providing a fascinating insight into the hearts and minds of these redoubtable adversaries.

'These are poems of love and war and friendship and tell us more about Afghanistan than a million news reports. Anybody claiming to be an Afghan expert should read this book before giving their next opinion.' — **Muhammed Hanif, author of** *A Case of Exploding Mangoes* **and of** *Our Lady of Alice Bhatti*

To purchase this book at a discounted rate of £12.00 please order through the following channels, quoting reference CMPOTT:
> email: rob@hurstpub.co.uk > tel: +44 (0)20 7255 2201 > post: address below

41 GREAT RUSSELL ST, LONDON, WC1B
WWW.HURSTPUB.CO.UK
WWW.FBOOK.COM/HURSTPUBLISHERS
020 7255 2201

FAITH IN LOVE

Suhel Ahmed

Julian takes purposeful strides through the street. He is desperate to reach Anika's house so that he can see her and, more importantly, speak to her uncle. Evening has fallen and the pavement glitters with frost, creating a fine cushion that crackles beneath his trainers. His walk soon breaks into a run and his breaths become sharp, forming cloudy bursts that reveal the chill in the night air.

It is a piece of bad news that propels him towards this showdown with Anika's guardian. Julian received the message on his mobile phone while sitting in the library. The message had hopped from mobile to mobile, spreading among their college mates until eventually it pinged on Julian's phone. He had to read it twice because the first time it made his stomach lurch so violently that it left him nauseous. Anika had dropped out of college. She was heading back to her country to get married. Immediately Julian tried to call her but she didn't answer. This set his mind racing in all sorts of despairing directions: *Why didn't she call him? Had she left already? Would he ever see her again?*

Fear soon gave way to anger leaving a single thought searing on his mind: the need to confront her uncle. It was impossible for Julian to accept that his relationship with Anika had ended not because they had fallen out of love, but because they had fallen in love.

Their affair was never meant to grow into a relationship. 'Just a bit of fun', they had agreed after their lips touched for the first time. It had happened at the start of term when, befitting a true gentleman, he walked her to the bus stop after a college social event. She was dressed in a ruby-red frock with matching shoes, and in the muted light of an idle, overcast day, looked like a lozenge of colour in the otherwise grey surroundings. The breeze flirted with her sleek, dark hair and lifted the perfume off her neckline. Her large bracelets jangled and gave music to her boho-chic look. Truth be told, he'd been smitten with her from the moment he first set eyes on her, picking her out from the other students and tracking her beauty from a distance until the afternoon of the social event when he managed to edge close enough to strike up conversation (helped by a few drinks which fuelled the courage and dampened the nerves). She had smiled brightly at his jokes and responded to his flirtations with coquettish head tilts and hair flicks. On the other hand, her sentences were polished, her manner composed, and her eyes attentive. Like an invitation. The ease with which she could switch back and forth from a giggling girl to a woman with a worldly aura attested to her feminine wiles. Hers was a personality that could put any man under a spell. And so under the bus shelter, encouraged when she had slipped her arm through his, Julian took the opportunity to gaze deeply into her eyes and stroke her honey-brown face before leaning in for a kiss.

But, over time, 'fun' had given rise to feelings, and feelings opened his heart to the possibility of a future together. It was his first love, and as such he found himself completely consumed by her, believing in that state of virginal innocence that she was the other half of his soul. He planned days for her. He took her on picnics, to music gigs, art galleries and museums, to his favourite café with its oak tables, smoky atmosphere and walls plastered with French film posters. He organised a day trip to the botanical gardens in Kew and then a night out to a West End show for which she dressed up in a satin dress that clung to her contours. They went on long walks by the canal, hand in hand, and Julian didn't care about the sharp edges of Anika's rings digging into his fingers, treating them as love bites of a more surreptitious kind. He would make these walks meander into all sorts of improvised directions to try to prolong their time together. In college he had to keep their romance a secret because she didn't want her uncle to find out. She was adamant that if word of their relationship ever got back to the family then she would be sent home immediately.

Everything was fine until, one day, a few weeks before they were due to break up for the Christmas holiday, Anika told him that the she could no longer see him.

'It could never be,' she had explained, gazing at him through the film of water that threatened to gather into a tear and make her mascara run.

'Why?'

'Because my family would never accept a non-Muslim.'

'It's the twenty-first century!'

'You don't understand.'

'What?'

'We're from different worlds. It would never work.'

'It is working. You want to be with me and I want to be with you.'

'It's not as simple as that.'

'Why not?'

Anika's expression turned hard.

'Just forget about us!'

Driven then by a lovesick fever, he entered the library the following day. He initially trawled the web but found it confusing when he was faced with the surf of conflicting and contradictory information, the sources of which were often dubious. He then visited the institution's Islamic studies faculty and harried the professor until the man wrote down a list of must-reads from his syllabus. Julian returned to the library and locked himself inside a carrel with a stack of books, connected to the outside world only by a narrow window offering a solitary view of winter's dark lid closing in on a December sky. A believer in God, but without a heartfelt allegiance to any faith, Julian sat down to take the fight to a religion that everyone knew advocated terror, misogyny and capital punishment, amongst other evils, and which also stood in the way of true love.

To his surprise, it became hard to stop when he started to read, exhilarated as he was by some of his discoveries. By the end of the session he revelled in the irony that, given the right spin, Islam could become his ally in the bid to win back his girl. He began devoting hours of each day in this labour for love, surrounding himself in multiple translations of the Book, reading the words of scholars and absorbing their meanings through the filter of his sensitivities. He learned about *Taqwa* — the moment of insight, *Shura* — the essence of democracy, and *Ummah* — the notion of a common moral purpose. He read about a religion that was plural and all embracing, pencil-marking passages that championed diversity. He read and reread the verse: *the noblest of you in the sight of God is the one who is most deeply conscious of Him*. The verse told him that Islam wasn't hung up on colour or creed, but a code of behaviour which he was willing to subscribe to. Two weeks later Julian sought to experience that spirit of community so he left his books and stepped inside a mosque for the first time to join in Friday prayers. No one raised a brow or batted an eyelid; he simply found himself as part of a communal organ absorbed in the harmony of worship. He came away feeling cleansed. For the first time in his life Julian felt he had found a faith to hook his spiritual being on to. And days later he bought himself a notebook and began scribbling down notes until his hand ached and his mind fizzed. He became so absorbed in the work, convinced that the words were speaking directly to him and promising to return Anika.

***

Julian has another mile to run until he reaches Anika's doorstep. The commuting hour is underway. The main road beside him is congested, the long stretch awash with headlights trying to bore their way through the evening traffic but only managing to press up against the blare of red tail lights and the fumes of puttering exhausts. The car windows he passes form a portrait gallery of faces in profile, all hunched over their steering wheels – lone people trying to get home to their loved ones, as he is trying to get to his. He is relieved not to be stuck inside a car. It suddenly occurs to Julian that he has never seen Anika's uncle, or her aunt for that matter. In the time they were together, Anika had never invited him round because 'it would cause problems'. He imagines her uncle as a proud, patriarchal figure, erect like a guard, and ready to defend the family's honour.

But the man needn't fear Julian's intentions. He himself has been raised by god-fearing souls, 'people of the book' as the Qur'an refers to them. He has two younger sisters towards whom he feels protective. He also understands what it's like to try to build a life in a foreign country, for his father is a working-class Polish man who was forced to endure all the brutal privations when he stepped foot inside Thatcher's Britain back in the Eighties. Julian wants to use the opportunity to appeal to her uncle's sense of compassion, find common ground, and show him that beyond the differences of religion, they share the history of being outsiders.

He knows Anika will be shocked to see him on her doorstep. She will try to stop him when he expresses his desire to speak with her uncle. Julian will hold her hand to his heart and promise to be calm and courteous. He will impress upon her his newfound knowledge by iterating that even the prophet Muhammad built kind relationships with non-Muslims all the time, in weakness as in strength.

Julian knows a shortcut. He turns off the main road, runs down several smaller streets, and through an alleyway adjoining playing fields which eventually opens out like the mouth of a river to a residential cul-de-sac. Three houses are hidden behind tall hedgerows. Each property is so grand that it is identified by a name. A plume of smoke rises from one of the chimneys, the breast of which is clad in a smiling neon Santa. The porch of another house is garlanded in flashing fairy lights. Anika's uncle's house stands mutely in the middle, as if scorning the spirit of festivity. For a moment Julian holds on to its wrought-iron gate, allowing his lungs to catch their breath and his thoughts to assume an order. He then gazes at the building and is struck by its stature. It is an Edwardian property with sash windows and quaint period features, which give it an old English charm. It stands over a driveway that can easily accommodate three vehicles. A black Mercedes takes up one of the bays, the chrome alloys of its wheels kissed by the security light, which has been tripped by his arrival. Julian looks up at the loft window jutting out of the roof. From past conversations he knows that it looks into Anika's room. His imagination turns the edifice into Rapunzel's tower and, despite himself, he scans potential footholds, the guttering and the trellis, tracing a route he can climb to reach her bedroom.

He shakes the thought out of his head and walks up to the door, his footfalls crushing the gravel as if sounding his intrusion. The wind blows hard making the stiff hedgerows behind him howl and judder. It is so eerie that he half expects a barking mastiff on a chain to leap out at him. He climbs the steps and presses the brass buzzer with a trembling finger. He dabs the sweat off his forehead and finger-combs his hair. He takes a step back and stands taut like an infantryman, his face packed with determination. The door opens soundlessly. It is a good sign, a pacific sign. For some reason he assumed Anika would answer the door, but it is an older man, the shape of whose mouth bears a familial resemblance to Anika's. It can only be her uncle. The two men lock uncertain eyes and Julian flashes his most charming smile – hoping the same smile that once attracted Anika will now endear him to her uncle.

'Assalumu alaikum, Mr Afzhal,' he says in a trite effort to sound familiar. But he trips over the words – words he has read in books many times before but has never said out loud – and his effort sounds more like ridicule than a mark of respect.

'Do I know you?' the man asks.

'I am Julian… Anika's… friend.'

There is a brutal pause as Anika's uncle scrutinises him with dark pupils that exude power through their sheer stillness. Julian tries to second-guess what the man is seeing: a tall, ashen-faced figure with a shock of curly hair, slovenly dressed in a thick duffle coat which is unbuttoned and hanging over a Tupac t-shirt. The self-appraisal leaves him feeling unsure. Though Mr Afzhal is a small man, his stature is elevated by the splendour of his home. The smell of his aftershave belongs to men who wear expensive suits and sit behind large desks, and who sign cheques with a flourish of the pen. Julian can feel his mouth drying and his confidence shrivelling.

'She's never mentioned me?' Julian asks.

'Anika's friend?'

'Yes.'

'What are you doing here?'

'I've come to see Anika.'

'She's not here.'

There is a pause.

'And to speak with you, if I may?' Julian says while shuffling on the spot.

Mr Afzhal smiles, a smile that is merely a veil for clenched teeth. He looks over Julian's shoulder, scans the vicinity before his eyes return to meet Julian's flinty pupils.

'How did you get here?'

'I walked.'

Mr Afzhal turns back indoors.

'Come in,' he says, almost as an afterthought.

Julian is slightly taken aback by the interior of the reception room he is led into. As much as the outside pays homage to a definite English era, the inside is something quite different. It is white, luxurious, with a high

ceiling from which dangles a Murano glass chandelier that throws shards
of light onto the walls. Yet the furnishings are touched by an array of
spicier colours: rich berry, saffron, cinnamon – an earthy palette that has
its roots in the East. The tall curtains are hand-embroidered with patterns
and beading. A wood-carved figurine of what looks like an Egyptian
artefact sits on the mantelpiece.

'Take a seat,' Mr Afzhal says.

Julian perches on the lip of a hefty armchair. Mr Afzhal sits in the one
opposite him. The two men are separated by a claw-footed coffee table.

'Tell me what it is you want.'

Although Mr Afzhal speaks softly, the words are ironclad. Julian sits up
and draws a deep breath. He wasn't expecting her uncle to be so well
spoken. There is no hint of an accent. In fact, there is an accent, best
described as Old Etonian. Julian looks around the room. He can hear
noises coming from some part of the house, the clatter of utensils, and
immediately turns his head in the offending direction. Mr Afzhal reads the
question in Julian's eyes, and also the thought behind it.

'That's the house maid. Anika has gone shopping with her aunt.'

There is a pause.

'Is it true that she is not returning to college to finish her course?'

'Yes.'

'She's going back to get married?'

Mr Afzhal nods.

'You can't make Anika marry someone against her wishes.'

'Who said it is against her wish?'

'We're in love.'

'Pardon?' Mr Afzhal says.

'Anika hasn't mentioned anything to you because it would cause
problems.'

Mr Afzhal takes a moment to consider his niece's transgression, the
possibility of her being so reckless in spite of knowing that any sort of
pre-marriage relationship is out of the question, never mind one with a
white man. Yet he also knows from the time his niece has spent living with
him that she is a spirited being, a city girl who has enjoyed all the trap-
pings of her father's success, not to mention an excess of affection.

'How long has this been going on for?'

'We've been together since the start of term.'

Mr Afzhal pinches the bridge of his nose. If word of this were ever to get back to his sister and brother-in-law, he'll be held culpable for dishonouring the family name by not keeping a watchful eye on his niece. Mr Afzhal is suddenly thankful that Anika has decided to return home. The girl must have come to her senses and stopped fooling around with the gora boy. He turns his attention back to the young man.

'How old are you?'

'Almost twenty,' Julian replies.

'I see. I can tell that you're a smart man. Love isn't what you see in the movies, it isn't what you hear in pop songs. And it isn't what you read in poems.'

'Please don't treat me like a kid.'

'Falling in love is the easy part. You only have to surrender your heart. But the rest is hard work, especially when there is a gulf of difference between the two people. You've chosen the wrong person to give your heart to.'

Julian finds himself getting more worked up. He is not here to listen to such highfalutin claptrap.

'Islam condemns forced marriages!'

Mr Afzhal balks from the force of Julian's words.

'What?'

Julian takes out a small notepad from his back pocket and begins rifling through the pages. A paralysing uncertainty forces him to want to dictate the course of this encounter.

'The story of Khansa Bint Khidam proves this.'

'Who? What? I'm not sure what you are trying to say.'

'She lived during the time of the prophet. Her father gave her in marriage when she was a matron and she disliked that marriage. So she went to the prophet Muhammad who declared that marriage invalid.'

The words come out in a tremulous torrent. All the mental rehearsal, the careful honing of words and phrases, hasn't prepared Julian for the overwhelming onslaught of nerves. It is as if he's stepped on stage with his lines in a muddle. But he forces himself to continue.

'It would be a sin to make Anika marry someone against her wish.'

Mr Afzhal holds up his palms gesturing the young man to calm down.

'There is no forcing of any kind. My niece is completely happy with the choice.'

'That cannot be right!' Julian snaps back.

'Are you saying that I'm lying?'

'No.'

'Then what?'

Julian rubs his face vigorously with his hand.

'You're protecting her!'

'From what?'

'From her feelings for me.'

'You are a friend of hers, no?'

'We are more than—'

'And you've been very kind in helping her to settle into college. I'm sure my niece appreciates this very much. But now she's decided not to continue with her course and is returning home. It's as simple as that.'

Julian realises that his nerves have made him come across hostile. He lowers his voice and tries to relax the muscles of his face.

'I understand why you wouldn't want someone like me to come into Anika's life, but I'm here to tell you that your reasons might be misplaced.'

Mr Afzhal shifts in his seat.

'Misplaced?'

'Sir, I was born into a Jewish family, and although I have no particular religious leanings, I've always believed in God. It's what keeps us humble. But I do think all religions offer sound moral guidance, be it Christianity, Judaism, Buddhism or Islam.'

'Jewish?' the older man repeats with a slight grimace as if the word has forced a sour taste onto his tongue.

'You'll find that the Qur'an regards both the Bible and the Torah as revealed texts,' Julian is quick to add.

Julian swipes at the pages, which Mr Afzhal notices are filled with handwritten notes. He watches Julian overshoot the page he wants and then leaf his way back, his eyes smarting and his head flitting frantically from side to side.

'Here it is, these are words translated from the Qur'an, ...*and those who are Jews and Christians and Sabaeans – all who believe in God and the Last day, and do righteous deeds shall have their reward with the Lord; and no fear shall be on them, neither shall they grieve.'*

He turns more pages and reads out other passages and quotes to prove his point. Julian is vibrating with intensity, jacked up by his scholarly endeavours and sounding like a deranged preacher who is fast losing his congregation. Every time he peers up, he sees the stupefied face of Mr Afzhal who seems to be getting further out of his reach.

'Jews and Muslims are closer to each other than you might think. Both have similar codes of conduct, laws and jurisprudence. The dietary rules of both religions are almost the same; and charity is an important feature of both.'

'STOP IT!' Mr Afzhal suddenly shouts. The sudden raising of voice causes the maid to come rushing out. She is a young woman – a brunette, dressed in a trouser suit, and clutching a Prada handbag. Her hair is slightly mussed up.

'What's happened, Waz?' she asks Mr Afzhal.

'Nothing! Just leave us alone for a moment.'

He waves her away. He then quickly turns back to Julian.

'That's enough,' he says, calm restored to his voice.

Julian can feel the heat of tears pushing against his eyes, burning the insides of his nose.

'I love her,' he mutters quietly.

'That is ridiculous. You've only known Anika for three months. You have no idea what you are saying.'

'I know what my heart is telling me.'

Mr Afzhal is rubbing his forehead.

'You're just responding to an impulse. You are behaving like a modern-day Majnun. You are too young to know any better.'

Julian looks up at Mr Afzhal with the face of a confused child.

'You're trivialising what we have.'

'All I'm saying is that you have attached too much meaning to this friendship with my niece.'

'You're only saying that because I am Jewish.'

Mr Afzhal sweeps his arms dismissively at the book Julian is clutching, which he's been raising slightly every time he's been consulting it as if it's a shield of some kind. Mr Afzhal notices Julian's fingernails for the first time. They have been gnawed into sore, jagged edges.

'All these notes you have made are biased. You have been picking quotes and commentaries like fruits from a tree. Writing the good ones, discarding the not-so-good. Not to mention pulling them out of context. Take it from me: any marriage between a Muslim girl and a non-Muslim man is forbidden in the Qur'an.'

'It doesn't matter. I am willing to convert because fundamentally I believe we are still praying to the same God. I am a good person, and that's all that matters.'

Mr Afzhal isn't sure how to respond to the young man's plea. He walks over to a cabinet and opens its doors, behind which stands a gleaming collection of bottles. He takes out a decanter and pours what looks like scotch into a crystal glass, and into which he drops two ice cubes from a small, silver bucket. They make a crisp, crackle as they rupture, cloud the glass and cool the drink. He swirls the glass in his hand and the liquid's colour lightens to a languid autumnal tint. He then takes a sip.

'Would you like something?' he asks.

'No thank you.'

Mr Afzhal returns to the armchair and sits leaning forward like a concerned parent.

'You're a very serious man, Julian. I'm sure you are aware that Anika was only meant to be here for a year anyway?'

'Plans change.'

'Yes they do. Now she's going home early.'

'Because you are forcing her to!'

Mr Afzhal grimaces. He puts the glass on the coffee table. He then crosses his legs and smoothes down the material of his trousers over his knee. He is beginning to feel a little sympathy for Julian.

'You are being irrational.'

'What?'

'Have you spoken to Anika?'

'She broke it off several weeks ago because we come from different religious backgrounds. She's never mentioned anything about a wedding. It's clear that this wedding has been thrust upon her. I can't let this happen to her.'

'Anika isn't a village girl. She is educated. She has made her choice. You should respect that and move on.'

'Once I convert to Islam there should not be an issue.'

Mr Afzhal takes a deep breath.

'Let me explain: in our culture we have a social system. It's called biraderi. The word roughly means clan. One's primary loyalty is to one's clan. One always stands by their biraderi, lives and marries among their biraderi. You are naïve to think that by embracing the same faith, you will be embraced by the family.'

Julian finds himself all at sea because what he is hearing does not reconcile with all that he has learnt in the last few weeks. Julian recalls reading in one of the translations of the Qur'an that believers should embrace difference. He remembers writing down a verse that filled him with hope. He leafs through the pages once again. He finds it and locks eyes with the middle-aged man for one final entreaty.

'That goes against the very grain of Islamic principles, Mr Afzhal. Listen to this: "O humankind! We have created you male and female, and made you nations and tribes, that you may know one another." Those words are in the Qur'an. So what you are saying is... is... sacrilegious!'

Mr Afzhal is now getting irritated.

'I am not Anika's father so I'm sitting here tolerating your crazy behaviour. If Anika's father were here he would have had you beaten up and thrown out of the house by now!'

'Why?'

'Because you are not the kind of groom their family is looking for. Even if you were to convert. You're simply not the right...' Mr Afzhal stops short of saying the word.

'I don't understand.'

There is a pause.

'What do your parents do?'

'My father is a taxi driver and my mother works part-time as a school assistant.'

'I see. And what plans do you have for your life?'

'Well, I'd like to be a youth worker.'

There is a long silence. Then Mr Afzhal begins to talk. His voice has receded to a whisper as if he is an informer.

'Anika is the only daughter of my older sister, whose husband, my brother-in-law, is a wealthy businessman. Being the only daughter, Anika has never been deprived of anything in her life. You can say that she's been cosseted. She also represents the honour in my brother-in-law's life. He isn't going to give her away to the first person who happens to turn her head.'

'It's more than that,' Julian stresses.

'The man Anika is marrying is the son of a Nawaab who owns some of the largest marble quarries in the country. His son is studying an MBA in Harvard. Both sets of parents want to put the marriage forward so he will go home next month and the couple will wed before he returns to finish his studies. He will eventually take over the mining business. The families belong to the same biraderi.'

'You're trying to pull the wool over my eyes so that I leave,' Julian says.

'Anika has been engaged to him now for over a year. She was engaged to him before she came to Britain. She implored her father to let her study abroad for a year so that she could do something useful with herself while waiting for her fiancé to return.'

'What? You're lying!'

'Have you not seen the ring on her finger?'

The blood drains from Julian's face. He blinks his mind back to all the boho jewellery Anika's fingers were adorned in. It never occurred to him that one of those was her prenuptial band. It was the diamond that used to bite into his hand whenever he threaded his fingers through hers during those long romantic walks along the canal.

'You can speak with her tomorrow. I'll tell her you called,' Mr Afzhal suggests.

Julian's resolve has crumbled. He feels cheated. He feels foolish for having been so sure about their relationship and for confronting Anika's uncle with such conviction.

'You can speak with her,' Mr Afzhal repeats.

Julian shakes his head.

'Fuck! She lied to me!' he mutters.

'Excuse me?'

Julian peers up, stares wildly at Mr Afzhal holding his alcoholic drink. He remembers the young woman with the mussed-up hair hiding behind the kitchen door. He then looks at the notebook in his hands and lets it drop to the floor.

'Fucking lies, all lies!' he starts repeating, the expletive coming out with such force that spittle shoots out of his mouth.

'I think you'd better leave,' Mr Afzhal says.

Without saying another word, Julian does as he is told.

It would be months later on a glorious spring morning while Julian was sitting in the café staring at a film poster of the gorgeous Cardinale that a waitress would interrupt him. She would hand him a red sweater which Anika had left behind on the couple's last outing together. He would bury his nose inside the soft garment, smell her perfumed presence and feel an electric charge of emotion shear through him. And on his walk home, after donating the sweater to a local Bernardo's, he would begin to acknowledge the demonic powers of his erstwhile obsession. Despite the accusations he'd been hurling on that fateful night, he would finally accept the truth that he'd been lying to himself all along. It was his faith in love that had been misplaced.

PARK51

Michel Abboud

The Park51 project, originally called Cordoba House, is a planned community centre located in Lower Manhattan, New York. When it was first
reported in *The New York Times* in December 2009, the project was not seen
as contentious. It received some coverage but nothing controversial, with a
couple of conservative commentators giving it a relatively positive mention.
But when the plans were presented to the local community board review in
May 2010, the situation changed drastically. The mild, even-handed
response to a local project was immediately transformed into an international controversy. Due primarily to the campaign of an organisation called
Stop Islamization of America (SOPA), the terms 'Ground Zero Mosque' and
'9/11 Mosque' proliferated throughout the media. Reductive and misguided representations of the project were thus projected both on national
and international level.

The context of the debate is important. It occurred in a Congressional
election year, fanning the flames of the polemic and leading to the politicisation of the project. As such, the controversy escalated throughout the following summer and autumn prior to the election in November. The term
'Ground Zero' directly linked the project to the September 11 attacks and
its perpetrators, and the notion of a mosque. The project was born in this
context; and would evolve within this context.

The first point to note is that the project is not located on Ground Zero.
It is located at 45–51 Park Place, New York City. The site is a typical mid-
block property, flanked by adjacent buildings on either side, a few blocks
from the World Trade Centre Site. There is no direct or indirect line of sight
to or from Ground Zero. Along with Lower Manhattan, it is in the neighbourhood of Ground Zero.

Although the site itself is not a part of Ground Zero, the conditions at the World Trade Centre Site at the time of the controversy undoubtedly exacerbated the debate. In the summer of 2010, the future of the World Trade Centre redevelopment was certainly not set in stone, with only one of the proposed seven buildings complete. The uncertainty of the World Trade Centre redevelopment coupled with the seemingly rapid development of Park51 also bolstered the opposition.

The second, equally important, point is that this is not a mosque. The proposed project does not seek any historical references, nor does it dwell on manipulation and recombination of past symbols and forms. The team at SOMA, the architects where I am the principal, has not done exhaustive research on the history of mosques nor did we attempt to reinterpret the type in modern forms or materials. We have addressed the project as we do all projects: with no preconceptions and a candid will to respond to a given site, propose a workable programme, and create a unique identity for the project.

The project is a mixed use facility, with a 500-seat auditorium, theatre, performing arts centre, fitness centre, swimming pool, basketball court, day care, art gallery, bookstore, culinary school, and food court. The true challenge, however, was to create an architecture that would create a platform for the mediation of social, cultural, and political differences, in one coherent environment that would cater equally for all parties.

The controversial programme of the building spawned a media war of images, and our first responsibility as architects was to propose a standalone image of a building: an image that would enter the world's collective imagination and replace the associations of classical mosques. The strong physical, social, political and urban constraints have led our design process to attempt to reverse their effect and utilise them as key design features. The abstract pattern on the facade is projected into the building to become floor plates that connect the exterior façade and the building's internal programme, as an intricate, sponge-like endoskeleton. This process creates a series of interior voids, which start at the prayer spaces in the sublevel and end at a 9/11 memorial on the top floor. The geometries forming the building's skin have been spawned by the interior program and create a self-supporting structural and dynamic interface with the urban realm, resulting in the building's street front.

Most importantly, however, the image of the building is one that reflects its intent to provide a platform for the mediation of differences. It is open, light, and transparent. As Philip Kennicott of the *Washington Post* notes, 'it is porous, open and bright, which is to say, it is literally an enlightened building.'

The design, derived from an interpretation of culturally significant motifs, is an attempt to merge meaning through pattern. The use of repeated and interlocking motifs was seen as a way to re-broadcast the Islamic doctrine of *tawheed* — variously translated as 'Unity of God' or 'unity in multiplicity'— by contemporary means. The transformation is inherently captured in the density of unique elements tessellated and atypically repeated. The densities were affected by the organisation of the interior programme allowing closure at elements of privacy and openness in areas requiring daylight.

This modern *musharabyeh* is designed to demonstrate signs of the transformation and transparency which is required on all sides — both around this building, and the place of Islam in the USA. This series of manoeuvres is an intentional, literal and conceptual exhibition of the building, with the clear message that the building is transparent. It promotes a message of openness and integration of the Muslim community with the city of New York and its various communities of faith.

As with most polemics, the release of our most recent images seems to have entrenched both opponents and supporters of the project. The ambiguous reading of the facade from both camps is fascinating. Some see the building as an abstraction of an Islamic pattern, while others envisage a crumbling Star of David and desecrated Christian Crosses. It is in this misreading in the face of controversy that the building begins to position itself. But as the controversy surrounding the project evolves, so would the reading of the façade — from conflict to resolution.

DOGGY BISCUIT BORDER

Anita Sethi

A little boy whips cattle before a sun that sinks into the city below Murat camping site which lies at the foot of a palace reached by a rocky hill. All evening members of our group have been stumbling up the rocky hill to try and reach the palace. Some have made it, some faltered mid-way, some not tried at all. I stump my toe mid-way as I walk up with Natasha and tell her to go on without me as I settle on the hill, finding it offers a glorious view of the red-bruise sun and if I crane my neck behind, the great palace. The whole of Dogubayazit, nick-named 'Doggy Biscuit', the border town between Turkey and Iran, seems to fall away below into the growing darkness. I shelter from the fierce dust and watch the son who has been tending the cattle reunite with his father as the night begins to darken and the town in the distance lights up. It is a shock to notice the town all of a sudden, as I flick my eyes to the urban landscape far below it, the sun draining away. Now, to the naked eye, half the world is in shadow; spin round, the other half is still light.

I make my way back to the campsite where members of the group have already put up their tents for the night. A bony dog sniffs around the camp as the cooks of the group throw chicken on the sizzling pan. The dogs' eyes fix on one girl who stares him out. Of all of the group she and I love our solitude. So she has come to the tent for some time alone whilst the others are in the shelter, drinking, the sounds of them growing ever more raucous. I need my time alone, she says. To be in my own world. She is sitting in her tent which flaps like a red skin around her, a little world sealing her away, her chrysalis. She has put headphones in her ears so is sealed away from the sounds of the outer world. She is not scared of the dog at all. 'If you stare them in the eyes,' she tells me, 'they get scared of you.' James has put on his new Turkish CD which is drowned by the wind growing harsher as it whips against tents.

I am drawn back to watch the boy and the man and walk closer to them, but when the boy turns towards me with his eyes gleaming in the darkness, I skulk back. I prowl along the other side of the road where there are no people in sight, just the ochre hills stretching far into the horizon.

Near the tents is a simple building. Inside there is a long wooden bench and chairs and in the far right hand corner a man is serving drinks to forty Western tourists who are drinking, glasses clattering on the wood and raucous laughter echoing around the room. I am the only brown face in our tourist group of forty and as our journey has taken us overland, from London towards the East, I have grown more conspicuous. Tomorrow, we cross the overland border into Iran. In Iran, they will not, they have been warned, be able to indulge in the nightly drinking which has been the norm hitherto. Our tour guide has warned us of what might happen if we continue to drink, or if we smuggle any alcohol through the country. She has warned us about trying to obtain drink there. We will no longer be a member of this little community we have built on our bus, we will be cast out from its care. We will be alone, fending for ourselves. She will make a telephone call to a person of our choice back home for us but that will be it. The penalties once we are over the border for being caught drinking, she warns us, include a public flogging, death by stoning, or, if lenient, jail.

Inside the shelter, members of our group sit playing cards, passing the Queen of Hearts from palm to palm, the King of Spades squeezed between sweaty thumbs. I walk back outside and lose myself among the tents and growing darkness.

All around there are rustles, scuttling, what sounds like boots stomping. I am too weary to set up my own tent. The thought of hammering those long, silver poles into the stubborn, hard earth, of negotiating the mass of yellow canvas which is now all tangled like a sad, dead butterfly, is enough to make me ask James if he can help me set it up.

'Sleep in my tent,' he insists, before going back to join the group inside and continue drinking. And so I explore the empty tent. His tent is an entirely different world from mine. His is cavernous and the kind of green of the lush rainforests. It has two sections, the smaller, outer one where it is possible to stash your belongings, wet dirty shoes or smelly clothes, all things which I have been keeping inside with me. His has an extra buffer to the great outdoors and all their cruel elements. This tent is on the very edge of the campsite.

The road which curves just a few inches from this safe haven of a tent is apparently scoured by Kurdish rebels. I lie alone inside the tent as the wind batters the canvas and listen to the scud scud scudding noise grow louder and recede as if a pair of large black boots were stomping through the campsite and there is a shrill howling sound. The stomp-stomping and howling seems to grow more aggressive, as if whatever is making it can smell my human flesh and I creep to the edge of the canvas, move the zip with a creaking that sends my fingertips ice-cold, and stick my head out into the cool night air. I peer around at the campsite. Far away the sound of laughter echoes. I want to return to the group and their laughter and what, in comparison to this, now feels like safety, the safety of sheer numbers, at least, physical safety even if not psychological. But shadows dance over the earth and I can barely make out the ground in the pitch black.

I feel around for the torch but can't find it. The only light I have is the wan gleam given off by my mobile phone whose battery is leaking away fast since it has been ushered into multi-function as a phone, torch and calcula-tor. The battery signal shows that there is but a trace of energy left as I have not had chance to fill its slight, overworked body up with energy, so any moment now this precious sliver of light will cut off into a total blackness.

The smell of cooked animal from the camp-fire dinner of chicken and vegetables is still pungent. The scrawny dog whines excruciatingly and I hear it rummaging amongst the waste, I see its white body darting like a tortured ghost, its wet eyes gleaming. It will be scared of you and leave you if you are not scared of it, isn't that what Alison said? If you stare at the thing of terror, look it right in its eyes, keep staring and do not be the one to shrink away, it will get scared of you, it will leave you alone. Do not be scared of it.

I zip myself back into the canvas, snuggle down into the sleeping bag, and lie straight and still and practise deep, slow, quiet breathing, lying so still that no dangerous creature outside of these canvas walls will be able to hear me even if I can do nothing to stop them smelling my blood. I lie straight, on my back and feel how soft the ground beneath me is in James's tent since, unlike mine, it has extra padding. I have been using only a sleeping bag through which you can feel the press of the hard earth beneath you. I sink into the kind of semi-consciousness so common to this trip, where the mind is too alert to dangers, attuned to strange frequencies and worries to sink fully asleep and yet so utterly exhausted that it hangs in a sort of limbo world. I feel my straightened body move into its usual sleeping foetal curl then almost fall asleep, for how long I don't know.

Do not let it know that you are scared, isn't that what she said? Alison, the kindest person in our group, also knows a lot about animals, since she has worked to protect and care for threatened and maltreated ones. She has also become adept at capturing them on camera. She knows how to become so still and let all fear from her being vanish so that she can get close to them in order to capture them. She can get close to the bird as it perches on a branch preening and capture the tiny marks and veins of its body. She can get close to the falcon, the pheasant, the dog, and also to small, frightened children. She has a knack for holding and positioning a camera just so, so that the image comes out wondrous and beautiful and any lethargy in the mind vanishes as you look upon the world afresh. Don't be scared, says Alison.

The zip wheezes open suddenly, the smell of tangy beer reaches to the back of my throat, and then a body is pressing against mine, hot breath is on my skin, hands are on my waist teasing and coaxing, flesh hard and erect is pressing onto the lowest curve of my back and a deep voice groaning. I move away, mind faint with tiredness, unable to understand this hard thing pressing against me, these hands on my waist, coaxing. The body moves closer, sighing and moaning. I move away until my face is pressed against the green canvas. Then I unzip the canvas and end up spending the long, cold night in the small bit of the tent, the bit for possessions such as smelly trainers or damp hoodies, the bit for possessions and not really for people. Soon enough, the sound of snoring begins emanating from the main part of the tent which I have just forsaken.

The hungry dog howls all night.

Next morning, I am a 'flapper' — not the 1920s glamorous type of flapper, but the ones that stand with their arms stretched wide on a border town of Turkey and Iran wildly waving until there is not a drop of moisture on the dark green plastic plate. I am draped in a headscarf, the navy pashmina I brought with me stitched with a tulip red border I tuck away, and a long silky skirt which trails on the earth, dampening at the fringes in the morning dew if I don't keep yanking it up. There are hot beans for breakfast for the early birds and bread for the rest. I was meaning to wake early and make a dash for the beans, the thought of them gnawing me into a deeper hunger, but my head is groggy from the troubled night and I make it just in time for the cold food. The memory of what happened the night before is still vivid when I awake, but the rapid pace of the gruelling trip this morning means there is no time to ruminate. Coloured headscarves emerge from tents, scarves in every primary shade; bright blues and yellows and pinks. There are several ex-army boys on the trip, used to the strict regime. It is indeed military: there are now 'police flappers' to monitor the dryness of the green plastic plates we eat off each day.

What do you call this? asks the police flapper on duty inspecting my plate. It's still wet. KEEP FLAPPING.

And so I keep waving my arms wildly bidding the stubborn moisture beads on the plate to vanish, for the group are now dismantling their temporary homes, gathering up the damp skins, packing away silver poles, loading bags onto the bus.

The garish tour company sign had been stripped off the bus that morning and so its body is now all white, a white that now seems dirty and off colour, slightly ill, although it has been scrubbed clean. The colour has vanished from the coach's body because it is important that the vehicle is not conspicuous as it carries us through terrain unsafe for tourists. During the journey so far, we have declared our presence gleefully, enjoying the looks of amusement that have accompanied the coach as it cruised through villages. But this is terrain in which we need, we are told, to blend in. The forty bright scarves nod, as if they have understood.

6:30am and the wheels are growling towards the Iranian border. We sit on metal chairs whilst our tour guide collects our passports and we fill out immigration forms. Four hours waiting at the border, during which we stock up on sweets in the shop on the first floor of the border offices. Andrew leans over me with widened eyes until I am collapsed into unstoppable giggles.

I'm going to change my Facebook photo, so I'm staaaarring, he says.

I gaze at the plastic containers filled with brightly wrapped sweets galore, piled onto shelves and men with pale brown skin gazing on at us bemusedly.

'Indian?', one asks me with a frown, 'Pakistani?'

'British!', I insist

He looks unconvinced, glancing at my fellow passenger Andrew for reassurance.

'She's English!', he says. 'She's with us!'

I ponder exactly what it I might be as I take out the burgundy bruise of a passport ever at the ready. It's the 'three second rule' instilled by our tour guide that we can find this precious thing within three short seconds, so often on this trip do we need to identify ourselves to conduct any number of transactions. I open its pages and show them the BRITISH and they smile and nod and continue to stare. Being the only brown face on the bus, they seem to need evidence that I have not been kidnapped, or smuggled in, or am not from the country just across the border with which there is enmity.

'But parents? Pakistan?' They frown again.

'British!', I say, as I have been told to say to avoid trouble, and they seem almost pacified as they hand over the bags of boiled, chewy, crunchy sweets that I squirrel away for the long hours on the road. Next we must change money and our thin American dollars or pounds sterling are returned in their equivalent form, after the cashier scribbles elaborate calculations onto paper, numbers multiplying into figures which exceed the bounds of my comprehension. The world of figures grows in this economy as does the prevalence of paper money. The slim Western monies are returned for huge wads of green notes so many that they will not even squash into my handbag and amongst ourselves we swap information about the exchange rate which I don't give myself much hope of remembering. Money and food, accomplished.

Then we are greeted by a lady with wide-rimmed sunglasses on her patterned headscarf and visible make-up — a hint of pink lipstick and lashing of black mascara framing her large eyes which betray worry even as her face smiles.

Finally, we are through the border procedures, all forty of us checked and verified. We are speeding across the border and into another country.

REVIEWS

FOUR LIONS

Claire Chambers

What does it mean to be a young person from a Muslim background in Britain today? The question has been explored in a number of films that have represented second-generation British Muslims over the last decade or so. In all of these films — such as Damien O'Donnell's *East is East* (1999) and Andy De Emmony's sequel *West is West* (2011), Ken Loach's *Ae Fond Kiss* (2004), Kenny Glenaan's *Yasmin* (2004), Dominic Savage's *Love + Hate* (2005), Penny Woolcock's *Mischief Night* (2006), and Sarah Gavron's *Brick Lane* (2007) — the central British Muslim character is presented, to a greater or lesser extent, with a choice between sacred and secular modes of living, almost in a 'clash of civilisations' model. Each of the directors represents the choice as being between two sexual partners, one representing a religiously inflected lifestyle, the other a secular one. For the most part, however, the films come down on the side of Westernisation, 'freedom', and an apparently uninhibited sexuality.

In contrast, Chris Morris's subtle and well-researched *Four Lions* (2010) offers a totally different take on the sacred and the secular. It is the story of the five would-be martyrs, who are soon reduced to four after their bomb-making specialist, Fessal, trips over a sheep and blows up. The remaining jihadis are led by Omar, the brightest member of the group and the only one shown to have a family and steady employment. His followers are the public school 'wannabe' Hassan ('the Mal') Malik; Omar's best friend, Waj, who is described in the script as being twenty years old 'and built like a fridge'; and the white convert Barry, the closest thing the film has to George W. Bush's description of 'pure evil'. Following Omar's and Waj's ignominious militant training in Afghanistan (which is actually filmed in Andalucía) and various arguments and rifts, the group decides to stage suicide bombings at the London Marathon. The attacks don't go to plan, and what begins as a hilarious sequence of accidental detonation set pieces becomes a chilling and

185

thought-provoking reflection of what happens when an intense combination of religion, politics, and friendship spirals out of control.

In *Four Lions*, Morris represents the sacred and the secular as being far from 'pure' and discrete entities. Rather, they have porous borders that blur into each other. He reminds his audience that even seemingly unequivocal religious and materialist philosophies and practices are highly diverse amalgamations, which are constantly shifting and interpenetrating. This is evident right from the film's opening scene, in a line spoken by the intellectually-challenged Waj: ''ey up you unbelieving *kuffar* bastards'. Mixing Yorkshire dialect with classical Islamic doctrine, profanity with an assertion of faith, Waj brandishes a replica AK47 in what he hopes will be a threatening jihadi video. His audience, consisting of his fellow militants Barry, Omar, and Fessal, criticise him for the weapon's miniature size, but he remains unfazed, arguing that if he brings it nearer the camera 'that'll bigger it'. The scene immediately locates *Four Lions* in terms of genre as a comedy that inter-textually references the American movie about a British heavy metal band, *This is Spinal Tap* (1984), in which a design mistake leads to Spinal Tap having to use on stage a risible prop of Stonehenge which is only 18 inches tall.

It was a risky and controversial decision to depict terrorism through comedy, and the families of many of the 7/7 victims boycotted the film, which was widely publicised in the media. However, the ineptitude of attempts to bomb Glasgow airport and Tiger Tiger nightclub in London, and the dark slapstick easily discernable in the Detroit pants-bomber debacle, demonstrate that not only is the subject ripe for satire, but it also abounds with physical humour, screwball, and character comedy. Indeed, Jesse Armstrong and Sam Bain from successful British character-led sitcom *Peep Show* are co-writers with Morris of the screenplay. In an unwittingly prophetic comment early on in the film, Omar personifies terrorism failures in the figure of the 'stupid nutter Muslim who blows a bagful of nails into his own guts in the toilets at TGIs', possibly a reference to Saeed Alim, a Muslim convert with learning difficulties who in 2008 injured himself when he accidentally detonated his homemade nailbomb at a restaurant in Exeter. Morris has said that his film was inspired by the inept Home Guard men portrayed in the BBC comedy series *Dad's Army*, but it is also worth comparing *Four Lions* to other British comedies on similar post-9/11 themes, such as the British stage show *Jihad! The Musical* and David Baddiel's film *The Infidel* (both 2010). However, the US puppet movie *Team America World Police* (2005) is perhaps Morris's most relevant cinematic forebear; this film and *Four Lions* both take a scattergun approach to humour, satirising targets across the political spectrum, and (unlike the musical and Baddiel's film about Islamic-Jewish relations) they contain no trace of moralising or uncritical stereotyping.

Four Lions is in many ways a quintessentially British movie: it is low-budget at £2.5 million, and its humour is eccentric, dark, and scatological. The film is also quite narrow, even claustrophobic, in its concentration on domestic spaces as settings, which hints at the ghettoisation experienced by many Muslims in Britain, and is characteristic of the British Asian film. The film's few outside scenes focus on fairly bleak Yorkshire scenery and even the Marathon scenes were shot in Sheffield: these are claustrophobic because of the bustling crowd scenes and hectic tracking shots which indicate the characters' paranoia. Chris Morris's use of genre and cinematic technique in Four Lions, therefore, reflects the impurity and mixed-up nature of the film's themes of the sacred and the secular, suggesting both contamination and cross-fertilisation between different influences.

Perhaps unsurprisingly, given Morris's past work in the groundbreaking 1990s' news satires *The Day Today* and *Brass Eye*, *Four Lions* also evinces great interest in another genre than the British Asian comedy: the jihadi video. Because of their violent content and status as the most horrific type of reality television, these videos have been subjected to content analysis rather than film studies criticism. Yet, Morris is not the only writer to have shown an interest in the genre. Hanif Kureishi's short story 'Weddings and Beheadings' (2010) is written from the perspective of an aspiring film-maker in an unnamed country (probably Iraq), who is coerced into filming footage of beheadings, which he disseminates on the internet. At the end of the story, he expresses his desire to make an art-house film, 'maybe beginning with a beheading, telling the story that leads up to it'. Mohsin Hamid's recent story, 'A Beheading', written for a *Granta* special issue on Pakistan, takes up this challenge, writing such a narrative from the perspective of a Pakistani victim who is taken from his house by jihadis and driven to a dilapidated house, where his murder is filmed. Iraqi writer Hassan Blasim's 'The Reality and the Record', a story from the collection *The Madman of Freedom Square*

(2009), centres on a refugee who claims that he was forced to make a jihadi video which was so convincing that he was sold from gang to gang to make more. He testifies that he was compelled to act variously as an officer in the Iraqi army, a murderous member of the Shiite Mehdi Army, a Sunni Islamist, 'a treacherous Kurd, an infidel Christian', and so on. However, it is never clear whether this story 'for the record' is genuine or merely a way of securing asylum in Fortress Europe because, after spinning this pungent tale of kidnapping, murder, and duplicity, the protagonist suffers mental collapse and tells psychiatric workers his 'real' story: 'I want to sleep.'

Rather than sharing Kureishi, Hamid, and Blasim's focus on filmed murders, Morris is interested in the posturing and explanations of a martyrdom video recorded prior to an attack and intended to be played posthumously. The main reference point here is probably Mohammad Sidique Khan's famous video statement, broadcast on al-Jazeera television several months after 7/7 on 1 September 2005. In the video, Khan declares that the attack on London was a military operation against citizens of a state currently at war against, as Khan puts it, 'my people'. He justifies the attacks on the grounds that those citizens were, consciously or not, complicit with their government's participation in a war that involved the bombing and illegal invasion of countries with largely Muslim populations. Morris takes this argument to its logical extreme when he has Barry tell bomb-maker Fessel that it's morally acceptable to bomb the mosque his father attends: 'has your dad ever bought a Jaffa orange? Well, then! He's buying nukes for Israel – he's a Jew!'

In a West Yorkshire accent very similar to that of the 'fictionary' Waj, Khan intones:

I'm going to keep this short and to the point, because it's all been said before by far more eloquent people than me, and our words have no impact upon you. Therefore I'm going to talk to you in a language you can understand. Our words are dead until we give them life with our blood. I'm sure by now the media's painted a suitable picture of me; its predictable propaganda machine naturally will try to put a spin on things to suit the government and to scare the masses into conforming to their power- and wealth-obsessed agendas. I and thousands like me have forsaken everything for what we believe: our driving motivation doesn't come from tangible commodities that this world has to offer. Our religion is Islam — obedience to the one true God, Allah, and following the footsteps of the final prophet and messenger Muhammad (salAllahu 'alayhi wasallam) — this is how our ethical stances are dictated. Your democratically elected governments continuously perpetuate atrocities against my people all over the world. And your support of them makes you directly responsible, just as I am directly responsible for protecting and avenging my Muslim brothers and sisters. Until we feel security, you will be our targets. And until you stop the bombing, gassing, imprisonment and torture of my people we will not stop this fight. We are at war and I am a soldier. Now you too will taste the reality of this situation.

Morris takes many elements of this partly eloquent, partly muddle-headed, and entirely violent and ethically indefensible statement. For example, he reproduces the video's sartorial statements: Khan ties a red and white *kuffiyah* unconventionally as a bandana, and pairs this with a combat jacket, fusing traditional Arab clothing with elements of militarywear and street style to fashion a specifically young British Muslim code of dress conveying a political statement. Waj and Omar sport similar outfits: a direction tells us that Waj 'wears camos, a black headscarf & behind him a rug is pinned to the wall', while Omar looks even more like Khan, with whom he shares a surname, as he has a red and white *kuffiyah* around his neck, and sports a neatly trimmed beard, grey t-shirt, jeans, and a combat jacket. In many ways, this hybrid look is the male equivalent of the layering of modest women's clothing (both subcontinental clothes such as the *shalwar kameez* and *kurta*, and British clothes from high street chains such as Primark and Topshop) to create a 'visibly Muslim' ensemble. The curiously secular patterned curtain and the bleeping of a car reversing suggest a British location for Khan's video, and Morris replicates the backdrop in the 'blanket pinned to the wall', indicating that the film's several martyrdom videos are almost entirely shot in Yorkshire. Khan's self-conscious rhetorical gestures such as clearing his throat during the speech and polemically pointing his finger are also adapted in Morris's jihadi videos.

Perhaps the most interesting thing about the quoted passage is the emphasis on language, on eloquent speech and failure to listen, the need for simple, straightforward language, and the ominous phrase 'our words are dead until we give them life with our blood'. In the film, the jihadis' words are dead, but they are not vivified by the ensuing bloodbath. The emptiness of language is emphasised in the jihadis' last words: Waj's poignant statement, 'I'm sorry lads, I don't really know what I'm doing'; Barry's wordless death when he is blown up after an unsuspecting passerby gives him the Heimlich manoeuvre as he chokes on Omar's sim card; Hassan's abortive attempt to give himself up to the police, 'I'm real, but not any more' ; and Omar's instruction to his colleague Matt to tell people he last saw him with a smile on his face, as this 'could be important'. Omar's last words may be based on Robert Fisk's report that when a Hezbollah suicide bomber killed 241 US servicemen in Beirut in 1983, a witness said, 'All I remember …is that the guy was smiling'. In *Four Lions*, the suicide bomber's triumphalist smile morphs into Omar's grim rictus, masking his tears as he blows up Boots — a pharmacy he had always been against attacking — to the accompaniment of the haunting piano duet 'Avril 14th' by Aphex Twin.

Of course, Tony Blair and other New Labour politicians furiously tried to disavow that British foreign policy had anything to do with 7/7 and other terrorist attacks. But in his video Khan indicates in 'short and to the point' form that this was in fact a prime motivating factor for the minority who became violent. Additionally, Khan also makes vague and empty fulminations against the media and consumerism, which Morris memorably satirises, but also pushes further in order to indicate why these relatively impoverished young men are so alienated as to get involved in the jihad. A good example comes in Omar's speech:

We have instructions to bring havoc to this bullshit, consumerist, Godless, Paki-Bashing, Gordon Ramsay Taste the Difference Speciality Cheddar, torture-endorsing, massacre-sponsoring, look at me dancing pissed with me nob out, Sky One Uncovered, who gives a fuck about dead Afghanis Disneyland.

Here Omar juxtaposes religious ideas with distaste for consumerism and the media. The partial insight he sheds on foreign policy abuses in Afghanistan sits bathetically alongside vague lifestyle jealousies, which are underlined when Waj responds, 'Fuck mini Babybel!' Yet all the members of the cell are to varying degrees complicit in the consumerist culture Omar condemns here, as when Waj compares the number of people he kills to Nectar points for heaven. Again, it is not so easy to separate the West from the non-West, 'tradition' from 'modernity', and the sacred from the secular: rather we need to explore the ways in which these constructs intertwine.

Although the film is set in Sheffield, where there is a dominant white working-class population, there is also a lot of interest in its northern neighbour Bradford. Morris has undertaken more promotion in Bradford than anywhere else, holding the national premier of *Four Lions* there and organising a special screening followed by a Q and A with cast and crew to raise funds for the Pakistan floods. The actors' voices, expressions, and attitudes seem to emanate less from South than West Yorkshire, whose vernacular can be accurately described as a cross between the north of England and Lahore. The overwhelming majority of Bradford's large Black and Minority Ethnic population is Pakistani in origin and, more specifically, Mirpuri. Many families migrated to the city in the 1970s due to the construction of a huge dam in the Azad Kashmir region of northeast Pakistan, which led to the flooding of several hundred villages and the displacement of their inhabitants. Britain needed menial labourers and movement within the Commonwealth was relatively easy at this time, enabling the migration of thousands of Mirpuris to Bradford, a city which needed workers for its then thriving textile industry. In Pakistani-British writer Moni Mohsin's novel *Diary of a Social Butterfly*, adapted from Lahore's *Friday Times* newspaper column of the same name, the rich and indolent protagonist muses during a trip to England in 2007:

Vaisay I think so the monsoon has come here also. In their Northern Areas tau there has been theek-thaak flooding-schlooding. Places like Badford and Leads and pata nahin kya. Where their Taliban types live. You know, the ninjas in their burqas and trainers and the mullahs with their beards down to their knees, who say, 'khuda hafiz, innit?'

This is the alien yet comic view of the north of England that we also see in *Four Lions*, which contains a similarly hybrid mishmash of religion, politics, and fashion with links to Pakistan.

The film begins with an extreme long shot of a building which anyone who knows the area would instantly recognise as Sheffield's Meadowhall, a well-known shopping centre. However, several viewers unfamiliar with the north of England have assumed the building to have symbolic overtones; for example, in his begrudging review for the *Observer*, Philip French writes, this 'mall, in the movie's one striking visual joke, is lit at night by neon strips that from a distance give it the appearance of a giant mosque'. But the film could have been produced in several different northern cities, and the decision to shoot in Sheffield was as much a pragmatic choice as anything else, because Warp Films, the company behind *Four Lions*, is based there. Morris described Mark Herbert, the chief executive of Warp, taking him to an evening of *nasheeds* (Islamic songs) in Sheffield's Town Hall, attended by about two thousand Muslims, and pitching the city to him as an ideal location four years before Four Lions came out. A *nasheed* makes it into the final soundtrack: from the album *Jihad Nasheeds: Songs of Arabic Struggle*, it features staccato gunshot and is a great deal more radicalising than anything Morris would have heard that night in 2006.

Another reason Sheffield is an ideal location is that tongues of countryside enter the city on the backs of hills, meaning that sheep graze peacefully in semi-rural areas near the city centre, facilitating the crucial scene in which Fessal is blown up in a field by Barry's allotment. In a remark that suggests a degree of concession that the city is a stand-in for its West Yorkshire counterpart, Morris said, 'what with the 2001 riots, I thought poor old Bradford, but I felt Sheffield could take it'. Indeed, the film continued to play in South Yorkshire longer than anywhere else, and the Sheffield branch of the Kebabish chain kept its old livery when the national company changed theirs because that was the one used in the kebab shop explosion scene — so in several ways the film was embraced.

The jihadis are preoccupied with cameras, camcorders, and cameraphones, and *cinéma vérité* and shaky hand-held camera techniques are often used. Waj and Hassan shake their heads vigorously on leaving their improvised bomb-making factory to ensure that any CCTV mug shot would be too blurry to identify them. During the shooting of his jihadi video, Barry imagines himself being interviewed by 'mister newsman, in the newsroom', and Fessal's death is later reported on rolling news, with a caption ticker giving the headline, while a reporter explains in true *Day Today* style, 'Steven Fap discovered the Asian man's head when it nearly fell on his dog out of a tree'. Even the more sensible Omar has one eye on his posthumous reputation, worrying about embarrassing 'bloopers' or outtakes from the group's footage. From the opening scene onwards, the jihadi videos' drama and polemic is punctured by mundane fears that batteries will run out or their cameraphones will run out of credit. There are cameras everywhere, from the panoptic bank of monitors Omar scrutinises in his job as a security guard, to the lens orthodox Fessal hides from by wearing a box on his head, because he believes the human image to be *haram*.

Hassan, the 'fifth jihadi', who enters the cell late in the day and is never quite accepted, films the group at every opportunity, leading Omar to fear he is a 'TV Paki or a coconut spook'. Hassan is significantly depicted as a Media Studies student, whose radicalisation is partly fuelled by his A-level teacher's belittling of him, and who performs extremist dub poetry (which Barry disparages as 'thingy thingy rap rap'). At a lecture ironically entitled 'Islam: Moderation and Progress', he stands up and intones the infantile lyric, 'I'm the mujahideen and I'm making a scene / Now you're gonna feel what the boom boom means / It's like Tupac said, "When I die, I ain't dead" / We are the martyrs, you're just smashed tomatoes'. To the audience's alarm, he shouts, 'Allahu Akbar!' and sets off party streamers from an imitation suicide belt. In this way, Morris draws parallels between hip hop and Islamism (rap stars such as Wu-Tang Clan and Brand Nubian, for instance, propagated Five Percenter ideology in their lyrics). Hassan and Waj dance to the song 'Aag ka Dariya' ('River of Fire': this is also the title of a neglected classic by Pakistani novelist Qurratulain Hyder and a Bollywood film of the same name from 1953), doing traditional moves such as *thumkas* and extended prayer poses, as well as miming each other's brutal murders. The track is by Dr Zeus, a Birmingham-based Sikh music producer who blends Punjabi bhangra music with hip hop and R and B influences, and has a raunchy and bling-filled video that was banned in India because of the near nudity of the featured singer, Czech starlet Yana Gupta. Rather than the contraposition of the sacred and secular which Islamism and hip hop at first appear to be, both concerned with identity assertion.

As well as cameras and the media, Waj in particular is obsessed by other technologies, exemplified in his naïve aim to 'blow up the internet', his 'Prayer Bear' which performs *namaz* for him, or the instance when he takes a call from a terrorist negotiator and thinks he may have won an iPhone (mobile phoneshops with their animal packages are also lampooned). Members of the group also eat their phones' sim cards with the intention of making themselves harder to trace. For communication, the cell uses the Puffin Party children's social networking (which evokes Disney's similar site Club Penguin). They receive emails from the address 'hillaryclinton55@ hotmail.com' inviting them to attend a wedding in Pakistan, code for joining the jihad. This is in part a simple reflection of Morris's own satirical media background, but also mirrors some Islamist groups' striving for e-jihad in online environments. Morris's jihadis prove themselves no strangers to more mainstream shoot-'em-up games, as when Waj says, 'I've got hostages and everything, like X-Box Counter Strike!' This preoccupation with new ICT, filming, and simulacrum, is also an attempt to counter stereotypes and iterate the current British Muslim concern about being under surveillance and reported or researched to excess. Morris is under no postmodernist illusion that the simulacrum is all that exists; indeed his jihadis make this category mistake to their mortal peril.

In one scene a jihadi video is shown in full-screen; the camera then pans out to show the images playing on a laptop in a cosy living room, with Ikea furniture and children's toys cluttering the floor. In my interview with him, Morris explained the reason for this juxtaposition:

If you go into people's houses, it's a jumble. Quite strict Muslims may have houses in which there are no figurative representations on the wall, but when the kids come home, if they've been good at Qur'an school, they can play Grand Theft Auto or watch television. [...] In the evidence in a court case concerning guys accused of doing a reccy for the 7/7 attacks; they had footage of Mohammad Sidique Khan in his house, taking the piss and introducing the people in the room from behind a video camera. It was a very straightforward domestic setting, so why wouldn't it be like that in the film?

Here Morris shows alertness to the 'jumble' or lack of separation between apparently pure and impure modes of living. The Muslim 'brothers' depicted in the film have a cut and paste approach to Islam and obviously don't know much about the Qur'an, which they selectively quote. Although they pepper their sentences with qualifiers such as '*insha'allah*' and '*masha'allah*', these are mixed with extremely British expressions, as when Hassan pronounces, '*Alhamdulillah*, bro. We skilled it'. They are autodidacts in religion, rejecting centuries of Islamic scholarship and chafing against the restrictive scholarship of Omar's possibly Tablighi brother, Ahmed, with his endless *fatwas*, or religious opinions.

This brings us to the issue of radicalisation. The film contests the simplistic binary thinking about Muslims, especially evident in Tony Blair's and George W. Bush's policies, but continuing in David Cameron's rhetoric of 'muscular liberalism', which he prefers to the so-called 'passive tolerance of recent years'. This kind of dualistic thinking has produced the notions of 'good Muslim', viewed by the dominant culture as being the authentic voice of Islam, and 'bad Muslim', interpreted as having transgressed religion's fundamental principles. Barry satirises this dominant myth in his line, 'yeah, a good Muslim keeps his mouth shut: yeah'. It is dangerous to accept the good Muslim/bad Muslim divide, even when the person doing this empha-sises the 'good' side of pluralism and tolerance within Islam. Unless these stereotypes are dismantled altogether, they can easily be reversed, whereby the 'bad Muslim' is taken to be the 'real' voice of Islam and the 'good Mus-lim' becomes somehow inauthentic. The convert character Barry is the main proponent of this view in Four Lions, and his circular reasoning leads him to punch himself in the face to demonstrate how 'moderate' Muslims will be radicalised if the jihadis bomb an ordinary mosque rather than tar-geting so-called '*kuffar*' or 'slag' utilities.

If Barry is taken to be representative of Muslim converts in Britain as a group, then to some extent Morris's demonisation of him is questionable. Barry is sexually deviant, as he makes Hassan 'put a bean up the end of his nob' and Waj urinate in his own mouth in bizarre initiation rituals. There is also the suggestion of mental disorder, which is especially apparent in the paranoia that leads him to believe a milk float is being driven by undercover intelligence agents and a mother with a pram is an MI5 operative. However, his delusions are not strong enough to consider him 'psychotic' (as some critics have argued), as he is in no mental distress; psychosis is often used as a lazy and inaccurate shorthand for 'evil', when it is actually a symptom of severe psychiatric illness. Morris rightly suggests that converts often find they cannot escape their ethnic origin, despite the fact that no credence is supposed to be given to race in Islam. The other jihadis taunt Barry about his lack of knowledge of Urdu, and for the fact that, whereas Omar has an uncle in Pakistan who can help the group make contact with Afghan training camps, Barry's uncle lives in the innocuous town of Maidstone in Kent. Yet when Waj and Omar go to Afghanistan, they experience a similar disloca-tion when they find themselves unable to communicate with the 'Afghan Arabs' at the training camp and are reduced to the stereotypes of 'James Fuck Bond' and 'fucking Mr Beanz'. Barry's alias is 'Azzam al Britani', the first name is an Arabic word meaning 'determined, leonine', which seems appropriate for this stubborn, hardline 'lion', and 'al Britani' ('the Briton') is a common suffix for British-born or -raised jihadis, such as Dhiren Bharot and Abu Abdullah al-Britani. Although there is some evidence to suggest that converts make more unhinged jihadis (Richard Reid is a good example), it should be noted that the vast majority of converts (or 'reverts' as they are sometimes unattractively labelled) give their allegiance to Islam out of spiritual longing, love for a Muslim partner, or both.

Notwithstanding the plethora of so-called bad Muslims in *Four Lions*, it is not so easy to identify a 'good' one. Omar's brother Ahmed is religious, and it would have been an easy option to make him a sympathetic 'moderate' Muslim, but Morris doesn't take it, making him boringly obsessed with fatwas, comically playing football under umbrellas with other brothers, misogynistic, and with an annoyingly pious face (Omar criticises him for doing the 'floaty face of the wise bird hovering on a million different quotes about to do a massive wisdom shit on my head'). Yet there is real sympathy for Ahmed at the end when the authorities mistakenly think he's involved in his brother's plot, and he is clearly about to face torture by Egyptians' in RAF Mildenhall, which hints at logged records that CIA flights passed through this airbase as part of extraordinary rendition. Here *Four Lions* hints at the securitisation policies of the Blair-Brown years and initiatives like the CONTEST agenda, with its Pursue, Prevent, Protect, and Prepare strands. One of the main problems in the film is that the security forces (derogatively characterised by Omar as 'Dibble') get it so spectacularly wrong, bickering about whether wookies and honey monsters may be categorised as bears, shooting the wrong man at the Marathon, and inadvertently insulting Waj as an 'arse man' when trying to negotiate with him. Along with the post-9/11 foreign policy, the context of such wrongful shootings, heavy-handed surveillance initiatives, detention without trial, ethnic profiling, and the brutal treatment in detention of Muslim suspects have substantially contributed to radicalisation. In interview, Morris remarked, 'tricky as anti-terrorist legislation is, it's shot through with mistakes. Quite what the acceptable level of incompetence is, I don't know'. British actor, Riz Ahmed, who plays Omar, had a taste of this in 2006 when he and two fellow actors were held at Luton Airport under the Terrorism Act during the making of a previous picture (ironically, this was Michael Winterbottom's film about the Tipton Three, *The Road to Guantanamo*).

But what is 'radicalisation'? It is best characterised, I would argue, as a process in which an individual becomes increasingly convinced that society can only be improved by dramatic and swingeing change (not unlike Britain's current coalition government). The terms radicalism and radicalisation are not inherently negative, and many different forms of radicalisation exist, very few of which are violent. Furthermore, radicalisation is not a uniquely Muslim problem, an assumption that was conspicuous in many journalists' initial Islamophobic assumptions about the Norway shootings of 2011, which were in fact perpetrated by the Norwegian right-wing extremist Anders Behring Breivik.

Attempts to explain radicalisation tend to rest on three approaches: a sociological methodology, which searches for a common social background among terrorists; the psychological attempt to look for a radical 'type'; and a communitarian approach looking at group dynamics and social situation. This first social explanation was discredited as it emerged that the stereotype of young, brainwashed men from deeply deprived backgrounds in the poorest parts of the third world did not tally with the higher than average levels of educational attainment, aspirational, cosmopolitan, and well-travelled backgrounds of many members of the global Salafi jihad. Few terrorists, apart from those from the distinctive Indonesian network, had attended *madrasas* or had unusually religious upbringings, and the majority of jihadis are married, often with children, rather than being the lone wolves identified in social explanations.

The psychological approach also has problems, for example because there is no evidence to suggest that jihadi terrorists have any higher instances of mental illness than the wider population. Fanaticism isn't a mental disorder, but a deeply held belief, and even suicide bombing, the facet of terrorism with the clearest link to mental illness, is part of this belief, and shares more with the Japanese practices of *kamikaze* or *seppuku* than with self-harm born out of mental distress. Nor is there evidence to suggest that a higher than average proportion of jihadis had experienced childhood trauma that, according to a Freudian psychoanalytical approach, may have sent them down the route of violence. Writers such as Martin Amis (who is aptly described by Morris in a *Guardian* Comment is Free article as 'the new Abu Hamza' because of his dogmatic hatred and absurdity), have tried to link jihadis with personality disorders such as pathological narcissism, which allegedly allow their sufferers to kill because the world is divided into 'me' and 'not-me' (in Amis's story 'The Last Days of Muhammad Atta', the epony-mous 9/11 ringleader believes himself to be 'not like the others'). This psychological trend is also typified in the commercial if not artistic success of Ed Husain's *The Islamist* (comprehensively subtitled 'Why I joined radical Islam in Britain, what I saw inside and why I left'), which has contributed to the development of a mini-subgenre which documents the (usually male) author's flirtation with extremist Islam, often while at university, and his growing disillusionment and eventual departure from the movement.

One example of this subgenre is *Human Being to Human Bomb* in which British Bangladeshi Russell Razzaque describes his brush with Hizb-ut-Tahrir during study at the University of London. Like Husain, Razzaque is British by birth with parents from Bangladesh, but, unlike Husain, he never became seriously involved with this Islamist group. He is now a consultant psychiatrist in East London for several mental health and addiction treat-ment centres. His film, *Halal Harry* (2006), is, alongside *Four Lions*, one of the more nuanced attempts to represent British Muslims in film and, to my knowledge, the only such by a director who is himself of Muslim heritage. What distinguishes *Halal Harry* from the other films I mentioned is that while Razzaque uses the overworked trope of a Muslim falling in love with a non-Muslim, he positions the male, non-Muslim protagonist converting to Islam in a fairly smooth and happy process, rather than a difficult choice being posed to a Muslim character about sacred and secular lifestyles.

In his less convincing, and sensationally-titled book, which is variously subtitled '*The Conveyor Belt of Terror*' and '*Inside the Mind of a Terrorist*', Raz-zaque outlines a psychiatric multiple choice test he has pioneered in order to profile people who are likely to be ripe for radicalisation, and thus pre-vent or reverse the process. If one scores highly on having an obsessive personality, authoritarian tendencies (which Razzaque suggest are likely to have come from a strict and distant father), and a scientific bent of mind (likely careers include medicine, engineering, and IT), then *Human Being to Human Bomb* claims that this means one would be susceptible to radical arguments. However, the problem for Razzaque is that while some radicals fit this profile, as Mohamed Atta does to a certain extent, others, including at least two of the 7/7 bombers, emphatically do not.

Morris himself rejects Ed Husain's and Russell Razzaque's pathologisation of jihadis as sons of absent fathers, sexually frustrated, jealous of the West, and so on. In his research, he saw many different types of jihadi. To take only the 7/7 bombers, Mohammad Sidique Khan was a husband, father, and classroom assistant, previously very Westernised and known as 'Sid'. Shehzad Tanweer was a sports science graduate from my own institution, Leeds Metropolitan University, who hadn't yet established a career; he loved cricket, and his parents ran a fish-and-chip shop. Jamaican-born Germaine Lindsay was unemployed, and the youngest, Hasib Mir Hussain, was still a student. They were not 'technical' people, and their parents on the whole seem loving and unexceptional.

The desire to find a way of identifying potential terrorists is understandable because it's hard to believe that 'normal' people would kill civilians, but Morris suggests that the search for a radicalisation type or push factor 'overcomplicates it'. Instead, he depicts his protagonists from all walks of life: Omar, the family man and leader; Waj, the simple(ton) lover of gadgets, women, and his friends; the nihilistic convert, Barry; the middle-class student, Hassan; and Fessel, who is the only one of the five with any technical aptitude. Morris has talked about the jihadis' activity as representing a kind of male homosocial bonding, with the repeated dream of martyrdom as being like jumping the queue at Alton Towers to enter the heavenly world of 'rubber dinghy rapids'. Yet perhaps a weakness of the film is that it stops short of explaining why certain characters are drawn more than others to the intense friendships and banal bickering of such cells. Apart from Fessel, whose father is implied to have mental health problems (he eats newspaper and moths and has started 'seeing creatures that's not there'), they seem well integrated in mainstream society, especially Omar, who is married to a beautiful nurse, Sofia, with whom he has a lively, intelligent child; a nice house; and a wide circle of friends and family. The 7/7 bombers were integrated to varying degrees too, but the South Leeds areas where three out of four of them lived are more run-down than the Sheffield suburb depicted in the film, and several of them attended the Iqra bookshop and Hamara youth centre in the area, where it is likely their radicalism was exacerbated in a two-directional process.

The film's title *Four Lions* derives from a scene after Fessel's accidental suicide when the four remaining conspirators comfort themselves by describing themselves as 'four lions', brave warriors in the service of their understanding of jihad. Lions have potent significance in the Indian subcontinent, where names such as 'Singh' and 'Sher' denote this majestic feline. In England, of course, the royal coat of arms features three lions, which are also displayed on the pound coin and the Football Association shirt, suggesting the warriors' unwitting immersion in consumerism and thuggery. In *Them: Adventures with Extremists*, journalist Jon Ronson describes Al Muhajiroun leader Omar Bakri Mohammed as an incongruous yet ardent fan of the Disney classic, *The Lion King*, who listens to 'Hakuna Matata' in order to relax. 'They call me the Lion', he tells Ronson, 'the great fighter'. Like the characters in the film, in Ronson's rendition, Omar Bakri Mohammed mixes frightening homophobia, misogyny, and anti-Semitism with comic ineptitude (his Scottish convert colleague plans to release 'a swarm of mice' into the United Nations headquarters). It is surely no coincidence that Morris has his character, also called Omar, tell the comforting story of *The Lion King* to his young son after returning in disgrace from a jihadi training camp in Afghanistan, where he had inadvertently fired an anti-aircraft missile at the terrorists' emir. In the sanitised bed-time version of this debacle, Omar refigures himself as the naïve but loveable Simba; positions an American warplane as the villain, Scar; and casts the terrorists' emir (who, it transpires, is Osama bin Laden) as wise Mufasa, tragically killed by his own son. Like Ronson's reporting of Omar Bakri Mohammed, the film's extremist characters are foolish lions, reminiscent of the Sanskrit animal fables, the *Panchatantra*, and more cartoon-like than leonine. Rather than lions, in the Marathon scenes at the end of the film, the characters are dressed in absurd fancy dress. Omar is a honey monster, a costume which expresses his sweetness and yet monstrosity; Waj is a man riding an ostrich (he buries his head in the sand); Barry dresses as a teenage mutant ninja turtle (he is the most violent of the four, and with distorted, juvenile attitudes); and Hassan is an inverted clown (signaling his joker role that nonetheless leads to violence).

Four Lions provides largely nuanced accounts of the apparent 'clash' between sacred and secular worldviews, and examines secular practices with as satirical an eye as it does religious worldviews, showing that the two are not easily separable. Morris has described it as a 'good-hearted film', and certainly the reception from Muslim communities in Britain has been very warm. However, there is also an undeniable pessimism which Morris acknowledges: 'If you make a film about this [terrorism] you have to have consequences.' Both Omar and Waj have second thoughts about the ethics of what they're doing and think about abandoning their mission, but go through with it.

Finally, it is rather problematic that the most positive character in the film is Omar's (admittedly naïve) non-Muslim security guard colleague, Matt. He has the last word in the film and his voiceover proclaims disbelief that Omar could have been involved in the plot: 'When we talk about the so-called terrorist attack on the London Marathon, we should remember one thing, most loud bangs are not bombs, they're scooters backfiring.' After recent terrorist acts, the incredulous, loyal friends have usually come from the Muslim community, indicating both the ghettoisation of Muslims and the fact that most members of the community have no idea about this violence; however, none of these voices are heard in *Four Lions*. While I applaud Morris's decision to destabilise good Muslim/bad Muslim binaries, it is a little disappointing that the nearest thing the film has to a 'good' character comes from the white, non-Muslim community.

MUSLIM ANTI-SEMITISM

Muhammad Idrees Ahmad

Five thousand Jews left Afghanistan in 1948 to settle in the newly-created State of Israel. In 1979, as Soviet tanks rolled down the Salang Pass, most of the remaining Jews also emigrated, some to India, some to Central Asia. By the time Afghanistan was reinvaded in 2001, only two Jews remained. In January 2005, when Ishaq Levin, the caretaker of the Kabul synagogue died, it left Zebolon Simintov as Afghanistan's sole surviving Jew. Simontov's former wife immigrated to Israel with his two daughters a long time ago. But this seemed to have done little to diminish his spirits In January 2012, when Channel 4 News's Alex Thomson caught up with Simontov, at fifty-one, he was rambunctious as ever. In a brief interview, the irrepressible Simontov denounced Karzai, NATO, the Afghan warlords and, inevitably, the Taliban. It is astonishing that this outspoken man survived the funda-mentalist Taliban regime.

The Arabs and the Holocaust: The Arab-Israeli War of Narratives by Gilbert Achcar, London: Saqi, 2009.

It was tough for him under the Taliban, said Simontov, but then it was tough for everyone. However, that did not prevent him from dealing with them in his characteristic irreverent style. When some Taliban would ask him to convert to Islam, he would instead offer them the choice of conversion to Judaism. 'They just laughed and left it alone,' he said. But the prospect of the Taliban's return does not please him. He fears the vacuum that a NATO withdrawal would leave in its wake that might, once again, turn the region into a lethal playground for proxy grievances. For the sole survivor of a community that had resided in Afghanistan since the eighth century, perhaps the example of Iraq is all too vivid.

Jews had resided in Iraq far longer, since the time of the Babylonian captivity in 538 BC. But by 2007, only eight remained. Alone and desperate, they were without a community to protect them from the bloody and indiscriminate civil war that engulfed Iraq. As in Afghanistan, the once large and flourishing community had dwindled after the creation of Israel. More deeply rooted and less willing to leave than Jews in other places, it took sabotage and intimidation by Zionist agent provocateurs to finally spirit the Iraqi Jews out (A similar campaign also succeeded in precipitating the flight of Egyptian Jews to Israel). As hostilities between Israel and the Arabs grew, Iraq under the Baath regime became less and less hospitable to those who remained. In the end, it was the two American-led wars that achieved what even the Mongol invasion, and everything in-between, had failed to do. Thus collapsed one of the world's oldest Jewish communities which, among other things, was responsible for producing the Talmud, Judaism's second-holiest book.

The treatment of Jews who have remained in the Muslim world is no better or worse than that of any other minority. Since the founding of Israel, their numbers have dwindled. Except for countries like Iran, where a substantial Jewish population still thrives, few in the Muslim world ever encounter a Jew. Most know Jews only through scripture or news reporting on the Israeli-Palestinian conflict. All Jews as a result have been cast unwittingly as adversaries by a conflict with which most of them have no connection, which many even oppose.

There is little doubt that anti-Semitism exists in the Muslim world today and that Holocaust denial is not uncommon. This is deplorable. But as the Lebanese-French scholar Gilbert Achcar notes in *The Arabs and the Holocaust,* the anti-Semitism of the Muslim world is an epiphenomenon of a political conflict; it does not have social roots. Achcar cites Yehoshafat Harkabi, the leading Israeli scholar and former head of the military intelligence and no friend of the Arabs, as saying 'it is functional and political, not social'. For most Muslims, anti-Semitism is a function of ignorance and unfamiliarity; it is also an abstract means of participation in a conflict where Jews have been cast as the oppressor by virtue of a state which adorns its instruments of war with Jewish religious symbols. In this respect it is quite different from European anti-Semitism; it does not involve any actual contact with a Jew. It is also different in so far as it comes from a position of weakness, whereas European anti-Semitism was born of strength and directed against a vulnerable minority. It is comparable less to the racism of the Ku Klux Klan than to the reaction of the Black Panthers. Both kinds of hatred were totalising, but only the former existed without a stimulus. Harkabi again: 'Arab anti-Semitism is not the cause of the conflict but one of its results; it is not the reason for the hostile Arab attitude toward Israel and the Jews, but a means of deepening, justifying and institutionalising that hostility. Its rise is connected with the tension created as a result of Zionist activity, and especially of the traumatic experience of defeat…Anti-Semitism is a weapon in this struggle.'

This might explain the attitudes of the majority, but it does not excuse the minority of voices who have shamelessly borrowed from the tired tropes of European anti-Semitism. The notorious anti-Semitic forgery, *The Protocols of the Elders of Zion*, was first translated into Arabic by a Maronite priest named Antun Yammin in 1925, and has remained in circulation ever since. Many of its ideas have been assimilated into the writings and pronouncements of some leaders, priests, and intellectuals. This is sometimes combined with more virulent forms of hatred of Jews, as a tit-for-tat response against Zionists who are seen as being at war with Muslims. As Zionists have sought political advantage by trying to erase the distinction between Zionist and Jew, some Arab-Muslim reactionaries have obliged by being equally impervious of those differences.

Achcar gives an example from an article published in the Saudi daily *Al-Bilad*. The writer, Hilmi Abu-Ziyad, responded to the capture of Adolp Eichmann in 1960 by congratulating the Nazi henchman for the killing of millions of Jews. Though a marginal position, Abu-Ziyad's is precisely the type of reactionary provocation that has produced a whole genre of books dedicated to exposing the anti-Semitism that is supposedly part of the Arab-Muslim social fabric. That the Eichmann trial itself had a propagandistic purpose is well attested to in Hannah Arendt's stellar reporting for the *New Yorker*. But if David Ben Gurion had aimed to use the Holocaust as a justification for the creation of the Jewish state, then his success has been compounded by the kind of reaction which made the Jewish genocide itself the focus of its ire.

Arendt was not the only person to warn about the political uses of the Holocaust. The eminent Israeli diplomat Abba Eban was himself known to quip, 'There is no business like Shoah business'. Scholars and intellectuals such as Raul Hilberg, Peter Novick, Avraham Burg, Norman Finkelstein and Tom Segev have all documented and deplored this abuse of the memory of Holocaust victims. But this misuse of the Holocaust as a political tool does not negate the nature and scale of the genocide. Muslims and Arabs are right to complain that the Palestinians are paying a price for crimes committed by others. But anticipating this argument, the Israelis have tried to paint Arabs themselves as complicit in Nazi crimes. They have made much of the Grand Mufti of Jerusalem Amin al-Husseini's collaboration with the Nazis while ignoring the well-known working relationship between the Nazis and some Zionists. Achcar sees no reason to cover up for the Mufti's execrable moral and political choices — he rejects the hackneyed 'the enemy of my enemy is a friend' argument — but nevertheless wants to keep things in proportion. He notes that while the Mufti's reprehensible misdeeds are fodder for numberless Zionist propaganda tracts, no attention is paid to the hundreds of thousands of Arabs, including many Palestinians, who fought and sacrificed for the Allies.

But since the Holocaust is bandied about as a justification for the creation of Israel — and the dispossession of the Palestinians — some Arabs have assumed that the legitimacy of this enterprise could be undermined by questioning the Holocaust itself. Instead, writes Achcar, such partisans merely display an inhumanity which undermines their own cause, painting opposition to Zionist colonisation as being based on anti-Semitism rather than in sympathy for its victims. Achcar notes that these attitudes, which have hardened as the conflict between Israel and the Arabs has escalated, sit in striking contrast with the Arab reactions contemporaneous with the Nazi genocide. He quotes many Arabs denouncing the genocide and professing sympathy for its victims, even as they affirmed the Palestinians inalienable political and national rights. Some even expressed a willingness to accept more Jewish refugees so long as the rest of the world was willing to accept their share.

All of this, however, has been erased from memory in no small part due to the Arabs' own willingness to forfeit this admirable legacy. As Arabs and Muslims have abandoned this tradition in favour of clumsy flirtations with anti-Semitism, they have made it easier for their detractors to paint them as later-day reincarnations of the Nazis. Trying to fight one alien import, Zionism, with another, anti-Semitism, was never likely to succeed. They seem to have overlooked the fact that the former always relied on the latter for its survival.

In his exhaustive study, Achcar is unsparing in his criticism of Arab anti-Semitism and attempts by some to deny or minimise the Holocaust. But unlike some Arab intellectuals who play exclusively to the Western gallery, his interest is primarily intellectual. His distribution of blame is not geared for personal or political advantage. Achcar reports borrowings from *The Protocols* by Rashid Rida, the celebrated reformer of Egypt, the Grand Mufti's collaboration with Nazis, and the preponderance of anti-Semitic language in the earlier literature of Hamas and Hezbollah. But he does not flinch from pointing out that the nature and scale of these associations are exaggerated and the context elided. His book offers a thorough and scholarly refutation of Zionist writers who have thrived on the subject. His greatest contribution is in restoring proportion and fairness to a debate which is generally charac-terised by hyperbole, vituperation, distortion and partisan apologia. In the preface, Achcar claims that his aim was to produce a work of objectivity and critical distance. He succeeds.

But Achcar's otherwise systematic, thorough and fair-minded work fails to give any reason other than the Israeli-Palestinian conflict for explaining why anti-Semitic views prevail in places which have little investment in the con-flict. Why did even an astute politician like Gamal Adbul Nasser find it neces-sary to refer to *The Protocol*? Might it be because discussions of Jewish power are so suppressed that people simply don't know how to talk about it and inevitably resort to myth? There is a large disparity between Jewish political influence in the most powerful Western states and the amount of attention it gets in mainstream discourse. Consider the American electoral process: while it is commonplace to hear about the excessive influence of corpora-tions over politicians, or the deleterious effect of the Citizens United legisla-tion which allows corporations to donate unlimited amounts of money while enjoying all the protections of individual citizens, the fact is rarely men-tioned that the largest donations that both political parties, Democrat and Republican, receive come from Jewish donors, Sheldon Adelson and Haim Saban respectively. Both donors are on record saying that the issue they are interested in most is Israel and both have supported intransigent policies in the Middle East. Yet few people even know their names. Why this silence? Is it the fear of being labelled an anti-Semite? Is it dogma, which recognises no agents, only structures and processes?

Every time the US president is brow-beaten by an Israeli prime minister or Israel's American allies, political discipline mandates that the mainstream intellectuals should not notice; but ordinary people do. However, unlike the intellectuals, they are not equipped with the analytical tools necessary to assess this skewed balance of power. It is not entirely surprising then that some of them end up indulging in anti-Semitic conspiracy theories ascribing mythical powers to Jews, who are treated as an undifferentiated and coherent social bloc. The only way to disabuse them of these notions would be to present them with an analytically sound, sociological explanation which recognises both the sources and limits of Jewish power and accepts the diversity of their class, cultural, and political affiliations. Some American intellectuals, such as John Mearsheimer, Stephen Walt, and Tony Judt, have done this with insight and rigour. But Achcar makes a single, somewhat disparaging, reference to the former two and does not discuss the Israel lobby at all. This is unfortunate since a scholar of Achcar's calibre could have elevated the debate. This quibble notwithstanding, Achcar has made an invaluable contribution, and Muslims would do well to make a gift of his book to anyone who makes another reference to *The Protocols*.

ET CETERA

THE CATALYST FOR KNOWLEDGEABLE GENERATION

SELANGOR FOUNDATION

For further details, kindly contact us at :

Corporate Affairs Unit
Menara Yayasan Selangor, No 18A, Jalan Persiaran Barat
46000 Petaling Jaya,
Selangor Darul Ehsan,
Malaysia.
Tel : +603 - 7955 1212
Fax : +603 - 7954 1790
Email : Info@yayasanselangor.org.my
www.yayasanselangor.org.my

ASSESSMENT

IRSHAD MANJI

Peter Morey

Irshad Manji is a hard woman to ignore. Rising to global prominence at a time when all aspects of international Islam were called into question in the wake of the 9/11 attacks, Manji personifies that breed of commentator looked to particularly by a non-Muslim media keen for an authoritative 'inside perspective', whose number also includes Ayaan Hirsi Ali, Wafa Sultan and Ed Husain among others. The tendency to look for Muslim spokespeople who can articulate an already approved position has become a key weapon in the battle to discredit radical Islamist positions. If articulate and reputable Muslims can be shown to have mulled over the weighty issues facing their faith and come to the conclusion that Western versions of modernity and progress must be championed against backwardness and insularity, then this is taken as a way of clinching the argument. Because of this — and quite aside from a general fascination with matters of Muslim motivation prompted by War on Terror framing — the press, media and publishers are always on the look out for fresh Muslim voices prepared to 'tell it like it is'. Indeed, entire careers and considerable amounts of money can be made on the basis of performing what could almost be described as an important public service. These Muslim spokespeople are essentially in the business of framing themselves (as enlightened, frank and fearless) at the same time as they frame many other Muslims as timid or complicit. Whether the persona promoted is one of clear-sighted rebel who refuses to be cowed by orthodoxy, or prodigal sojourner who once counted himself among the enemy, 'true stories' of Muslims who dare to speak out are dependable money-spinners and ratings winners. Closer examination of Manji's role as one such spokesperson can reveal more about how this framing, sometimes tinged with self-mythologising, takes place.

It is important at the outset to acknowledge that Irshad Manji is a very brave woman. Her call for a reformation within Islam has seen her become the target of insults, vilification and even death threats. Some critics argue with her interpretation of the Qur'an and Islamic history; others are angered at her depiction of Muslims as the authors of their own misfortune; still others are outraged that a small, plucky Canadian lesbian should have the temerity to stand against clerical diktats and established practices. Quoting her favourite sura — 'God does not change the condition of a people until they change what is in themselves' — Manji regularly appears on mainstream news and discussion programmes to push for a rejuvenation of ijtihad, the Islamic tradition of critical questioning she claims has been subdued by a numbing, and dumbing, orthodoxy. Her book *The Trouble with Islam Today* was published in 2003 and instantly catapulted Manji into the front rank of those so-called experts on Islam courted and showcased by channels such as CNN, CBS, Fox News, PBS and the BBC. I want to consider here in some detail the content of this book, along with an accompanying documentary, *Faith without Fear: Irshad Manji's Quest*, produced by 90th Parallel and the National Film Board of Canada, and Broadcast in the United States on the PBS channels as part of their 'America at a Crossroads' series in 2007.

The Trouble with Islam Today is a partly autobiographical tract, charting in its first chapter Manji's journey to adulthood and her difficulty reconciling the tenets of Islam as taught at her madrassa in Richmond, Vancouver — emphasising obedience and passivity — with her questioning spirit and the opportunities presented by the West more generally: 'Call it my personal clash of civilisations' (page 11). This feeling of being at odds with the official representatives of her religion led her to develop a personalised, informal type of faith and worship, eschewing conventional ritual and observances. The same spirit prompted her to carry out her own research into the history of Islam, this time challenging received versions about a once-proud and powerful civilisation beaten down by Christian perfidy. Instead, Manji presents the reader with what she takes to be an overlooked story in which a golden age of Muslim intellectual, cultural and artistic freedom — running from around the eighth to the thirteenth centuries CE and reaching its apotheosis in Moorish Andalusia — marked by mainly tolerant interaction with other faiths (most notably Judaism), was lost not to warlike Crusaders but to the purveyors of an intolerant, purist brand of Islam who gained a stranglehold on the faith and outlawed critical questioning. The inheritors of this narrow, punitive strand, who include the Muslim Brotherhood of the mid-twentieth century and, in our own day, Al Qaeda, have succeeded in imposing a cowed quietism on the Muslim world, leaving themselves a free hand to sow the seeds of fundamentalism and violence. Even more controversially, according to Manji, Muslims need the West to intervene to enforce values they themselves ought to have defended more resolutely in their own lands.

Manji's answer to the current Muslim malaise is 'Operation Ijtihad', a return to that tradition of individual critical questioning smothered by the blanket of what she calls 'Foundamentalism': a brand of 'desert Islam', based on tribal collectivism, a slavish mentality and the oppression of women, which aims to preserve the perceived values and practices of Islam's seventh-century founding moment. Against the foundamentalists, Manji's Operation Ijtihad works by 'liberalising Islam', in both the social and economic senses of that term. She advocates a three-pronged attack based on 'God-conscious, female-fuelled capitalism'   the empowerment of long-oppressed Muslim women as businesspeople through small start-up loans; a necessary proliferation of independent television channels in the Muslim world allowing access to divergent views and debates; and an interfaith hajj to open up the holy places of Islam to followers of the other Abrahamic faiths too, in the way that the holy sites of both Christianity and Judaism are open for others to visit. She testifies to the excitement her suggestions have caused, especially among women and young Muslims looking for another way to engage with the world without giving up their religious identity.

Manji's excoriating indictment of a faith she sees as having become mired in injustice and backwardness scores some palpable hits. She advocates 'literacy', rather than 'literalism', 'interpretation' instead of 'imitation' in understandings of the Qur'an, emphasising the ambivalent and sometimes openly contradictory messages contained in different suras (32, 36). For her, the Qur'an is a conflicted, ambiguous (and, crucially, imperfect) text, and believers ought to be allowed to engage critically with it instead of abdicating responsibility to a self-perpetuating clerisy. Elsewhere, she points to the hierarchical founders' privilege by which some Arabs usurp the position of 'real Muslims' and lord it over 'converts' from other parts of the world: points out how Wahhabism and a Saudi national consciousness grew up together; and takes pot-shots at the kind of wet-liberal relativism which causes some non-Muslims to stifle or compromise their criticism of objectionable Muslim practices — as in the facile comparisons sometimes drawn between enforced acts of gender oppression done in the name of religion and the peer pressure culture of female fashion in the West.

On the face of it, then, Manji appears a breath of fresh air in the stale and predictable discussion of relations between what are often tacitly assumed to be two separate entities, Islam and the West. In an era when the loudest voices frequently seem engaged in acts of cultural re-entrenchment, Manji dares to be different. Her overall position, including the decision to remain a Muslim in spite of the shortcomings she identifies, is summed up well when she says on page 210, 'Religion has compelled me to bow to no one but the God dwelling restlessly in my conscience, a precious skill to develop in an era of boundless spin. Better, religion has taught me not to confuse authoritarianism with authority.'

One would expect the same fiery, uncompromising spirit to be on display in the documentary, *Faith without Fear*, narrated by Manji and written with the help of her director, Ian McLeod. To be sure, the searchlight is again turned on reprehensible Muslim activities across the globe and the same argument for ijtihad advanced. However, it turns out that the filmic grammar of *Faith without Fear* is composed of stereotypical imagery and associations. Its anthropological animus is made clear by the frequent cuts between Irshad Manji enjoying her Western freedoms, chatting with 'Mom' and making a friendly meal for an adversary from within the Canadian Muslim community, and parts of the world where a strict Islamic code is enforced and where people are treated (and, by implication, behave) like mindless robots. In its editorial juxtapositions and use of stock imagery, the film shares an ideological consistency with the most simplistic, undifferentiated views of Muslims which, in fact, runs throughout Manji's work. The visual correlatives found for her hypercritical narrative include a scene in a Yemeni classroom where scores of women sit, clad from top to toe in full abayas. Their unity through uniformity is contrasted with the individualism embodied in the only colourfully dressed woman in the room, our author and guide on this surreal trip. Later she herself wanders awkwardly through the streets in an abaya, the better to prove its stifling qualities. At another point, she encounters Osama Bin Laden's former driver who cheerfully admits he would be proud to see his young son die a martyr's death for the cause: a shocking confession which we are invited to judge against the enduring and affectionate relationship Irshad shares with 'Mom'. This shuttling to and fro between the West where, as she puts it, 'we have all these precious freedoms', and an undifferentiated 'Muslimland' comprising interchangeable shots of baying mobs chanting for the death of Salman Rushdie or the blood of injudicious Danish newspaper editors, recalls those tactics Edward Said, writing in *Covering Islam*, sees in Steve Emerson's rabble-rousing 1995 film *Jihad in America*: 'In scene after scene — all of them isolated from any real context — we are regaled with fulminating, bearded imams, raging against the West and Jews most especially, threatening genocide and unending warfare.' And if Western freedom is too nebulous a concept for the viewer to get any purchase on it can easily be reduced to totemic soundbites such as sexual licence or free speech. Holland, it would seem, is no longer defined by the windmills and tulips of yore, but by those guarantors of a good time, 'pot and prostitution', both readily available on Amsterdam's streets. That a firebrand film director and descendant of Vincent van Gogh came one day to be lying dead on one such street with a letter detailing his offences against Islam skewered to his chest can only be an indictment of a misguided multicultural complacency through which European societies have allowed intolerant Islam to gain a toehold. Even 'at home' in Canada, Muslims are not without ingrained secrecy and paranoia. On a visit to her mother's local mosque, Irshad and 'Mom' are confronted by three burly men who insist they stop filming. 'Why?' we are being invited to ask, 'What have you got to hide in there?'

Part of the effectiveness of the argument comes from the style, which is accessible and arresting. However, it is this very mode of address – with its folksy references to 'Mom' and implicit assumptions about the documentary viewer's values — which hides the most glaring quality in her account of the present state of Islam: that is, the complete absence of a sense of context. In truth, the arguments of both book and film say next to nothing about the global geopolitical causes that might lead to Muslim feelings of injustice and hostility that, in turn, could fuel fundamentalist sympathies. Muslims in the East are dupes and dullards, deprived of the means to improve their lot by cruel overlords who hoard the material and cultural wealth of their countries, whereas Muslims in the West are insufficiently appreciative of the freedoms they enjoy. (A grasp of the relative poverty, ghettoisation and disenfranchisement suffered by many Muslim communities, especially in Europe, is conspicuous by its absence, as if such factors could not be significant at all.) When it comes to the documentary — otherwise chock full of the carnage caused by Muslim violence around the globe — Manji's support for the 2003 Iraq War perhaps explains the absence of images of Muslims killed in this, and the Afghan conflicts. Such pictures might dilute the impact of the rallying cry to Muslims to reform by gesturing toward legitimate grievances. In the same way, while her take on Qur'anic indeterminacy and Muslim history is distinctive and attractive, what is missing from her individualistic reading is any notion of the kinds of strategic power plays and special interests that have bedevilled relations between developed and developing nations since the era of colonialism. These may or may not press on the daily lives of believers in the Ummah, but how they can still be used to orchestrate violent responses to deeply felt historical injustices should not be underestimated.

Writing from her home in Canada, Manji claims she wants to reach the entire Ummah — or at least those open to her message — and force a rethink about the shape and direction of contemporary Islam. Indeed, she begins her book, and ends her documentary, with an invocation to 'My Fellow Muslims'. In fact, her addressees will for the most part probably be found much closer to 'home': those elements in Western societies suspicious of too much accommodation with an Other whose integration is constantly posed as a problem. The relentless focus on Islamic wrongs, while admirably fearless, runs the risk of confirming prejudices, while her refusal to explore the socio-economic dimensions of her own position as a comparatively prosperous and privileged Muslim in the West, means that her ability to communicate with less materially advantaged Muslims elsewhere is likely to be limited, the distance between them being one her breezy reformist optimism may be unable to span.

This willed blindness to certain features in the current international landscape, and the determination to consider only Muslim brutality and guilt, make Manji easy prey for critics. However, they are at the same time central, not simply to her argument but to her worldview and self-projection. She consciously stands outside and above the specificities that characterise Islamic cultures in their various forms: Shia or Sunni, South East Asian or North African, for example. Instead, it serves Manji's purpose to by-pass such divisions and take on the general mantle of 'Muslim dissident', since her appeal is supposedly to all Muslims equally. This is a problematic stance, not least because it tends to replicate the same type of undifferentiated portrait of Muslims beloved of simple-minded government strategists. Indeed, Manji arguably confirms convenient neoconservative framing of Muslims in a number of ways that can be summarised as follows. First, she homogenises. All Muslims (singular and undifferentiated) are inevitably tainted either through their actions or in their silent complicity with a dogmatic, joyless 'mainstream Islam' (likewise singular and undifferentiated). Schismatic and doctrinal differences become comparatively irrelevant in this account, as does the cultural and political soil in which they grew. Similarly, history has been distorted and misused by Muslims themselves. Her own attractive, broad-brush version, purged of Muslim special pleading, is the right one, but has conveniently been buried by dogmatic power-hungry factions. Yet, at the same time, too obsessive a fixation with the past and its perceived injustices (mostly self-inflicted) is what holds Muslims back. This then taints their view of more forward-looking nations, such as Israel and the United States, whom they secretly admire even while condemning them. (Note the slippage here from the idea of modern day Muslims as citizens of the world to a more conventional — one might almost say civilisational — idea that they are 'out there' looking on enviously at the jamboree of Western democracy and freedom.) In *The Trouble with Islam Today*, this leads to the conclusion, on page 115, that Muslims hate 'us' because 'they' really want to be like 'us' — 'It's not jealousy so much as unrequited camaraderie' – thereby echoing the more insular and self-regarding answers to the 'Why do they hate us?' question which preoccupied America in the aftermath of 9/11. It follows naturally from this that the Bush doctrine of pre-emption is right and many Muslims really want more of it, especially in a scenario where the UN and Old Europe are either impotent or untrustworthy — an idea Manji seems to borrow straight from Donald Rumsfeld. At one point she recalls attending a victory party after the toppling of Saddam in 2003 where pre-emptive war by America was warmly endorsed. She muses: 'There will always be a contingent of anti-Americans and isolationists, Muslim and not, who want Washington to butt out. However, many young Muslims I talked to even before this party want Washington to "butt in" — and follow through — on behalf of human rights.' (It would be

unsporting to condemn Manji for being unable to foresee a future in which
the Bush administration itself might find it convenient to temporise about
human rights, and in which Washington might appear to be 'following
through' on behalf of less lofty concerns such as Halliburton's share price or
Blackwater's profit margins.)

In Irshad Manji's world, honest plain speaking can cut through the flum-
mery of Islam's vested interests. But it also brings her close to some conclusions that many in the Muslim world would be hard-pressed to accept. Once
such conclusion is about the State of Israel. Manji acknowledges the centrality of the Middle East conflict to the current tension between Muslims and
'the West'. However, her wholehearted support for the Jewish homeland is
articulated in terms which leave no doubt about where the real culpability
lies. In two chapters of *The Trouble with Islam Today*, 'Gates and Girdles' and
'Who's Betraying Whom?', she unpacks the Israeli-Palestinian standoff in
breathtakingly simplistic terms. On the strength of a 'fact-finding' mission
she has made, we learn that Israel is a utopia of openness and self-scrutiny
in the dark, tyrannical Middle East. The impositions it makes on the Palestinians in the Occupied Territories are regrettable but less harsh than 'emotional' left-wing arguments make out, tending to be temporary and not
unreasonable in a situation where Israelis live every day in fear of attacks.
Israel's progressive transparency contrasts with the unreasoning, blinkered
victim mentality and martyr complex of the Palestinians. The biggest concession to lives disrupted by surveillance and restricted movement is tame
and parenthetical; we are told at one point that roadblocks, checkpoints and
security barriers 'can't be good for the Palestinian economy'. Moreover, a
piece of disquieting sophistry explains away a situation where 'an eighteen-
year-old Ethiopian Jewish soldier can request the identity card of a sixty
year old Arab' when we are told: 'When it comes to citizenship, Israel does
discriminate. In the way that an affirmative action policy discriminates,
Israel gives the edge to a specific minority that has faced historical injustice.
In that sense, the Jewish state is an affirmative action polity. Liberals should
love it' (page 112). So pleased is Manji with this conceit that she repeats it,
not bothering to consider whether a nation set up specifically as a haven for
one religious group might not more honestly be termed 'majoritarian'; in
what sense does 76 per cent of a population require affirmative action? This
is the kind of technique by which Manji repeatedly aims to take the wind

from the sails of radical criticisms of Western policies towards Muslims in the Middle East and elsewhere: turning the language and structures of naive but well-meaning liberalism back on itself to suggest that if its adherents had any real commitment to the freedoms they champion, such gentle souls would immediately see the rightness of the pro-Israeli position.

This is not a minor point for Manji. Nor is it unconnected with another, more sinister turn in the argument where the undoubtedly widespread anti-Semitism among Muslims links them quite directly to Hitler, both through the irate splutterings of modern extremists and the alliances of mad mullahs in the past, some of whom sided with the Axis powers in World War Two. 'Many Muslims hitched their futures to Hitler' we are told on page 102. The breathtaking force of Manji's frankness is, presumably, supposed to prevent us from noting her wholesale dishonouring of the memory of thousands of Muslim troops who fought and died for the Allies, and from requesting some solid figures. It is enough to let the idea of Muslims as Nazi collaborators sink in and do its work. Axis Powers. Axis of Evil. The word association games can begin. As one would expect from a journalist, Manji is, throughout, very sensitive to words and their effect, so such juxtapositions can hardly be accidental. The idea of present day Islam as some kind of totalitarian enemy that can slip easily into the shoes of more familiar historical foes, has, we can now see, been all along implicit in the refusal to differentiate between ideologically quite separate and even warring movements.

It is also there in Manji's preferred designation as a 'Muslim Refusenik' or 'Muslim Dissident', both immediately recalling those victims of another totalitarian horror show, the Soviet Union. As with the other homogenising that has gone on, the term 'dissident' suggests a monolithic, statist entity called 'Islam' from which one is dissenting, and conjures the spirits of other much put-upon but finally vindicated dissenters, like Sakharov, Solzhenitsyn and Bukovsky. The crucial difference, of course, is that these Russian figures did not self-identify as dissidents, the term was applied to them by others. When the likes of Manji or Ayaan Hirsi Ali assume the mantel of dissident, the emotive power of the appellation is designed to underline their moral courage and head off potential objections, it is actually unclear what they are supposed to be dissenting from. In the absence of a singular entity called Islam which can be opposed in this way, the terms 'refusenik' and 'dissident' in this self-designation become meaningless. Her position relies heavily on what Salman Rushdie, in conversation with Manji at New York's 92Y cultural centre in 2009, shrewdly identified as a dubious distinction between the benevolent impulses of the faith, to which her work seeks a return, and something more pervasive, sinister and inherent. Recalling the distinction made by Western socialists in the Cold War era between the Actually Existing Socialism of the Soviet Union and the benevolent face of real socialism which, if actually applied somewhere, would turn out very differently, Rushdie argues from an atheist perspective that the same equivocation is there in the claims of those, like Manji, who believe that a reformed Islam could be a force for good. The pertinent point Rushdie did not go on to make, however, was that Actually Existing Islam — in the sense of a statist, centralised ideology governed by a power elite — can be, and has been, erected in different places at different times through War on Terror rhetoric. Actually Existing Islam, in the sense of a threatening enemy with internationalist aspirations, appeared, for the Bush administration at least, to exist everywhere and nowhere — a moveable feast involving Afghanistan, Iraq, Iran, Syria and so on as policy required — taking little or no account of tensions between Sunni and Shia, military and clerical, or elite and popular interests in these places. When Irshad Manji constructs a 'mainstream Islam' that needs forcible cleansing, these are the simplifications with which she is identifying.

So in the end there is nothing neutral about Manji's preference for ethics over politics, challenging Muslims directly to get past the intellectual gatekeepers to ask their own ethical questions. This is because, without history, those ethics exist in a vacuum. Instead, everything is reduced to questions of individuality, both that of the Muslim inspired by Manji to ask awkward questions of his or her faith, and that of Manji herself. All is personalised through her self-mythologisation as an embattled speaker of truth to Muslim power. Standing outside any denominational allegiance allows Manji to beat back all objections from her fellow Muslims as instances of the kind of small-minded dogmatism to which she is opposed. It also allows for the continuation of the Manji bandwagon on television news programmes and talk shows; if she does not represent one or other of the fractious strains of contemporary Islam she can never, as it were, go out of fashion when one of them disgraces itself in the eyes of the Western media. Reliance on individual refashioning and the absence of a complex understanding of history, including those religious power struggles as Islam ebbed and flowed, place *The Trouble with Islam Today* in the tradition of self-help books, rather than serious political or theological treatises. Yet its directness is, at the same time, the secret of her success. In her writings and in personal appearances, Manji often talks of the threats she regularly receives which range from the absurd to the blood-chilling. Yet she also talks of the support and encouragement she receives, often from anonymous Muslims who have been inspired by her ideas but who have yet to take enough courage to speak out and face the consequences.

Yes, Irshad Manji is a very brave woman: as one who speaks out against tyranny and indoctrination must be. And, moreover, it is important that we, her readers and viewers, are always aware of her bravery — the fact that she refuses to have a bodyguard, for example — since this is absolutely central to her persona. From an ugly necessity, Manji crafts a virtue that adds credibility to her otherwise somewhat outlandish reading of modern world affairs. Of course, a little colour never goes amiss, especially on television. How much better for ratings if the inconvenient truths she tells in the end confirm the rightness of our defensive western mindset?

Contextualising **JIHADI THOUGHT**

Jeevan Deol & Zaheer Kazmi (eds)

9781849041300 / Jan. 2012
£22.00 paperback / 416pp

'If you want to understand the origins, ideological and political worldviews of what is popularly referred to as transnational jihadism, then Jeevan Deol and Zaheer Kazmi's *Contextualising Jihadi Thought* is the book to read. A masterful and accessible global perspective that will be welcomed by academic experts, policymakers and students alike.' — **John L. Esposito, University Professor, Georgetown University and author of *The Future of Islam***

Contextualising Jihadi Thought aims to transcend the dominance of security-studies approaches in the study of militant groups by creating a broader framework for understanding the varied intellectual histories, political engagements and geographies of jihadi ideas. Contributions to the volume span a range of academic disciplines and areas of policy research including history, anthropology, political science, religious studies and area studies. Challenging prevailing policy understandings of a single jihadi ideological narrative, the book's chapters study militant currents of thought and the responses to them in Afghanistan, Yemen, Somalia, India, Pakistan, Egypt, South-East Asia and Europe as well as the global contexts within which transnational jihadism has been developed and propagated.

41 GREAT RUSSELL ST, LONDON, WC1B
WWW.HURSTPUB.CO.UK
WWW.FBOOK.COM/HURSTPUBLISHERS
020 7255 2201

TOP 10 'PLEASE-GOD' GADGETS

Thanks to the wonders of technology, delivered courtesy of Western civili-sation, Muslims can now fulfill their religious duties with relative ease. There are all sorts of brilliant gadgets out there, designed to ease the bur-den of the pious and ensure they face the right direction, perform their ablutions properly, read the right duas (prayers) when entering or leaving the toilet, pronounce the Arabic words correctly, and fulfill their numerous rituals according to prescribed tradition. So here is our selection of ten pieces of kit no self-respecting Muslim should be without.

1. Bismallah
Muslims should start every act by uttering *Bismillah*: 'in the name of God'. This neatly and nicely designed app for smart phones, from app designers Appovation LLC, takes the effort out of reciting these words. Press a but-ton, and your phone will say them for you.

2. iPray
Never miss your prayers again. iPray displays the next prayer time as well as the complete prayers timetable for your current location. It even calls the *Adhan*, and warns you not be neglectful with Adhan alarms and push notifi-cations – which could be handy in case you are in the company of the *kuffar* (unbelievers). Settings allow for adjustment to timezones, prayer calcula-tion methods and calendar corrections.

3. Automatic Wudu Washer
This genius of an invention is designed to assist believers in the art of ablu-tion (*wudu*) which is required before prayers. The state-of-the-art user-friendly technology from Australia fulfils all your wudu needs; and makes *wudu* 'a cleaner, convenient and more pleasant experience'. Different parts of the machine, all with helpful indicators and signs, wash your hands, face, and head – and dry them with hygienic blasts of hot air. When you are ready

to wash your feet, place them in the right slots (alas, it does not roll up your *toupe* or *shalwar*) and they will be washed according to religious dictates. Operating with infra-red sensors, it has in-built nano-technology features that take care of germs and bacteria. It has a few drawbacks such as lacking a device to sort out the nose blowing operation. However, it provides just the right amount of water — the measure is called *mudd*, the water which is held by two hands cupped together — for every step, and helps in the conservation of this vital natural resource. Do check it out for yourself: http://www.youtube.com/watch?v=976UJL1JxDY.

4. MeccaLocator

Automatic wudu completed, you are ready for prayer. But there is still the perplexing task of finding the direction to Mecca. Fear not, MeccaLocator from Appovation will tell you which way to face. Alternatively you can get the Pro version (which we presume is meant for professional Muslims) of iPray, which also includes a useful Qibla direction finder. Or you can go low tech, and get a prayer mat with a built-in compass. Unfortunately, none of these devices are of much use when you are travelling on a plane. Religious authorities are not quite sure where to turn on this issue. But in an article in *Arab News*, widely available on the web, the Saudi-based Islamic scholar and newspaper columnist Adil Salahi advises us to 'offer it normally, next to the catering area, standing up and prostrating'. Moreover, we need to board 'the plane before the prayer is due' and 'be certain that its time range will have lapsed before we can offer it at our destination' — time zones not-withstanding. Some problems are just too complex for modern technology to solve.

5. Quran Hakeem and iQuran III/iQuran Lite

During prayer you will have to read some verses from the Qur'an. The helpful Quran Hakeem app from SHL Info Systems provides the experience of reading 'as if from the *Mus'haf*' (codex). You are guaranteed a pleasant reading experience in Arabic with clear script and aesthetically-pleasing layout. But if you want to understand what you are reading, turn to iQur'an, which contains the complete text alongside a selection of multi-language classical translations and six downloadable audio recitations.

6. Fortification of the Muslim

To further strengthen your *iman* (faith) turn to this obliging free App. It provides readymade *duas* (prayers) for every occasion, emotion and feeling. For example, when climbing up the stairs you should say, 'Allah is the Greatest', when descending you should say, 'How perfect Allah is'. If you hear a barking of a dog or braying of asses at night: 'seek refuge in Allah for they see what you do not'. But 'if you hear the crow of a rooster, ask Allah for his bounty for it has seen an angel'. If you feel amazed say: 'Allah is the Greatest'. If you have doubts, say: 'I renounce that which is causing such doubt'. Original Arabic is provided with an English translation so you can say it in Arabic too, just to ensure that God is listening and understands.

7. Highly Superior Istanja machine

Sooner or later there will be a need for *istanja* — Muslims, are, after all humans. But what is *istanja*, the uninitiated may ask. The Pakistani website, 'Haq Char Yaar' ('Truth, Four Friends', who are the four Rightly Guided Caliphs; http://www.kr-hcy.com/index2.shtml) provides a very useful definition: 'getting rid of un-cleanliness, which one gets when one excretes is called *Istanja*'. And it offers some useful tips for performing the ritual: 'after urinating dry the urine with a clean piece of mud or toilet paper and then wash with water' and 'after excreting faeces clean the private part with three or five clean mud pieces or toilet paper and then wash'. In these days of high technology, a better alternative than keeping a bucket of clean mud or the *lota*, the spherical vessel used to store water for ritual cleaning, is to use an *istanja* machine. There are several on the market. All replace the accursed paper, used and wasted so profusely by decadent westerners, with fresh jets of water providing convenient wide cleaning. Some have deodorizers, remote controls, pulsating seats and even provide a soothing massage. Heaven on earth! Or you can go for low tech option developed, in the days of old, when knights were bold and toilet paper had not been invented, by the canny Ottomans: it consist of a normal commode with a hole for a nozzle. Superior than a bidet, which requires you to stand up, move sideways, and then sit down again, creating an almighty mess; and damn sight better than the 'Muslim shower', also known as *shattaf* or hand-held bidet spray, which tends to refresh the face as well as the posterior, and spreads water all over the place.

8. Islamic Car

Refreshed from face to posterior and full of *duas*, you are ready to venture out in the world. Why not continue in a state of peace and submission inside the Islamic car? Built by the Malaysian company Proton in collaboration with Iran Khodro, it is the first car of its kind, unlike any other car it 'acts in line with Muslim values'. It calls the Adhan, has compartments for your copy of the Qur'an and that all-important headscarf, and a compass to indicate the direction of the Qibla, no matter where else you might be going. It will be in showrooms throughout the Middle East and parts of Asia and Africa by the end of 2012, priced between $8,700 and $12,000.

9. Zabihah

Equip your Islamic car with Zabihah, a useful free app from Halalfire Media LLC. It utilises a massive online database of halal stuff and provides listings and reviews of halal restaurants, markets and mosques near your current location. It has listings from around the world, making it useful for travellers. You will never be too far from halal burgers and chicken.

10. The Hajj and Umra package

The fifth pillar of Islam, the pilgrimage to Mecca, began as a once-in-a-life-time journey full of hardship, danger and sublime experience. Not any-more. Thanks to the hajj and umra holiday packages, available widely throughout the world and throughout the year, you can go on hajj every year, and for a quick umra, the lesser pilgrimage, anytime you chose. Better than a holiday in the Bahamas; just as relaxing and rewarding but with more shopping opportunities. A divine bargain!

Apps to come

The i-Phone imam

Prayers need to be led by the most pious in a group. But if you can't decide who is closest to God, why not get the all new i-Phone imam app. Settings will include the 'Islamic-ometer', in which a fingerprint scan will reveal, using the latest biophysical technology, which among you is privileged to be the leader. If that could be tricky, for example if you're in a group of friends, why not try the 'digital-imam' setting. At the appropriate time just form a prayer-line, place the i-phone in front and press the green button marked 'lead'. The device will then lead the prayers. Version1 will be equipped with Sunni and Shia modes. Other traditions will be catered for in subsequent releases. Please note that an imam-enabled i-Phone is inappropriate for members of the Ahmadi, Ismaili and Druze communities and should be kept well beyond the reach of children and women.

CITATIONS

Introduction: What We Fear by Merryl Wyn Davies

A new edition of *The Ugly American* by Eugene Burdick and William Lederer was published by W W Norton in 1999. The novel, originally published in 1958, represents several real people with pseudonyms and was made into a film in 1963 starring Marlon Brando. The term 'ugly American' is now associated with loud and ostentatious individuals. Michael Hirsh's 'Bernard Lewis revisited: what if Islam isn't an obstacle to democracy in the Middle East but the secret to achieving it?' appeared in *Washington Monthly*, November 2004; available from http://www.washingtonmonthly.com/features/2004/0411.hirsh.html; Rajiv Chanderasakaran, *Imperial Life in the Emerald City: Inside Baghdad's Green Zone* (Bloomsbury, 2008).

Neocon Orientalists by Abdelwahab El-Affendi

The neo conservatives mentioned include: Paul Berman, *Terror and Liberalism* (W W Norton, 2004); Bernard Lewis, *What Went Wrong? Western Impact and Middle East Responses* (Oxford University Press, 2002); and 'The Roots of Muslim Rage', *The Atlantic Monthly*, September 1990, pp. 47–60; Samuel P Huntington, 'The clash of civilizations?' *Foreign Affairs*; 72: 3 (1993), pp. 22–49; Norvell B. De Atkine and Daniel Pipes, 'Middle Eastern Studies: What Went Wrong?', *Academic Questions*, Winter 1995-1996, www.campus-watch.org/article/id/558; Martin Kramer *Ivory Towers on Sand: The Failure of Middle Eastern Studies in America* (Brookings Institution, 2001); Martin Kramer, editor, *The Islamism Debate* (Tel Aviv University, 1997) – his quotes are from pp171 and 172; and Robert Satloff, 'Islamism Seen from Washington,' in Kramer, pp 101–2.

All the quotations from Edmund Burke III are from his 'Orientalism and World History: Representing Middle Eastern Nationalism and Islamism in the Twentieth Century,' *Theory & Society*, 27: 4 (August 1998), pp. 589–607; the quotes form Richard Rorty, *Philosophy and Social Hope*, (Penguin, New York, 1999) are from pp 16–17 and p181; and the quotations from Ziauddin Sardar's *Orientalism*. (Open University Press, Milton Keynes, 1999) are from pp78 and 92. The comments on Kramer are from F. Gregory Gause III, 'Who Lost Middle Eastern Studies?' *Foreign Affairs*, 81: 2 (2002).

Other works cited: *The 9/11 Commission Report: The Full Final Report of the National Commission on Terrorist Attacks Upon the United States* (W. W. Norton & Co. (26 July 2004); Zachary Lockman, 'Behind the Battles over US Middle East Studies', *Middle East Report Online*, January 2004; Joshua Teitelbaum and Meir Litvak, 'Students, Teachers, and Edward Said: Taking Stock of Orientalism', *Middle East Review of International Affairs*, March 2006; Shmuel Bar, 'The Religious Sources of Islamic Terrorism', *Policy Review*, no. 125, June 1, 2004; Joshua Micah Marshall, 'The Orwell Temptation: Are intellectuals overthinking the Middle East?' *Washington Monthly*, May 2003 (accessed on 23 December, 2004 at: http://www.washingtonmonthly.com/features/2003/0305.marshall.html).

Defending Civilization: How Our Universities are Failing America, and What Can Be Done About it was published, in November 2001, by American Council of Trustees and Alumni, established by Lynne Cheney, Saul Bellow, Joe Lieberman and others. See also *The Professors: The 101 Most Dangerous Academics in America* by David Horowitz (Regnery Publishing, Washington, 2006), where you will find M Shahid Alam, Hamid Algar, Miriam Cooke, Hamid Dabashi, John Esposito, Yvonne Haddad, Ali Mazrui and *Critical Muslim's* Vinay Lal. It's good to be 'dangerous' in the neocon universe!

The quote from Bhikhu C. Parekh is from *A new politics of identity: political principles for an interdependent world* (Palgrave, London, 2008, p99.)

I would like to thank the ESRC and AHRC for their support for my current research.

Bernard Lewis by Peter Clark

The latest revised editions of books by Bernard Lewis mentioned in the article: *The Emergence of Modern Turkey* (OUP, New York, 3rd Edition, 2001); *Music of a Distant Drum* (Princeton University Press, 2001, Reprint edition 2011); *The Political Language of Islam* (University of Chicago Press; 2nd edition 1991); *The Assassins* (Phoenix, 2003, reprint of 1967 edition); and *Islam in History* (Oxford Paperbacks; new edition of 6th revised edition 2002). Alas, there is no revised version of Lewis's Islamophobia.

Twenty-First-Century Crusaders by Arun Kundani

The following works have been mentioned in this article:
Wajahat Ali, Eli Clifton, Matthew Duss, Lee Fang, Scott Keyes, and Faiz Shakir, *Fear, Inc.: the roots of the Islamophobia network in America* (Center for American Progress, August 2011). Jamie Bartlett and Mark Littler, *Inside the EDL: populist politics in a digital age* (Demos, 2011). Anders Behring Breivik, 2083 — *A European Declaration of Independence* (2011). Matt Carr, 'You are now entering Eurabia', *Race & Class* (Vol. 48, no. 1, 2006). David Edgar, 'Racism, fascism and the politics of the National Front', *Race & Class* (Vol. 19, no. 2, 1977). English Defence League mission statement, available at http://englishdefenceleague.org. Richard Hofstadter, *The Paranoid Style in American Politics* (Vintage, 2008). Paul Jackson, *The EDL: Britain's 'new far Right' social movement* (Radicalism and New Media Research Group, University of Northampton, 2011). Alana Lentin and Gavan Titley, *The Crises of Multiculturalism: racism in a neoliberal age* (Zed Books, 2011).

Hindutva's Sacred Cows by Vinay Lal

The quotations from Swami Agnivesh are drawn from his article, 'Religion: Ready to Kill, but Reluctant to Live', on www.swamiagnivesh.com/rel. htm, and from his book *Religion, Spirituality and Social Action* (2nd ed., Delhi: Hope India Publications, 2003), pp27–29; for his views on Islam and terrorism, see the *Hindu*, 1 June 2008; for Amarnath, see http://www.dailyindia.com/show/441120.php (accessed 1 January 2012); and for his general outlook, see his book *Hinduism in the New Age* (Delhi: Hope India, 2005).

The views of Hindutva's principal ideologues are best accessed through the following texts: V. D. Savarkar, *Hindutva* (1923; reprint ed., Delhi: Bhartiya Sahitya Sadan, 1989); Volumes VI and VII (in Hindi) of *Samagra Savarkar [Collected Works of Savarkar]* (1963; Delhi: Prabhat Prakashan, 2009); M. S. Golwalkar, *Bunch of Thoughts* (various editions, among them this one: Bangalore: Sahitya Sindhu, 1996); and M. S. Golwalkar, *We or Our Nationhood Defined* (Nagpur: Bharat Publications, 1939). A recent scholarly study partly focused on Savarkar is Aparna Devare, *History & the Making of a Modern Hindu Self* (Delhi: Routledge, 2011).

On Hitler's popularity in India, see Monty Mumford, 'Indian business students snap up copies of *Mein Kampf*', *Daily Telegraph* (20 April 2009); Zubair Ahmad, 'Hitler memorabilia attracts young Indians' (15 June 2010), at http://news.bbc.co.uk/2/hi/south_asia/8660064.stm; and http://www.mid-day.com/news/2010/oct/021010-Mein-Kampf-Adolf-Hitler-Mahatma-Gandhi-margin-Navajivan-Trust.htm. Bose's years in Germany are covered in Rudolf Hartog, *The Sign of the Tiger: Subhas Chandra Bose and His Indian Legion in Germany, 1941-45* (Delhi: Rupta, 2001).

The 15 November ceremony in Pune is reported in Indian newspapers most years. As an illustration, see the coverage in the *Indian Express* (2007 & 2008), online at: http://www.indianexpress.com/news/quietly-in-a-pune-plot-they-meet-to-remember-the-assassin/239711/0 and http://www.expressindia.com/story_print.php?storyId=386592.

The quotation from Har Dayal appears in B. R. Ambedkar, *Thoughts on Pakistan* (Bombay: Thacker and Co., 1941). Raymond Brady Williams, *An Introduction to Swaminarayan Hinduism* (Cambridge University Press, 2001), is a good beginning. I have drawn upon the various BAPS websites, especially www.mandir.org/introduction; www.chicago.baps.org.introduction; and http://atlanta.baps.org. The exhibition catalog, *Understanding Hinduism*, is published by the BAPS Shri Swaminarayan Mandir (Neasden, n.d.). *The Protection of Cow-Clan* is one of several pamphlets published on behalf of the RSS by Suruchi Prakashan, New Delhi, 2000.

Taking Liberty by Gordon Blaine Steffey

For the thoughts of father and son Falwell, see Jerry Falwell, *Falwell: An Autobiography* (Lynchburg, VA: Liberty House Publishers, 1997); and Jonathan Falwell, *One Great Truth: Finding Your Answers in Life*, (New York: Howard Books, 2008). The works of their disciples include Ergun Mehmet Caner and Emir Fethi Caner, *Unveiling Islam: An Insider's Look at Muslim Life and Belief*, (Grand Rapids, MI: Kregel Publishing, 2002); and Kevin Roose, *The Unlikely Disciple: A Sinner's Semester at America's Holiest University*, (New York: Grand Central Publishing, 2009).

On the controversy surrounding Caner's background, see his 'Statement', *SBC Today*, 25 February 2010, at http://sbctoday.com/2010/02/25/statement-from-dr-ergun-caner/; 'Ergun Caner Guilty: Removed As Dean From Seminary', *Liberty Student News*, no date specified, at http://www.libertystudentnews.com/?p=520; 'Ergun Caner named dean of Liberty Baptist Seminary', *Baptist Press*, 17 February 2005, at http://www.sbcbaptistpress.org/bpnews.asp?ID=20171; 'Ergun Caner trains US Marines (Base Theatre)', *Viddler*, video uploaded by jsin on 1 August 2010, at http://www.viddler.com/explore/jsin/videos/1/; 'Ergun Caner trains US Marines (o-club)', *Viddler*, video uploaded by jsin on 1 August 2010, at http://www.viddler.com/explore/jsin/videos/2/1241.37; Bob Allen, 'After investigation into claims, Liberty University demotes Ergun Caner', *Associated Baptist Press*, 28 June 2010, at http://www.abpnews.com/content/view/5284/53/; 'Ergun Caner moving to school begun by J. Frank Norris', *Associated Baptist Press*, 18 May 2011, at http://www.abpnews.com/content/view/6405/53/; and Jessica Tuggle, 'Students catch on to Starbucks conversation starters', *Florida Baptist Witness*, 26 February 2008, at http://www.gofbw.com/news.asp?ID=8474.

On the Creation Museum, see A. Larry Ross Communications, 'Online Newsroom', *Creation Museum*, no date specified, at http://www.alrcnewskitchen.com/creationmuseum/index.htm.

I have also cited text from http://www.creationcurriculum.com.

Other works cited include James Davison Hunter, 'Fundamentalism and Relativism Together: Reflections on Genealogy', in Peter L. Berger (ed.), *Between Relativism and Fundamentalism: Religious Resources for a Middle Position*, (Grand Rapids, MI and Cambridge, U.K.: Wm. B. Eerdmans Publishing Co., 2010). See also, James Davison Hunter, *To Change the World: The Irony, Tragedy, & Possibility of Christianity in the Late Modern World* (New York: Oxford University Press, 2010) and Vincent Jude Miller, *Consuming Religion: Christian Faith and Practice in a Consumer Culture*, (New York and London: Continuum, 2005). The Phew 'Global Survey of Evangelical Protestant Leaders', carried out by the Pew Forum on Religion & Public Life on 22 June 2011, can be found at: http://pewforum.org/Christian/Evangelical-Protestant-Churches/Global-Survey-of-Evangelical-Protestant-Leaders.aspx.

You have probably guessed. My fellow explorer of the Falwell universe was Ziauddin Sardar. See his essay 'Welcome to Postnormal Times', *Futures 42* (2010) 435–444.

Lot's Legacy by Shanon Shah

The Joseph Massad quotation is from his article 'Re-Orienting Desire: The Gay International and the Arab World' *Public Culture*. 14:2. 2002; and queer theorist Jasbir K Puar's from 'The Center Cannot Hold': The Flourishing of Queer Anti-Occupation Activism. *Huffington Post*. [Online] 3 Octoberr 2011; available at: http://www.huffingtonpost.com/jasbir-k-puar/the-center-cannot-hold-th_b_991572.html.

Ziauddin Sardar's comments on LGBT are from his paper, 'The Language of Equality' (Equality and Human Rights Commission, London, 2008); and Tariq Ramadan's opinion is from his website: http://www.tariqramadan.com/Islam-and-Homosexuality,10683.html?lang=fr. News stories mentioned in this essay include: 'Cameron threat to dock some UK aid to anti-gay nations', BBC Online, 30 October 2011, available at: http://

www.bbc.co.uk/news/uk-15511081; 'Hillary Clinton declares gay rights are human rights': http://www.bbc.co.uk/news/world-us-canada-16062937 ; John F Burns, 'Cameron Criticizes "Multiculturalism" in Britain. *New York Times*, 5 February 2011, available at: http://www.nytimes.com/2011/02/06/world/europe/06britain.html ; Chris McGreal, 'Military given go-ahead to detain US terrorist suspects without trial', *The Guardian*, 15 December 2011,http://www.guardian.co.uk/world/2011/dec/15/americans-face-guantanamo-detention-obama; and Yow Hong Chieh, 'Anwar backs Seksualiti Merdeka's right to expression', *The Malaysian Insider*, 8 November 2011, available at: http://www.themalaysianinsider.com/malaysia/article/anwar-backs-seksualiti-merdekas-right-to-expression/.

Both the hadith cited are from *Sunan Abu Dawud*, Book 38, Number 4447, and Book 41, No 5106.

Sectarian Gulf by Fanar Haddad

The *Al Arabiya* report deconstructed in the article, and comments on the report, can be accessed at: http://www.alarabiya.net/articles/2011/09/24/168359.html.

Tottenham Riots by Gary McFarlane

Following the writing of this article the *Guardian* newspaper, partnered with the London School of Economics, produced an exhaustive report called 'Reading the Riots: Investigating England's summer of disorder' (http://www.guardian.co.uk/uk/series/reading-the-riots) on the disturbances in Tottenham and elsewhere in August 2011. Many of the points highlighted in this article were affirmed in the testament of participants recorded for the project and the subsequent conclusions of the researchers.

News sources quoted in this article, in order of appearance: Owen Bowcott, 'Magistrates were told to send rioters to crown court, emails show', *Guardian* (14 September 2011), www.guardian.co.uk/uk/2011/sep/13/

riots-sentencing-justice-system-emails; Stafford Scott, 'Interview with Tottenham activist Stafford Scott' (transcript of live Sky News broadcast), http://bat020.posterous.com/interview-with-tottenham-activist-stafford-sc; footage of the alleged attack on the young women can be seen at www.youtube.com/watch?v=1odqMZJ9hFo; Zoe Williams, 'The Psychology of Looting', *Guardian* (9 August 2011), www.guardian.co.uk/commentisfree/2011/aug/09/uk-riots-psychology-of-looting; and Naomi Klein,'Daylight Robbery, Meet Nighttime Robbery', *Nation* (16 August 2011), www.thenation.com/article/162809/daylight-robbery-meet-nighttime-robbery (6) BBC Newsnight with David Starkey can be accessed at: www.bbc.co.uk/news/uk-14513517; the quote from the student is from BBC News, 9 December 2011, available online at www.youtube.com/watch?v=k1BsTl4QRjI. The 2010 IPPR report, 'Young people and the recession', can be accessed at: www.ippr.org/uploaded-Files/events/Youth%20unemployment%20and%20recession%20technical%20briefing.pdf. Finally, 'There will be riots' video is on the Guardian website,www.guardian.co.uk/society/video/2011/jul/31/haringey-youth-club-closures-video.

Four Lions by Claire Chambers

Hanif Kureishi's 'Weddings and Beheadings' is in *Collected Stories* (Faber and Faber, 2011); Mohsin Hamid, 'A Beheading' appears in *Granta* 112 ('Pakistan', 2010, pp191–196); and Hassan Blasim's 'The Reality and the Record' is in *The Madman of Freedom Square* (Comma Press, 2009)

Muslim anti-Semitism by Muhammad Idrees Ahmad

The Channel 4 interview with Zebolon Simintov can be seen at: youtube.com/watch?feature =player_embedded&v=r8vgEDnzV8M. See also Hannah Arendt's 'Truth and Politics' in the 25 February 1967 issue of the *NewYorker*; http://www.newyorker.com/archive/1967/02/25/1967_02_25_049_TNY_CARDS_000286116.

Irshad Manji by Peter Morey

Irshad Manji's film 'Faith without Fear' is directed by Ian McLeod (WETA/ PBS Home Video, 2007); and her book is entitled *The Trouble with Islam Today* (New York: St Martins Press, 2004). The quote from Edward Said is from *Covering Islam: How the Media and the Experts Determine How We See the Rest of the World* (London: Vintage, 1997, revised edition, p77).

Last Word: On Beards by Ziauddin Sardar

On how beards reflect certain traits, see Dan M. Kahan, 'Cultural Cognition as a Conception of the Cultural Theory of Risk' in S. Roeser (editor), *Handbook of Risk Theory*, Harvard Law School Program on Risk Regulation Research Paper No. 08-20, Yale Law School, Public Law Working Paper No. 222; available from http://papers.ssrn.com/sol3/papers. cfm?abstract_id=1123807#.

On the Japanese beard ban, see Justin McCurry, 'Japanese bureaucrats face up to the clean-cut look', *The Guardian* 20 May 2010: http://www.guardian.co.uk/world/2010/may/20/japan-isesaki-beard-ban?INTCMP=SRCH. The antics of Salafi MP, Mamdouh Ismail, can be viewed at: http://www.arabist.net/blog/2012/2/8/the-salafi-who-called-the-azan-in-parliament.html, and the Pumpkin Mullah at: http://www.youtube.com/watch?v=vcDIllRupqY. Shoaib Mansoor's *Khuda Kay Liye* (In the Name of God), released in 2007, is available on DVD. Amla's beard is all over the web, and its street value is increasing exponentially.

ON BEARDS

Ziauddin Sardar

On the top deck of the Number 32 bus, a group of Muslim teenagers took the seats in front of me. There were six of them, all in black hijabs, and very rowdy. They were simultaneously trying to balance their school bags and books in one hand, while holding onto mobile phones in the other; texting or surfing the web, giggling and getting worked up, all at the same time.

'Look at this,' one of them exclaimed, pointing to her phone. Other girls immediately tried to peer inside an impossibly small screen. 'She looks like a *hijra* [transsexual], innit?' They laughed. Another girl pointed to a picture from her mobile. 'It's me dad's new car; it's blue,' she said. 'But if someone says it's blue he gets upset.' She pulled at her hijab, and, pretending to sound like her father, said in mock-accented English, 'Why are you insulting my second wife? It's turquoise.' They all laughed again.

'Me mum wants me to marry this American geezer,' another of the girls said. The others all tried to snatch the phone from her hand. 'American Muslims are like *Tablighis*. They go around converting people,' one of them declared to the entire bus. 'Is he a man or an elf?', another asked. 'Dream on elf,' shouted another. 'Look at his beard! It goes all the way to his knees.' Everyone looked. 'He can say his *namaz* [prayer] starkers!' Then came a question that wouldn't be out of place in a philosophy seminar: 'God, He has a beard, innit?'

I suspect He does. He has created the world in His own image. That's why he has asked all those who worship Him to announce themselves with appropriate lengths of stubble. All the great prophets — Moses, Jesus and Mohammad — had beards. Those in charge of keeping the faith pure and unsullied — the rabbis, the priests and the mullahs — normally have beards. Some, such as Sikhs and Jews from the Hassidic tradition, do not even trim them. In Eastern Christianity, beards were recommended for the believers and mandatory for the priesthood. Certain Christian sects, such as the Amish and Hutterite men, never sever their beards. For pious Muslims, a beard is obligatory, a legally constituted entity with its own rights and needs. For the mystics of all varieties — the Sufis, the Yogis, and followers of Kabbalah — the beard is holy, the instrument that channels the grace of God (*barakah*) above, where God presumably resides, to the human soul.

My own soul, I am sorry to report, has not been very accommodating to beards. Like the vast majority of the inhabitants of the Japanese town of Isesaki, I find beards 'unpleasant'. In 2010, Isesaki, which is in Gunma prefecture, reportedly banned its public officials from 'displaying any manifestation of facial hair'. I wouldn't go that far. But I would prefer to stay away from beards. Some of my friends say my attitude displays classical symptoms of fear and loathing.

All I can say is that I express my dislike vigorously.

Part of my problem with beards is that they confer identity. And in most cases, identity decides who is right. Facts, reasoning, evidence do not matter. It's the shape and the length of the beard that clinches the argument. Now this is not a problem particular to Muslims. It's a universal phenomenon that is described by those who know, such as folks at Harvard Law School, as 'cultural cognition'. What it means is that people form opinions about what is right or wrong not from facts and evidence but in line with their existing prejudices and cultural types — of which beards are an integral part. In religious circles, a beard announces: 'You can trust what I say. I am pious. I share the same values as you. I will reinforce your self-image'. That's why beards only listen to other beards. Thus prejudice is reinforced.

My own fear and loathing of beards has, as you would expect, a personal history. I can pin exactly when my dislike of beards began. During my youth I was involved with various Islamic groups. Every other week we would gather at the house of a bearded 'brother', often a PhD student, to study and discuss religious matters. Later, after evening prayers, dinner would be served. But just as we were about to eat, another beard would inevitably ask: 'Is this fish halal?' And the bearded host would reply: 'Yes brother. We are Muslims. We only serve halal fish.'

After a string of such incidents, I deduced that in Muslim circles there was a causal link between beards and IQ. Somehow beards were soaking up grey matter. I experimented; I would start a serious discussion with a group of clean shaven friends and wait for a beard to arrive. Then I would try and measure, on a scale of one to ten, just how low the discussion would sink. A score of ten would be achieved at any point in the discussion in which some-one would seek to kill the conversation by quoting an alleged hadith. The point of this would be to declare the issue being debated *haram* — forbid-den. There was a time, just after I had finished studying physics, when I came very close to deciding that I should devote my life to pursuing research to prove my theory. Unfortunately, no one was willing to fund the research.

The connection between beards and fear is less difficult to confirm. Look at the beards of the Taliban and tell me they don't send a chill to your spine. Or look at the bearded outfits in Pakistan known as Jamaat-ud-Dawa, Lashkar-e-Taiba, Sipah-e-Sahaba, who have recently formed themselves in to the 'Defense of Pakistan Council'. Now these guys are serious about their beards – so serious, in fact, that if you had a beard that was unlike theirs, you would be a legitimate target for execution. They strictly believe that a human face can only support a single type of beard. Other varieties are deviations, innovations, perversions that cannot be allowed to mushroom. If these bands of holy warriors are going to 'defend' Pakistan, you know it is surely doomed.

But we don't have to go to extremist fringes to find fearful beards. They can be easily seen on any Muslim country's TV channel, of which there must now be as many as stars in God's heaven. You can easily recognise these channels because they are almost exclusively populated by pestiferous beards preaching hell and damnation. You know there are mouths some-where underneath these beards because foam is dribbling on the pelt. (The guy on Pakistan's Geo TV, who presents a programme called 'Aalim Online', has a rather smart beard — the kind I like. But the beard gets the better of him and he occasionally talks from the wrong orifice.)

Classical Muslim thinkers were passionate about classification. Everything had to be categorised: hence different types of hadith, levels of duties, varie-ties of social obligations, and countless classifications of knowledge. In the same spirit, let me offer my topology of Muslim beards. So when you are forced to utter 'here comes a beard', you know what it is actually saying.

Like the pillars of Islam, the beards of Islam are five in number.

1. The Tabligh

This is full, long, untrimmed, unruly and chaotic. Obligatory amongst the members of the *Tablighi Jamaat*, it is, following the rules of chaos theory, a fractal beard. That is to say it looks the same from all directions: absurd. The best example is Amla's beard. Hashim Amla, the South African batsman, is undoubtedly the finest beard in contemporary Islam; and second only to that of W.G. Grace in the history of cricket. Amongst cricketing fans, Amla's beard is endowed with supernatural powers, and attracts as much attention as his batting, which is truly remarkable. Unfortunately, the same cannot be said of his beard, replicas of which can be bought easily at any match involving South Africa. 'The optimum length for me, as a Muslim,' Amla told a *Guardian* journalist, 'is for the beard to be of fist-length'. Which makes you wonder: just how long is Amla's fist? 'I love it when guys ask me about Islam or my beard. To share knowledge is a duty,' he says. So for Amla, his beard is a kind of *dawa*, an invitation to Islam, all that is good and wholesome.

By all accounts, Amla is an excellent chap. His conduct, on and off the pitch, is immaculate. He is amongst the diminishing league of cricketers who will walk when they know they are out, even before the umpire's finger has gone up. So, one could legitimately ask: does Amla's beard not undermine my entirely prejudiced theory of beards of Islam?

I have two things to say in my defence. One, Amla is a very handsome chap. The beard makes him look like a medieval-era baker. However, to suggest that such a beard would invite people to the benefits of Islam is rather difficult to swallow. Second, Amla's head is clearly in control of his beard. But the Tabligh have uncanny ways of affecting the mind leading to an inability to distinguish the bat from the beard. One can end up playing with the beard instead of the bat. It can, for example, persuade you to go on *dawa* and start knocking on the doors of perfect strangers to ask whether they know how to perform their prayers according to a prescribed manner in the middle of a world cup. And, like the Pakistan cricket team, which, under the captaincy of Inzamam ul Haq, had more players supporting the Tabligh than a gathering at the Alpine Beard Competition, you can end up losing to Ireland. It happened in 2007 World Cup. It's a kind of death by beard. Not surprisingly, Inzy has been compared to several varieties of potatoes. Amla is the exception that proves my rule!

2. The Curtain

This is a thick, busy affair that shrouds the face. Shorter than the Tabligh, it is usually groomed and trimmed. It is de rigueur in Islamist circles. You will find it gracing the followers of Jamaat-e-Islami, some more pious members of the Muslim Brotherhood, the Salafis and the Deobandis. Like the hijab (and other variants such as *purdah, niqab, chador*), which hides a woman's beauty, the Curtain too hides something in men that should not be displayed in public: ugliness. This beard is more potent than the Tabligh as it can derive the person supporting the Curtain into a religious fervour bordering on madness. That's why these beards are very good at issuing fatwas such as the *samosa* is *haram* because it resembles a cross or women are not permitted to shave their moustache.

A fine example of the Curtain is provided by the Egyptian Salafi MP Mamdouh Ismail. During a recent session of Parliament, Ismail felt the uncontrollable urge to call the *Adhan*, the call to prayer. It wasn't time for prayer, and the members were deeply involved in discussing the violence inflicted by the Ministry of Interior on protestors. Ismail just got up and started proclaiming '*Allahu Akbar*'. The Curtain announces that 'I am more and better Muslim than you and, as such, it is my duty to put you in your place — by force if necessary.' A message that the Speaker, Saad al-Katatny of the Muslim Brotherhood, understood well. He told Ismail that he was no more Muslim than anyone else in the Parliament and if he wished to pray he could go to the mosque nearby.

The Curtain has an in-built biological on-off switch. When the switch is off, the Beard behaves as normal, and can even appear pleasant and amiable. But when the switch flips, it generates an uncontainable urge to display and flaunt the Beard's devotion to His will for all to admire and fear. In certain fundamentalist circles, the Curtain is seen as a sign of masculinity, higher status, religious authority and even wisdom. I see it as a general absence of refinement and rational thought.

3. The Mahmal

A combination of the goatee and the moustache, but the two are not connected. Sometime the goatee is as wide as the mouth, giving the illusion that it is the beard that does all the talking. The Mahmal hails from a part of Saudi Arabia known as Najd, where the Wahhabi movement began. It is found mostly in Saudi Arabia, and mostly on Najdi faces, but it has an international influence. The sculpted, sophisticated nature of the Mahmal symbolises wealth and power.

It is named after the palanquin that the Mamluk Sultans and Ottoman Caliphs sent to Mecca with each pilgrim caravan to assert their sovereignty over the holy places. Like the palanquin, which was designed for one person, the Mahmal reflects a single, correct and authentic view of Islam that, by the Grace of God, will become sovereign over the globe. And, like its namesake, it comes with largesse that is generously distributed to those who follow the Wahhabi path and equip themselves with appropriate mental and physical apparatus. I am reliably informed that there is beard farm in Mecca where it is grown in abundance. If the Wahhabis have their way, we will all be following their obscurantist path — but we will be, as lesser mortals, forbidden from wearing the Mahmal.

4. The Tashbih

Long and flowing, usually white, with a turban on the head. The Tashbih should not be confused with *tasbih*, which is a prayer bead; although I imagine hair in one's beard could also be used for enumerating the Beautiful Names of God. It is said to be 'a beard made of love' and can be seen gracing the faces of many contemporary Sufis, most notably the Sufis of the Naqshbandi *tariqa*.

The Tashbih, a Father Christmas-like rug, has two strong tendencies. The word itself means anthropomorphism; and the beard is meant to display human characteristics of God. The circles supporting Tashbih are full of stories of superhuman men with God-like powers — leading their devotees to accept them as their Masters, who, naturally, have a direct link to God, as manifested by the fine snowy quality of the beard. Some Masters, also known as *peers* in South Asian circles, specialise in exorcism, particularly of jinn. The most widely used method involves stuffing mouth of the person possessed by a jinn with chillies and beating the unfortunate victim with sticks. Some Masters are described as 'Cosmic Intellects' and preside over ceremonies where angels dance and the Virgin Mary makes regular appearances. The Tashbih also leans heavily towards neo-conservative politics. It is superb at fooling people. The devotees often discover that the beard is more real than the claims to special Divine knowledge of men sporting it. In more aware circles, these chaps are not known as Sufis or peers but as charlatans.

5. The BTINAB or the Beard That Is Not A Beard

It's like Duchamp's urinal which became a 'Fountain' when it was placed in an art gallery. In Southeast Asia, where the BTINAB is used to stand out from the *Kafiroon* (the unbelievers), it is simply a dozen or so hairs in agony. In other places it is nothing more than designer stubble used to express a particular mood: I am feeling like an intellectual. Despite its ramshackle appearance, the BTINAB requires a great deal of time and attention – it is not easy to get that illusiveness quite right. The BTINAB is popular with fashion conscious, liberal, young Muslims.

The girls on the Number 32 bus thus made the right deductions. But, I wonder, why is the Qur'an so conspicuously silent on the subject of beards? The Sacred Text has quite a few categorical statements and direct injunctions. For example, 'there is no compulsion in religion' (2:256); although the bearded one's have interpreted it to mean there is compulsion in religion — the very fact that you have to have a beard is compulsion enough, in my opinion. Or 'free the slave' (90: 13; 2: 177), which the bearded ones never did, much to the shame of Muslim civilisation. So the Qur'an could easily have said 'grow a beard'. Which it doesn't. Perhaps God is not so enamoured of beards as the visual evidence suggests and we have been led to believe.

The sanction for the beard comes from the traditions of the Prophet. There are sections and sections on the subject in *Sahih Muslim*. They contain hadith like: 'The Messenger of Allah (peace be upon him) said: "Act against the polytheists, trim closely the moustache and grow beards." Now according to *The Masail of the Hair*, which for the uninitiated is 'A Short Treatise Explaining the Laws of Hair, Nails and Dyeing of the Hair', a copy of which I was fortunate enough to acquire at my local Islamic bookshop, this is a universal command. 'The shaving or trimming of the beard is a major sin' and the beardless are doomed to hell.

However, it is probably worth mentioning that the seventh-century Hijaz was not a particularly diverse place when it came to modes of dress. Every-one — Jews, Christians, Muslims, the polytheists and the 'fire worshippers' mention in Sahih Muslim — dressed and looked the same. This was a bit of a problem when you had to distinguish the Muslims from non-Muslims. For example, when the Muslims were caught in a pincer movement during the Battle of Uhad, and the enemy approached both from front and behind, the Muslims were unable to distinguish who was who and started to fight each other. So it made sense for them to physically stand out from the pagan Quraysh. The facial furniture served the function of a military uniform. It made perfect sense in the specific context. I suspect that the Prophet would have provided his followers with military uniforms, if they were available. He loved perfume, which was available in Mecca and Medina, and asked the believer to use it. He would have advised his followers to use disposable razors, if they too were widely available.

Not everything the Prophet liked or disliked has universal import. If we follow this logic we end up in a surreal universe, as demonstrated so well by a Pakistani mullah, supporting a huge Curtain. The Prophet, the Mullah announced on Dunya TV, liked the pumpkin. As such, all Muslims are duty-bound to like the pumpkin. Those who don't, he declared, are not following *sunnah*, the example of the Prophet, not demonstrating their love for him, and therefore should be put to the sword. The pumpkin, the Prophet's favourite vegetable dish, is more valuable and sacred than human life!

Just how inhuman the beards can become is well-explored in the excel-lent Pakistani film, *In the Name of God*. The story involves a liberal religious scholar who is called to give evidence in court about the importance of beard in Islam. Played by Nasiruddin Shah, supporting an exceptionally long airborne Tashbih, the scholar clinches the argument by declaring: 'There is no Islam in beard but there is beard in Islam.' The first part of the statement is undoubtedly true. But I would argue there is beard in Islam as there is camel in Islam. The camels were, of course, the Prophet's favourite mode of transport. Alas, they have been consigned to history. It is time the beards followed.

CONTRIBUTORS

Michel Abboud is the principal of SOMA, the architects of the Park51 Islamic Cultural Center ● **Muhammad Idrees Ahmad** is Senior Lecturer in Journalism, Leicester University ● **Suhel Ahmed** won the Muslim Writers Award for Best Unpublished Novel ● **Claire Chambers**, Senior Lecturer in Postcolonial Literatures, Leeds Metropolitan University, is the author of *British Muslim Fictions* ● **Stéphane Chaumet** is the author of a novel on the Algerian War of Independence, *Même pour ne pas vaincre*, and three books of poems ● **Peter Clark** has translated Arabic fiction and is author of *Marmaduke Pickthall; British Muslim*, *Istanbul* and *Dickens's London* ● **Merryl Wyn Davies** is the Director of the Muslim Institute ● **Abdel Wahab El-Affendi** is Visiting Fellow at the Centre of Islamic Studies, University of Cambridge ● **Fanar Haddad**, a London-based analyst of Middle Eastern affairs, is the author of *Sectarianism in Iraq* ● **Arun Kundnani**, a former editor of *Race & Class*, is the author of *The End of Tolerance* ● **Vinay Lal**, cultural critics and prodigious author, is Professor of History at UCLA ● **Gary McFarlane** is a journalist, political activist, and the developer of the iPhone app iGaza ● **Peter Morey**, Senior Lecturer in English Literature, is co-author of *Framing Muslims* ● **Farouk A. Peru** is a Phd candidate and seminar instructor in Islamic studies in King's College, London ● **Ziauddin Sardar's** latest book is *Muhammad: All That Matters* ● **Anita Sethi**, writer and journalist, is recipient of a Penguin Decibel Prize ● **Shanon Shah** is yet another doctoral candidate at the Department of Theology and Religious Studies, King's College, London.